# ABSTRACTS OF WILLS, ADMINISTRATIONS, AND MARRIAGES OF FAUQUIER COUNTY, VIRGINIA 1759-1800

*With Cemetery Inscriptions, Rent Rolls, and Other Data*

J. ESTELLE STEWART KING

An Improved Edition

With a New Index by
Elizabeth Petty Bentley

CLEARFIELD

Reprinted for
Clearfield Company, Inc. by
Genealogical Publishing Co., Inc.
Baltimore, Maryland
2001

Originally published: Beverly Hills, California, 1939
Reprinted in an improved format
and with a new index by
Genealogical Publishing Co., Inc.
Baltimore, 1978, 1980
© 1978 Genealogical Publishing Co., Inc.
Baltimore, Maryland
All Rights Reserved
Library of Congress Catalogue Card Number 78-51004
International Standard Book Number 0-8063-0801-X
*Made in the United States of America*

## PUBLISHER'S NOTE

For this improved edition the text has been re-organized and re-typed. The entire work has been re-paged and a table of contents and a new index added.

TABLE OF CONTENTS

PROBATE RECORDS

    Will Book Number 1  1759-1783      1
    Will Book Number 2  1783-1796      21
    Will Book Number 3  1796-1803      33
    Wills from Miscellaneous Court Orders      43

MARRIAGE BONDS      45

CEMETERY INSCRIPTIONS      63

RENT ROLLS

    Fauquier County - 1770      71
    Prince William County - 1738      73

FEES - 1827      74

TENANTS OF THE MANOR OF LEEDS - 1777      75

PENSION RECORDS      76

INDEX      77

## NOTE

In the wills, the first date given is the date of the instrument, the second date, that of probate.

Few abbreviations have been used, and these are obvious: Wit. - Witness, Exr. - Executor and Executrix, Apprs. - Appraisers, Admr. - Administrator.

WILL BOOK NUMBER 1   1759-1783

BROOKS, William
Will dated 10th January 1767.
To daughter, Sarah, what she has already received from me. To daughter, Hannah, what she has already received from me. To daughter, Danckus, what she has already received from me. To daughter, Mary, what she has already received from me. To daughter, Ann, what she has already received from me. To daughter, Elizabeth, to have an equal portion with her sisters. Son, Thomas, to be content with what he has recieved until decease of his mother. Son William to have other plantation. Exrs: William Brooks, Thomas Brooks (sons). Wit: Peter Conway, George Threkeld. (p. 1)

SMITH, John
Date of will, 3 Sept. 1767. Hamilton Parish, Fauquier County.
To sister, Mary Manrony, 160 acres of land in County of Dunmore. To mother, Jane Smith, land in County of Dunmore; after her decease land to be divided between sister Hannah Smith and her son, Lewis Smith. Wit: Augustine Smith, James Smith, William Smith. (p. 2)

BULLITT, Benjamin
Deceased 9th January, 1767. Inventory.
Apprs: Jonathan Gibson, James Murry, William Ranson. (p. 2)

TULLOS, Richard
13 July 1758. 24 May 1759.
Peter Lawerence to have all my clothes. Edward Lawerence, Jr. to have my horse. To Teanny (or Feanny) Lawerence, money that is now in the hands of Martin Hardin; balance of money to her oldest son. "There is 4% in the hands of William Stewart that I have no account; crop at Seaton's to sister's oldest son. Friend, John Markham, to take charge." Wit: William Marshall, Thomas Conway. (p. 4)

REDMAN, Richard
28 June 1759. 23 Aug. 1759. Inventory.
Appraisers: William Underwood, Joseph Smith, Henry Mouffett. (p. 4)

FOOTE, George
31 May 1759. 28 June 1759. Hamilton Parish.
To wife, Mary Foote, plantation where I now live, after her decease to son William, if deceased to son Richard. To son, Henry Foote, 100 acres of land. To son, George Foote, 365 acres of land. To son, Gilson Foote, 640 acres, part of land in Prince William Co. To son, Richard Foote, 556 acres of land. To son, William Foote, to have plantation at death of mother. Wife, sons and daughters, Elizabeth, Frances and Bethelon, to have slaves. Wife and daughters to have household goods. Sons, Richard and William, to be educated according to satisfaction of sife. Exrs: wife and sons, George, Gilson, Richard and William. Wit: William Fletcher, John Burdell, George Russell. (p. 1)

SHADRACK, John
11 Aug. 1759. 27 Sept. 1759.
"Being very sick and weak." To wife, Elizabeth Shadrack, slaves, household goods and cash. To Thomas Johnson, who now lives with me, a tract of land in Culpepper Co. (640 acres) and his mother's ring that is now in my possession. Exrs: wife and Charles Morehead (friend).

BRADFORD, William
30 Sept. 1759. 28 Feb. 1760.
"Very sick and weak in bed." To son, Henry Bradford, 206 acres of land that I now live on; unborn child to have one-half of the 206 acres. To daughter, Ann Bradford, one slave. Wife, Mary Bradford, to have use of estate, both real and personal. Exrs: wife and Daniel Bradford (brother). Wit: Alexander Bradford, Henry Rector, Lazarus Taylor. (p. 8)

McCORMICK, James M.
    28 June 1759. 28 June 1760. Inventory.
    Apprs: John Duncan, Edward Willborn, Francis Tennill. (p. 9)

HOLTZCLAW, Jacob
    15 Jan. 1759. 29 Feb. 1760. Hamilton Parish, Prince William Co. To son, Joseph Holtzclaw, 374 acres of land. To son, Jacob Holtzclaw, 200 acres of land that I purchased of Harman Kamper and Harmon Button, also land that I purchased of Thomas Barton. Son, Joseph Holtzclaw, to have the liberty of taking as much timber off 150 acres as he has need for building a dwelling house. Son, Harman Holtzclaw, to have land that I bought in Prince William County of Thomas Stone. Grandsons, Henry and Joseph Holtzclaw, sons of John Holtzclaw (son). Grandsons: Henry Hall, Joseph Hall. To daughter, Eve Wiley (hus. Allen Wiley), 300 acres of land. To daughter, Elizabeth Miller (hus. Harman Miller), land. To daughter, Alice Katherine Hitt, 1 Negro boy. Grandson, Joseph Darnall, son of Jeremiah Darnall, to have 355 acres of land in Prince William County. Grandson, Jacob Fishback, son of Frederick Fishback, to have 1 Negro. Land in Augusta County to be sold and the money to be divided among all my children. Exrs: son Jacob Holtzclaw and Jeremiah Darnall (son-in-law). Wit: Peter Hitt, Thomas Marshall, Henry Kamper. (p. 10)

WEAVER, Tillman
    14 Dec. 1759. 27 March 1760.
    "Very sick." Wife, Elizabeth Weaver, to have use of plantation, being land I bought of Martin Hardin and taken up by John Hardin. After decease of wife land to go to son, Tillman Weaver. Slaves to be divided between sons Tillman, John and daughter Susannah Weaver. Wife to have livestock. Daughters: Ann Kemper (hus. John); Mary Hitt (hus. Harman) to have land in Culpepper Co. and slaves; Eve Porter (hus. Samuel) to have land I bought of Charles Taylor. Daughter, Elizabeth Weaver, to have 150 acres of land and slaves. Daughter, Catherine Weaver, to have 150 acres and slaves. Daughter, Susannah Weaver, to have 89 acres of land and slaves. Son, John Weaver, to have 150 acres and slaves. Son, Jacob Weaver, to have 200 acres and slaves. Exrs: wife, son Jacob, Samuel Porter (son-in-law). Wit: William Norman, Tillman Martin, Thomas Marshall. (p. 13)

WRIGHT, Joseph
    5 Nov. 1759. 27 March 1760.
    Daughters: Hester Jackman, Mary Russell, Catherine Bailey. Exrs: William Russell, Thomas Jackman. Wit: Lazarus Taylor, Richard McPherson, Elizabeth Butler. (p. 14)

TWENTYMEN, Edward
    12 April 1759. 22 May 1760.
    Son Benjamin Twentymen, to have 200 acres of land in Prince William Co. Son John Twentymen, to have 200 acres on home plantation. Daughter, Alender Twentymen, to have personal estate. Wit: William Jett, William Threlkeld and Jesse Threlkeld. (p. 18)

WRIGHT, Joseph
    27 Nov. 1761. Inventory of Joseph Wright's estate. (p. 25)

COOK, John
    5 Jan. 1760. 22 May 1760.
    Daughters: Elizabeth Page, Jane Pritchett and Sarah Cook. Exr: Sarah Cook. Wit: Isaac Shark, John Loman, William Marshall. (p. 19)

REDDIN, Timothy
    28 Aug. 1760. Inventory.
    Appraisers: Daniel Bradford, Jeremiah Darnall, H. (or A.) Bradford. (p. 21)

SPILLMAN, Jacob
    28 August 1760. Sale. Admr: Daniel Floweree.

CORDER, John
    25 Sept. 1760. Inventory.
    Apprs: William Dulin, David Darnall. (p. 24)

BROWN, John
    1 Oct. 1744. 26 Feb. 1761. Parish of Hamilton, Prince William Co.
    One-half of estate to son, John Brown, and other half to son, Dixon Brown. Personal property to be sold and the money divided among all my children. Exrs: son John and Will. Wit: Lazarus Taylor, William W. Delaney, John Corder. (p. 28)

ALLEN, John
    3 Nov. 1759. 26 March 1761.
    To son, John Allen, land in the Marsh Neck and slaves. To son, Thomas Allen, all land below Indian Springs. To son, William Allen, land that I bought from John Hopper, where Gerrard Edwards now lives. Sons, Joseph and James, to have land on which I now live. To daughter, Ann Merr (or Marr), 2 slaves. Exrs: wife and son Thomas. Wit: George Crump, Benjamin Crump, William McDaniel. (p. 29)

FINNIE, John
    15 Aug. 1760. 27 Nov. 1760.
    Wife, Ann Finnie, to have all estate during her life time, at her decease estate to be given daughter Hannah. Exrs: wife, John James (friend). Wit: Alexander Parker, Daniel Newlan, Jane Newlan. (p. 30)

LEGG, Davenport
    26 Feb. 1761. Inventory. (p. 31)

WYATT, William
    4 June 1761. Inventory. (p. 37)

BROWN, John
    27 Aug. 1761.
    Apprs: Alexander Bradford, John Butler, Thomas Smith. (p. 38)

SMITH, Alexander
    26 March 1761. Inventory.
    Apprs: William Reading, David Holder, William Preston. (p. 39)

OBANNON, Bryan
    4 Sept. 1760. 23 Feb. 1762. Hamilton Parish, County of Fauquier.
    "Sick and weak in body." To son, John Obannon and wife Sarah, land where he now lives, containing 212 acres, and slaves; mention is made of granddau. Sarah, dau. of son John. To son, William, plantation where he now resides, containing 212 acres. To son, Samuel, plantation and land in King George Co., containing 300 acres, and all wearing apparel. Daughter, Elizabeth Ambrose, to have 60 pounds of current money and horses. Daughter, Ann Miller, to have 100 pounds of current money. To grandson, Thomas Obannon, son of John, plantation where I now live, containing 220 acres. Grandson, William Obannon (son of William), to have remaining part of land I now live on. Grandson, Bryan Obannon, son of John, to have slaves. "I give to each of my grandchildren (27 in number) the sum of 10 pounds currency to be paid to them by my executors when they come of age." To Aaron and Francis Johnston, children of Margaret Johnston, my plantation and land in Frederick Co. I appoint Jacob Hite (son-in-law) and Elizabeth Hite (gr. dau.) to have care and management of said children until they come of age. To Aaron Johnston, a slave. Exrs: sons John and William Obannon and Jacob Hite. Wit: Elias Edmonds, Samuel Earle, James Rogers. (p. 41)

BEARD, Andrew
    26 Nov. 1761. 24 Sept. 1762.
    Apprs: Edward Humston, John Ashley, Maxmillian Berryman. (p. 47)

CHURCHILL, John
    27 Aug. 1762. Bill of sale. (p. 61)

SEAMAN, Thomas
    26 Aug. 1762. Inventory.
    Appraisers: E. E. Home and Martin Hardin. (p. 56)

BEECH, Alexander
    11 March 1762. --- No date of probate. Hamilton Parish.
    To daughter, Elizabeth Butler, 1 shilling, sterling, with what she is already possessed with. Children: Peter Beech, William Beech and Mary Beech, are to each have 1 shilling with what they have already received. Other children mentioned - Alexander, Thomas and Sarah Beech. Wife: Margaret Beech. Exr: John Barber (or Barbee). Wit: Henry Smith, George Smith, Henry Moseless (,). (p. 63)

STAMPS, Thomas
    8 July 1761. 26 May 1763.
    To son, Timothy Stamps, 150 acres of land where he now lives. To son, John, the remaining part of the aforesaid land. To granddaughter, Molly Stamps (dau. of son Thomas), 15 pounds curr. To son, William Stamps, ---- not of age. To son, George Stamps, 150 acres, land that I purchased of Lewis Tackett. Should son George die before becoming of age, property to go to children of daughter, Elizabeth Tackett. Daughter, Elizabeth to receive 10 pounds currency and 800 pounds of tobacco. Daughter, Mary Shackleford, to have 10 pounds curr. and 800 pounds of tobacco. Mary Shackleford now has 2 children. "I lend to wife, Mary Stamps, all moveable estate, both slaves and stock." Exrs: Timothy, John and William Stamps. (p. 67)

WOODS, Robert
    25 May 1763. Inventory. (p. 71)

READING, Timothy
    May 1763. Inventory.
    Admr: William Reading. (p. 72)

HARRILL, John
    25 Feb. 1764. Administrator of estate Account. (p. 80)

COPPEDGE, John
    27 March 1763. Division of the estate of John Coppedge, dec'd.
    Elizabeth Coppedge, widow of John, to receive -- 1 Negro man - 50 pounds, 1 Negro boy - 10 pounds, 1 Negro boy - 14 pounds. William Coppedge, Negroes and 35 pounds curr., John Catlett, guardian. To Sally Coppedge, 1 Negro boy and 30 pounds curr. To John Coppedge, 1 Negro boy and 60 pounds of curr. Wit: Gilson Foote, James Seaton, James Murray. (p. 75)

GARNER, John
    22 July 1762. Inventory.
    Appraisers: James Arnold, William Morgan, Paul Williams. (p. 80)

LUTTRELL, Richard
    27 Sept. 1764. 25 May 1766.
    To son, James Luttrell, 70 acres of land. To son, Michael Luttrell, 70 acres of land. To son, Samuel Luttrell, 70 acres of land -- where John Collier formerly lived. Son John to have 70 acres of land. To son, Richard Luttrell, my new patent of land containing 58 acres. Land to the following daughters: Unstips (?) Luttrell, Mary Luttrell, and Susannah Luttrell. The last named to have 80 acres of land. Son Robert to have the place on which I now live, furniture, my new gun, sword and coluck box. To daughter, Catherine Corum, a tract of land and 5 pounds curr. To daughter, Sarah Luttrell, a tract of land. Granddaughter, Mary Corum, to receive 5 pounds curr. Wife, Mary Luttrell, to have rest of moveable estate in her possession to enjoy during her widowhood. Exrs: wife and sons Richard and Robert Luttrell. Wit: Edward Lawerence, Sr., Edward Lawerence, Jr., Richard Lawerence. (p. 95)

GREEN, Duff
  May 1766. June 1766. Inventory.
  Appraisers: John Bell, Wharton Ransdell, H. Brooks. (p. 100)

DARNALL, Morgan, Jr.
  30 Sept. 1765. 29 July 1766. Nun-cupative will. (p. 105)
  To brother, Isaac Darnall, land and plantation containing 150 acres, horse, bridle, saddle and all wearing apparel. To brother, Waugh Darnall, 5 pounds due on the rent of my plantation and all debts due me in Carolina. To my mother and to my brother Waugh's wife, I give all money in my pocket book. To John Wood, son of Samuel Wood, as much money out of my estate that will pay for one year schooling. To brother John Darnall, rifle gun. Exr: Morgan Darnall (father). Wit: Jean Darnall, James Wheakley, Elizabeth Darnall.

MORGAN, Charles, Sr.
  3 Dec. 1758. 22 Sept. 1766. Hamilton Parish, Prince William County.
  Seven of my children have received their full parts in proportion of my estate, both real and personal: Charles, Simon, William, Benjamin, James, Alice and Mary Morgan. To "beloved wife", Anne Morgan, 1/3 of my personal estate, the other 2/3 to my son, John Morgan. Exr: John Morgan (son). Wit: John Edwards, Garret Edwards and James Edwards. (p. 107)

BULLITT, Benjamin
  3 May 1766. 27 Oct. 1766. (p. 108)
  To son, Joseph, all that is now in his possession and 2 shillings, 6 pence sterling, no more. To son Thomas Bullitt, a tract of land in the Province of Maryland, purchased of one Hutcherson, where my father, Joseph Bullitt, was buried. To daughter, Sith Combs and her husband, John Combs, 1 shilling 6 pence. To son, Cuthbert Bullitt, 1 shilling 6 pence. To daughter, Elizabeth Bullitt, slave, silverspoons, feather bed. To wife Sarah and six sons, slaves. Names six sons, viz: William Burditt (alias Bullitt), John, George, Benoni, Parmenas and Burwell Bullitt. Exrs: wife, sons Thomas and Cuthbert Bullitt. Wit: Jonathan Gibson, William Connay, Alexander Parker.

PICKETT, William
  26 Sept. 1766. 24 Nov. 1766.
  To daughter, Sarah Pickett, slaves and personal property, when she comes of age. Wife, Elizabeth Pickett, all estate except land that I hold in Caroline and Culpepper Counties - to go to son Reuben Pickett when he comes of age. Land that I hold in Caroline Co., after decease of my mother, to be sold and the money arising from sale to be paid Mary Ann Marshall. Daughter Sarah Pickett to have 70 pounds curr. After decease of wife property to be sold and divided among 3 sons - John, Martin and William Pickett, except should my sons George and Reuben Pickett not have as much as the others they shall be made equal. Exrs: wife and sons Martin and William Pickett. Wit: Henry Kamper, James Peny, Philip Kamper, Sarah Peny. (p. 110)

HAMPTON, Richard
  24 Nov. 1766. Dec. 1766.
  Wife, Martha Hampton, to have use of plantation during widowhood. Daughter, Elizabeth Hampton, to have slaves after decease of wife. Daughter, Sarah Hampton, to have land and slaves. Daughter, Martha Hampton, to have 5 slaves. Sons, William and Richard, to have 5 shillings each. Grandson, Richard Hampton, after decease of wife to have 2 slaves. Grandson, Gale Hampton, son of Richard, 1 slave. Land in Hampshire County to be sold after my decease and widow to pay my debts. To "my beloved wife" my riding chair and harness. Exrs: son William and Richard Lingham (son-in-law) Wit: Charles Morehead, Sarah Sinkler and John Bell. (p. 112)

SEAMAN, Thomas
  26 May 1767. Estate Account. Admr: Martin Hardin.

HOGAN, Margaret
  20 Nov. 1767. 20 June 1767.
  To great-grandchild, Frances Bannister, bed and buggy. To beloved daughter,

Mary Bannister, 1 large chest. Wit: John Williams, Ann Williams, Frances Moore. (p. 120)

NEAVILL, John
24 April 1767. 27 April 1768.
The following named sons are to receive 1 shilling each: John, Robert, Gabriel and Henry Neavill. The following named daughters are each to receive 1 shilling: Milly (?) Fitzgerald, Elizabeth Taylor, Sarah Redman, Mary Neavill. Rest of estate to go to son Thomas Neavill. Exrs: loving friends, George Neavill and John Buchanan. Wit: James Young, Mary Barratt, Alexander Parker. (p. 125)

TYLER, Mary
27 Aug. 1767. Inventory.
Apprs: Thomas Priest, Richard Luttrell, William Ranson. (p. 126)

DODSON, Abraham
Wife, Barbarey Dodson, to have slaves, household goods and stock. Daughter, Milly Holtzclaw, to have slaves, but should she die without issue then slaves to go to brother Jodeph. To Tabitha Dodson, slaves. To son, Enoch Dodson, slaves. To son, Greenham Dodson, slaves. To son, Grantham or Granthane, slaves. Exrs: wife and Jacob Holtzclaw. Wit: Absalom Cornelia, Elijah Dodson, John Bennett. (p. 135)

MOREHEAD, John
23 June 1768. 24 Oct. 1768.
The following named children are to have 5 shillings over and above what they have already received: Hannah Johnson, Charles Morehead, John Morehead, Mary Lawerence and Elizabeth Bristraw (?). Son, Alexander Morehead, to have 2 slaves. Son, William to have 15 pounds over and above what he has received. Son, Samuel, to have a tract of land, containing 90 acres and 50 acres. The land that wife now lives on to be divided between Alexander, William and Dressley. Exrs: sons Charles, Alexander and William. Wit: John Jett, William Macklan, Joseph Macklan. (p. 136)

DAVIS, Thomas
28 Nov. 1768. Inventory.
Apprs: Stephen McCormack, John Freeman, John Bell. (p. 139)

MATHIS, Robert
30 Nov. 1766. 23 Feb. 1767.
To wife, Elizabeth Mathis, land held by lease from Rev. William Stewart of Stafford County, and slaves. To son, John Dudley Mathis, land in Prince William County, left by brother, Griffin Mathis. To son, Chichester Mathis, land purchased of Benjamin Morris in Fauquier County. Following children to have 1 slave each: Robert, Alice and Sarah Mathis. The 3 youngest daughters: Elizabeth, Ann and Nancy Mathis. Exrs: wife, James Lane, Newman Mathis. Wit: Cornelius Kinchloe, James Hamrick, Maxmillian Haynie.

MAUZY, Mary
10 Feb. 1769. 25 Sept. 1769. (p. 152)
To daughter Sally, slaves and cash. Brothers: John and Peter Mauzy. Exr: Thomas Conway (uncle). Wit: Susannah Kenner, Betty Ranson, J.W. Markham.

MILLER, Simon
26 March 1769. 26 Feb. 1770.
To granddaughter, Ann Edmonds, 1 tract of land and household goods. To granddaughter, Betty Edmonds, tract of land, slaves, copper still, worm and casks. To granddau. Judith Edmonds, place where George Ford is overseer. To grandson, Elias Edmonds, 200 acres of land in King George County and slaves. To brother John, wearing apparel. To Joan Hughes, 100 pounds of curr. money the day she marries or when she reaches the age of 18 years. Exrs: Elias Edmonds, William Edmonds, John Obannon, George Bennett. Wit: James Craig, Thomas Mackie, Robert Scott. (p. 155)

BURGESS, Francis
  15 Nov. 1767. 20 March 1770.
  Wife Jane to have use of entire estate during her life. To daughters, Jane, Ruth and Ann Burgess, personal estate. Eleanor Elliott (hus. William) to have 20 shillings to buy a gold ring - no more as she has received her share. To son Dawson Burgess, lease of land where I now live and slaves. Granddaughters, Sarah and Ann Elliott, to have household goods. Exrs: John Suddeth and Francis Tupman (friends). Wit: Thomas Marshall, John Southard, Benjamin Elliott, Moses Congrove. (p. 157)

WATTS, Francis
  23 Oct. 1753. 28 Oct. 1769. Of Craven Co., S. C.
  Wife, Ann Watts, to have use of slaves and land during her life, after her decease to grandson, Francis Watts. Mention is made of other grandchildren, but they are not named. Exr: wife, but should she die then Benjamin Stone is to act as executor. Wit: John Dugan, Benjamin Stone, Ann Dargan or Dugan. (John Watts ordered the above will recorded in Fauquier County.) (p. 159)

WHITE, Pleasant
  28 May 1776. Inventory. (p. 164)

FOOTE, Gilson
  22 Oct. 1770. Inventory.
  Apprs: Richard Foote, Jr., William Alexander, Lynaugh Holm.

SINCLEARE, John
  21 June 1767. 22 April 1771.
  Sons William and John to have slaves. Son James to have 213 acres. To son, Robert, slaves and furniture. To son, Daniel, slaves and furniture. To daughter, Charity Sincleare, household goods. To daughter, Jimime Sincleare, feather bed, furniture and 5 pounds curr. All rest of estate to be divided between five daughters: Sarah, Mary, Elizabeth, Charity and Jimime. Exrs: sons John and William Sincleare. Wit: John Wright, John Kerrs (or Kerns), William Preston. (p. 178)

EDRINGTON, John
  27 May 1771. Inventory.
  Apprs: Charles Deane, Thomas King, William Pearse. (p. 179)

BAILEY, Carr
  7 Oct. 1770. 28 May 1771. (p. 181)
  To wife, Mary Bailey, estate during her life or widowhood, after her decease or marriage the estate to be sold and divided among children: James, Joseph, Betty, Carr, William and John. Exrs: George Rogers, Joseph Minters, Jr. Wit: Humphrey Brooks, William Hampton, Charles Morehead, Thomas Bailey.

CUMMINGS, Simon
  12 April 1771. 24 June 1771.
  To son, Alexander Cummings, plantation. Wife to have use of plantation during her life. To son, John Cummings, live stock. To daughter, Sarah Myoratt, stock. To daughter, Sinty Edge, stock. To daughter, Conty Birciram, personality. Son Peter and daughter Elizabeth Cummings. Exrs: wife (not named), sons John and Alexander. Wit: Daniel Harrilland, John Edge. (p. 182)

DARNALL, William
  28 Aug. 1771. 23 Sept. 1771. (p. 187)
  To Hannah Sears (or Lears), 10 pounds curr., saddle and bridle. To Sallie Rile, 10 pounds curr. Exr: Edward Ball. Wit: Sarah Jeffers, Alec Robertson.

STAMPS, William
  23 April 1772. 23 March 1772.
  Wife Ann to have use of estate during life, should she remarry the estate to be divided between children, including unborn child (children not named). Exrs: William Hunton, Robert Sanders. Wit: Richard Chichester, Peter He-

dengran, Margaret Metcalf. (p. 189)

BOGGS, Thomas
11 Dec. 1772. 23 May 1772.
Wife, Hannah Boggs, to have use of estate during her life time. Sons, Richard, Thomas and Jeremiah Boggs, to have slaves. Daughters: Magdalen Jackson, Elizabeth Maddox, Hannah Russ Watts, to have slaves. Estate to be equally divided among four youngest children after decease of wife. Wit: Moses Johnson, Betty Johnson, Eli Edmonds. (p. 197)

HITT, Peter
23 March 1772. 27 July 1772.
Wife, Elizabeth Hitt, to have estate during life. Slaves to sons, John Joseph and Peter Hitt. Daughter, Mary Rector, 100 acres of land. To son, Henry Hitt, 100 pounds of curr. money. Children: John, Joseph, Harmon, Peter and Mary. Exrs: sons Harmon and Joseph. Wit: Harmon Rector, Joseph Taylor, John Morgan, Harmon Rector. (p. 200)

RECTOR, John
5 July 1772. 22 March 1772.
Wife, Catherine Rector, to have plantation where I now live during her natural life, after her decease it is to be divided between children. Son Henry to have 224 acres of land. Sons, Daniel and Charles. Son Jacob to receive slaves. Son Benjamin to have plantation. Son Frederick to have slaves. To grandson, John Rector (son of John), to have land. To brother, Harmon Rector, land. After decease of wife household goods to be divided into six parts: sons, John, Daniel, Jacob, Charles, Benjamin, Frederick and children of daughter Catherine (dec'd.) and children of daughter Elizabeth (divided into 8 parts). Exrs: wife and son Henry Rector. Wit: Henry Rector, John Adams, Jacob Fanbeon (?). (p. 205)

MINTER, Jacob
21 Nov. 1772. 26 April 1773.
Wife to have the bed my father gave me and use of 2 slaves. Son (unnamed) to have schooling and maintained as thought proper by my executors till he comes of age. Exrs: William Settle and Hannah Minter. Wit: Francis Bronbaugh, Andrew Anderson, Edward Settle, John Edwards. (p. 207)

MORGAN, Randle
30 Feb. 1773. 27 May 1773.
Wife, Martha Morgan, to have plantation for her natural life, or until her remarriage, at her decease property to youngest son, Randle Morgan, Jr. Sons, Abel and Enoch Morgan, to have 10 pounds curr. money. Abraham Morgan (son-in-law) to have 10 pounds curr. money. Randle Morgan, Jr. will be 21 years of age on 5 October 1777. Daughters, Mary, Grace (dec'd.), her daughter, Sarah Carpenter, to have sum of 10 pounds curr. Exrs: sons Abel and Enoch Morgan. Wit: Michael Hennie and Nathan Banley (?). (p. 208)

QUARLES, Betty
9 Sept. 1773. 22 Nov. 1773.
To father-in-law, Thomas Harrison, slaves. (Thomas Harrison was stepfather). To Thomas Gibson (son of Jonathan), slaves. To brother, Benjamin Harrison, slaves - should brother Benjamin die, then property to go to Burr Harrison, son of brother William, and niece Susanah Humstead, slaves. To Benjamin Harrison (brother), Thomas Gibson, Susana Humstead, cattle, etc. To Burr Harrison (son of William) my bay mare. To sister, Mary Fowkes, a ring. To my brother John Quarles' daughter, Elizabeth Minor Quarles, ring. To brother, John Quarles, all my ready cash. Exrs: Jonathan Gibson (friend). Wit: William Coppedge, John Coppedge, Benjamin Jones. (p. 220)

STEPHENS, Robert
22 Nov. 1773. Inventory. (p. 221)

HARRISON, Thomas
26 Sept. 1773. 25 Jan. 1774.

To son William, 4 Negroes, land to be divided between him and his brother Burr. To son Thomas, 409 acres, personal property, money, wearing clothes. To son Burr, 480 acres, plantation house, slaves. Daughter, Susannah Gibson, 5 Negroes, 200 pounds curr. money, looking glass and my cloak. To daughter, Mary Fowkes, 4 Negroes and 150 pounds curr. money. To daughter, Ann Gillison, 2 negroes and 150 pounds curr. To grandson, Thomas Gibson, plantation. To grandson, John Gibson, 2 Negroes. Gr. dau., Ann Harrison Fowkes, a Negro. Jonathan Gibson (son-in-law) to have sum of money he is indebted to me - 79 pounds and 5 shillings. To Chandler Fowkes (son-in-law) to have sums of money I have several times lent to him -- about 70 pounds. Grandson, Thomas Harrison Fowkes, 1 Negro. Grandson, Burr Harrison (son of William), 1 Negro. To son, Burr Harrison, slaves. Granddaughter, Lucy Harrison (dau. of William), Negro. Gr. dau., Ann Grayson Gibson, a Negro. Gr. son, Catlett Gibson (Jonathan Catlett Gibson), a Negro. To son, Benjamin Harrison, the old plantation that I purchased of my father on Cedar Run, also other tracts of land, large number of slaves, household furniture, at his death this property is to descend to three grandsons, Thomas Gibson, Burr Harrison (son of William) and Thomas Fowkes. To friend and nephew, Cuthbert Harrison, 25 shillings to purchase a mourning ring. To four nieces, Sith Harrison, Frances Harrison, Ann and Sarah Harrison, the sum of 20 shillings to purchase mourning rings. To sons, William, Thomas and Burr Harrison, all cattle and hogs at the Mountain, also interest in a large number of slaves. To Jonathan Gibson (son-in-law) one dark horse. Exrs: William Harrison, Benjamin Harrison (sons) and Jonathan Gibson. Wit: --- Young, John Peters, John Shumate, Sr., John Coppage. (p. 231)

OBANNON, John, Sr.
18 Nov. 1773. 28 March 1774.
Wife, Sarah Obannon, to have use and benefit of plantation where I now live during her natural life. To son William land on the east side of Pigginutt Ridge and slaves; mentions a legacy left son William by grandfather, Bryant Obannon, 189 acres of land. Son James to have a good suit of clothes. Son Thomas to have a good suit of clothes. Son Samuel to have a tract of land and slaves. Son Andrew to have a Negro, in lieu of a legacy left by grandfather Obannon. Son Joseph, to have a Negro boy, in lieu of 50 pound legacy left by grandfather. To son, Bryant, one riding horse. To son, Benjamin, new saddle and bridle. To daughter, Sarah Foley, one Negro. To daughter, Caty Nelson, one Negro. Son Bryant to have plantation at death of mother. Exrs: sons William, Samuel and John. Wit: Thomas Elliott, Benjamin Elliott, John Moffett. (p. 237)

ASH, Francis
24 Sept. 1774. 25 April 1774.
To wife, Elizabeth Ash, Negroes. To son, George Ash, 11 Negroes. To son, Francis (eldest surviving son of wife Elizabeth), land, Negroes and blacksmith tools. To daughter, Dorothy Allsup, Negroes. To daughter, Elizabeth, slaves. To son, Uriel Ash, slaves. To son, Eon, slaves. To son, Littleton Ash, slaves. To daughter, Peggy Neaoble (or Neavill), slaves. Son William and daughter Molly. Nine children mentioned. Exr: Francis Ash (son). Wit: Robert Ashley, Enoch Ashley, John Adams.

NEAVILL, George
Wife, Mary Neavill, to have use of land and slaves. Daughters, Joanna Hathaway and Judith Barrett, to have land and slaves. Sons-in-law, John Roper (or Roser), Solomon Jones, Ambrose Barrett and James Hathaway, to have mill on Cedar Run. Daughters, Lucy Calmes, Ann Blackmore, Mary Barrett, Susannah Hampton, Letty Helms, Mary Roser and Betty Jones, to receive slaves. Dau. Lucy Calmes to have 120 acres of land. Mention is made of son-in-law, Richard Hampton, a slave. Gr. daughter, Ann Helms, to have 20 pounds curr. Gr. daughters, Charlotte and Joanna Hampton, slaves. Gr. sons, George and William Jones, 20 pounds curr. Gr. son, John Barrett (son of James) 20 pounds curr. Carpenter shop to sons-in-law. Exrs: wife, John Roser, Sol Jones, James Hathaway, Ambrose Barnett. Wit: Richard Chichester, Samuel Pharis, John Shurley. (p. 250)

SNELLING, Benjamin
    8 Nov. 1773. 27 June 1774.
    To wife, Elizabeth Snelling, the use of estate during life. Son Benjamin, other children mentioned, but not named. Wit: Daniel Bradford, Alexander Bradford, Edward Humstead. (p. 253)

MINTOR, Joseph
    12 Dec. 1772. 27 June 1774.
    Wife Mary to have use of estate during her life and at her decease it is to be divided between sons John and Joseph and grandson William Mintor (son of Jacob, dec'd.) to have 25 pounds. Exrs: Joseph Chilton, William Chilton. Wit: John Chilton, Will Chilton. (p. 253)

HALL, Richard
    1 March 1774. 25 June 1774.
    All Negroes to remain on the plantation of Mrs. Hannah Corbin until my debts are paid. Mention made of land purchased of Richard and William Hampton. Children: Elisha Hall Corbin, land and Negroes, dau. Martha Corbin land and Negroes, should they die their share to go to their mother, Mrs. Hannah Corbin. Sister Mary Williamson to receive legacy, also her son, James Williamson. Nieces: Martha, Mary, Hannah and Elizabeth Williamson (daus. of sister Mary Williamson). Exr: Mrs. Hannah Corbin of Richmond Co. Exrs. in Fauquier Co.: Wharton Ransdell, James Scott, Thomas Marshall, John Chilton. (p. 257)

BLACKWELL, William
    20 Sept. 1772. 26 Sept. 1774.
    Wife, Elizabeth Blackwell, to have use of land and slaves. Son William to have use of all land that I bought of Alexander Clement, Chris Marr and Thomas Evan. Children: John, Samuel, William, Joseph, Hannah, Sarah and Lucy. Exrs: wife, sons John and William.

LAWSON, Ann Stepham (Steptoe)
    1 June 1774. 28 Nov. 1774. (p. 268)
    To brother, Epaphroditus Lawson, all my Negroes. To brother John and wife a suit of mourning. To loving uncle Joseph Blackwell and Aunt Lucy Blackwell, a suit of mourning. To Cousin Betty Chilton a suit of worked muslin, not quite finished. Cousin Judith Blackwell to have my stone ring. To cousins, Elizabeth Lawson, Ann Steptoe Lawson, Harry Lawson, Elizabeth Gibson, wearing clothes. Sister Mary Lawson to have built a brick wall around the graves of mother and father. Exr: brother Epaphroditus Lawson.

PARKER, William
    3 April 1775. 22 May 1775. (p. 273)
    Brothers, Alexander and Richard Parker. All estate to be used to maintain father and mother. At their decease the estate to be divided between brother Richard and sisters Ann and Judith Parker. Exrs: brothers Alexander and Richard Parker. Wit: James Shackleford, William Allen, William Hardiwien.

HERMONS, John
    5 April 1775. 22 May 1775.
    To son, James Hermons, 5 pounds sterling, to be educated in English school for six years, to receive 1/4 of estate when he comes of age. Wife, Mary Hermons, bequeathed land. Daughters, Mary and Susannah, to receive 3 years education in English school. Exrs: wife, John Kinchloe. Wit: John Barker, William Kinchloe, John Kinchloe. (p. 274)

FOOTE, George
    15 July 1775. 27 July 1775.
    Wife Celia to have 1/3 of estate during life. Son Richard Helm to have all land. Daughter, Hester Foote, to have 1/2 of Negroes and chattels. Unborn child to share in estate.

BRAHAN, John
    No date of will. Proven 27 Nov. 1775. (p. 282)

Wife, Lettice, to have slaves and proper part of estate. Son Thomas to have tract of land where I now live. Sons, John, William and James, to have slaves. Mention is made of a daughter, but not named. Exrs: wife and Morris Hansborough. Wit: Morris Hansborough, John Nelson, Edward Ralls.

RENNOLDS, James
2 Feb. 1776. 25 March 1776.
Wife, Margaret Rennolds, to have entire estate. Exr: wife. Wit: Edward Settle, Rosanna Settle, Absalom Iles. (p. 286)

RANSDELL, William, Sr.
3 July 1776. 29 Oct. 1776.
Wife (not named) to have estate during her life. To son, Wharton Ransdell, mansion house and plantation. Sons, Thomas and William, to have remaining part of land. Mill to be kept for use of plantation and my 3 sons upon tract of land. Should son Thomas die his part of estate to go to sons Edward and Chilton. Exrs: sons, Wharton, Thomas and William Ransdell. (p. 389)

CORNWELL, Peter
2 June 1776. 26 Aug. 1776.
Wife, Sarah Cornwell, to have use of land during life or widowhood. Daughter Mary to receive personal estate. Sons, David and Jacob, each to have a horse. Sons, Simon and Jarvice, each to have a feather bed. Exrs: wife, son Simon, Mr. William Hunton. Wit: J. Moffett, John Dugarde, Anne Cockrell. (p. 293)

SINKLEAR, John
5 Aug. 1776. Inventory.
Apprs: Hez. Turner, John Adams, John T. P. Chunn. (p. 295)

JAMES, Thomas
9 April 1772. 26 Feb. 1776.
Wife, Mary James, to enjoy 1/3 of estate during her natural life and at her decease the property is to go to my sons, George and James. Daughters: Molly, Agatha, Margaret and Elizabeth James, to receive 250 pounds of curr. money. Mention is made of land in Spottsylvania Co., house and lot in Fredericksburg purchased of Warner Washington. Exrs: Charles Bruce, Thomas Hoard, Gerrard Banks, John James (brother). Wit: James Allen, John James, William Delaney, Benjamin Cramp (Crump ?), J. H. Smith. (p. 305)

BARBEY, Thomas
24 Feb. 1777. Inventory.
Apprs: Garner Burgess, Samuel Luttrell, Matthew Neal. (p. 307)

HALL, Richard
July 1774. Inventory.
Appraisers: Zach Lewis, James Wright, Jeremiah Darnall. (p. 308)

CARVELL, Sanford
8 April 1777. 28 July 1777.
Wife, Elizabeth Carvell, during widowhood, to have jointly with Silvester Welch the plantation on which I now live. Children: Anna, Dempsey, Porter and Sally Carvell. Exrs: wife and Capt. John Obannon. Wit: Thomas Bartlett, Silvester Welch, James Bartlett. (p. 308)

OBANNON, George
Date of probate 25 Aug. 1777. (This will was in form of a letter and probated.)
"Dear Mother and Brothers: I write to let you know that I am in good health, thanks to God for it, hoping this will find you all in health. Remember me to all my friends, not forgetting Cuzzen Elizabeth Carle - remember - my love to her. I don't expect I shall write any more and this is to let you know that we have been in no battle yet, but we are expecting it every day and night. We are on an island about fifteen miles long and two or three miles wide, and the innamy is all around the iland and we have no way to get off, we must fit our way off. Our men are fighting every day and night. The other night there

was a battle at King's Bridge where the town is on the iland. I am in grate hopes I shall see you all again but we expect a battle every day. I am in hopes the town will be burnt in a few days -- the English would have burnt it before this time, but they want it for barracks, but if they don't burn the town we shall. Now (no) more at present but your dutiful son, George Bannon." (Oath of James Foley as to writing) (p. 311)

DODSON, Greenhane
    8 Oct. 1776. 25 Aug. 1777.
    To brother, Enoch Dodson, several slaves. To sister, Tabitha Shumate, 1 Negro. To sister, Mary Shumate, 15 pounds curr. Estate to mother, Barbarby Dodson. Exrs: William Hunton, Daniel Shumate. Wit: Johnson Owens, Ajah Shirley. (p. 312)

METCALFE, Christopher
    March Court, 1777. Inventory.
    Apprs: James Murray, John Fields, Uriel Crosby. (p. 316)

WOOD, Samuel
    May Court, 1777. Inventory.
    Apprs: Champ Caram, Thomas Railey, James Luttrell. (p. 317)

CHILTON, John
    24 Aug. 1776. 24 Nov. 1777.
    Land purchased of Debutts to be sold and the money divided among the children they of age: Joseph, Lucy, George and Nancy. Executors to give children such education as the estate will afford. To son, Thomas, land given me by my father where I have lately lived. Exrs: Charles Chilton, Major Martin Pickett, Thomas Keith. Wit: Samuel Boyd, John Blackwell, John Ashby, Jr., Isham Keith, Joseph Blackwell, Jr. (p. 320)

BULLITT, Thomas
    17 Sept. 1775. 25 Feb. 1778.
    Executor to build a house for brother Joseph on land where he now lives. And that executor shall carry into execution an agreement made and entered into by me with Cuthbert Combs relative to sundry lands upon Kankawa River at the mouth of the Elk. To Sarah Bronaunt, 400 acres of land and slaves. To Sarah Bronaunt, natural daughter of Martha Bronaunt, a young Negro wench. To sister, Sith Combs, 15 pounds to purchase a mourning ring. To Mr. Benjamin Harrison, 2 colts. To Cuthbert Combs, a horse. Rest of estate to brother, Cuthbert Bullitt, who is also named as executor. Wit: William Blauset, John Blauset, Charles Grey. (p. 321)

MINTER, John
    Wife Mary to have 1/3 of estate during life or widowhood. After decease of wife estate to be divided between children, William, Elizabeth and Jacob. Son Anthony to have a tract of land left me by my father, Joseph Minter, also to have worm and still and a good country education. Daughter Elizabeth to be raised by sister Rogers. Exrs: Charles Chilton, Joseph Minter, George Rogers. Wit: George Rogers, Mary Baley, William Tomlin. (p. 322)

ETHERINGTON, Elizabeth
    29 Nov. 1776. 23 March 1778.
    To Cathering Nelson, 1 feather bed and personal property. All "Waring cloathes" to be equally divided between Catherine Nelson and Betty Allen and Catherine Duncan. To Benjamin Russell, 1 bed and personal property. To nephew, Thomas Obannon, son of Samuel and Stelle, 1 tam... (illegible) for use during life and Capt. John Wright to have use of same for life. Nephew Thomas to have slaves. Exrs: Elias Edmonds, Sr., Jeremiah Darnall. Wit: Henry Bramlett, Berryman Jennings, James Wright. (p. 323)

SHIPP, John
    19 Feb. 1778. 23 March 1778.
    Slaves are bequeathed to daus. Sukey Drummon, Polly Shipp, Nancy Shipp. Sons to receive slaves: Richard Wiatt Shipp, Laban and Colby Shipp. Exrs:

sons Laban and Richard Shipp. Wit: Thomas Lewis, Thomas James, William Donaldson. (p. 324)

CATLETT, John
    3 Feb. 1778. 28 March 1778.
    To son, John Catlett, 1 shilling. To son, William Catlett, the plantation where I now live - containing 179 acres. To daughter, Elizabeth Catlett, 2 white boys until they arrive at the age of 21 years, which boys were purchased for me with their father and mother of Mr. Hector Ross and the Indenture taken in the name of Alexander Catlett. To daughter, Jane Coppage, personalty. To granddaughter, Margaret Hume, weaving loom and gear belonging to old loom. To daughter, Bersheba Young, "Furniture and Bed I now ly on." Remainder of moveable estate to be divided between Mary Ann Hogan, Elizabeth Catlett, Jane Coppage, Bersheba Young, Isabbell Summers and Frances Priest. Exrs: Moses Coppage, John Hogan. Wit: James Holmes, James Dowdall, Original Young, William Pope. (p. 326)

BRONAUGH, John
    1 July 1777. 25 March 1778. Overwharton Parish, Stafford County.
    To beloved wife, Mary Ann, slaves and all estate, provided that she does not remarry. To son William, a tract of land in Prince William Co., where lives John Delgram, William Davis, Meredith Moss. To son John, 500 acres in Loudon Co. Daughter, Margaret Bronaugh, to have slaves. Dau. Mary Mason Bronaugh bequeathed slaves. A tract of land lying in Fairfax Co., bequeathed me by my mother, Sympha Rosenfield Bronaugh, to be sold. Exrs: wife and brother William Bronaugh. (p. 327)

DONALDSON, Stephen
    8 Aug. 1777. Inventory.
    Apprs: Painick George, Benjamin Robinson, William Roach. (p. 329)

DUGARD, John
    25 May 1778. Inventory.
    Apprs: William Norris, Rowley Smith, Joseph Taylor. (p. 331)

JAMES, John
    6 Nov. 1777. 25 May 1778. Hamilton Parish, Pauquier County.
    "Being sick and weak in body." To son, Thomas James, all that tract of land lying on the eastermost side of Spring Branch, which land came by his mother, as this is a small quantity of acres of land which came by her on the other side of Spring branch, I give to son Thomas in lieu of other land. His mother's land was 500 acres as a whole. Son Thomas not to possess the land until decease of mother. To son, Benjamin, plantation where I now live, after decease of mother. To son, James, a tract of land and slaves. To daughter, Susannah James, a horse and bridle, personalty. To granddaughter, Hannah Finnie, bed & furniture, cow & calf. To grandson, Benjamin James, horse and bridle, furniture, etc. To wife, Dinah James, residue of estate during widowhood, all land not bequeathed to children. Daughters: Sarah Hitt, Ann Tullis, Hannah Humes, Elizabeth Bradford, Mary Conway, Dinah Thompson, Susannah James. Exrs: wife and sons, Thomas, Benjamin, John James. Wit: William Grant, John Kerr, Jonathan (?) Markham, Marmaduke Brown. (p. 332)

MARR, Mary
    4 June 1776. Inventory. (p. 334)

LEWIS, Sarah
    4 Feb. 1778. 22 June 1778. Of Loudon Co., Va.
    To daughter, Silby West, 1 mourning ring. To daughter, Sarah Manly, 1 mourning ring. Rest of estate to daughter, Mary Peake, during her life, at her decease to her children. Exr: John Peake (son-in-law) Wit: William Whitely, Cleater Smith. (p. 336)

RUST, John
    22 June 1778. Inventory.

Apprs: Thomas Nelson, Benjamin Rector, Joseph Robinson. (p. 337)

CORNWELL, Peter
    22 June 1778. Inventory.
    Apprs: Thomas Maddux, Thomas Watts, George Kennard. (p. 338)

FOOTE, George (Gentleman)
    22 June 1778. Inventory.
    Apprs: Benjamin Harrison, John James, Jonathan Gibson. (p. 340)

WINN, Minor
    30 July 1775. 23 March 1778.
    To son, William Winn, a slave. To granddaughter, Martha Smith, a slave. To son, James Winn, a slave. To son, Minor Winn, my Great Big Bible, personalty, etc. To son, Richard Winn, slaves. To daughter, Margaret Johnson, slaves. To daughter, Mary Smith, slaves. To daughter, Susan Grant, slave. Forty pounds to be divided between children of daughter, Elizabeth Smith. Exrs: wife Margaret Winn, son Minor Winn. Wit: Stephen Tolle, Thomas White, James Fleming. (p. 343)

JENNINGS, Augustine
    13 Dec. 1776. 24 Aug. 1778. Of Hamilton Parish.
    Wife, Hannah Jennings, to have plantation during life. Son, William Jennings, to have 200 acres of land and all goods and chattells that he has received. The following named sons are to receive land and slaves: Benjamin, Baylor, George, Berryman, Lewis and Augustin. Daughter, Betty Jennings, to have 40 pounds curr. money. To daughter, Hannah, slaves. To daughter, Sally, 2 slaves. To daughter, Jemina Hudnall, all estate that she has received. To daughter, Nancy Weathers, 1 slave and 10 pounds curr. To daughter, Cloe Weather, 1 slave. Exrs: sons, Augustin and William Jennings. Wit: Henry Bramlett, Peter Barker, Lucretia Russell. (p. 348)

LUTTRELL, Michael
    16 March 1776. 24 Aug. 1778.
    To daughter, Franklin McKenzey, large pot. To dau. Hannah Luttrell, 1 bed & furniture. To son Abner, 1 sorrel horse. To daughter Lydia, 1 bed & furniture. To son Michael, 1 pair of stillards. To son Nathan, a Bell metal skillet. To daughter, Dinah Luttrell, 30 weight of feathers. To son Nathan, a Bell metal skillet. To son Richard, 1 hand saw. To daughter Sarah, 1 large and 1 small Pewter Basons. To daughter Dolly, black walnut chest. To son Lot, 120 acres of land. To daughter Mary, 1 sugar bowl. To daughter Betty, my trunk. To wife, Dinah Luttrell, all moveable estate to be by her possessed and enjoyed during her natural life and then divided among all my children. Exrs: wife, Richard Luttrell, John Luttrell. Wit: John Combs, Richard Coram, Robert Luttrell. (p. 351)

WEBB, John
    24 Aug. 1778. Inventory.
    Admrtx: Mrs. Judith Webb. Apprs: John Adams, Thomas Chunn, John Ashby.

WEBB, John
    4 Feb. 1777. 23 May 1778.
    Wife, Judith Webb, to have land and slaves during her life. Sons, John and William, to have slaves. Slaves to daughter, Priscilla Webb. A tract of land in Northumberland Co. bequeathed to wife. Exrs: wife, William Ballard, William Miskell, John Keith. Wit: John Keith, James Keys. (p. 355)

KENNER, Howson
    9 April 1778. 28 Sept. 1778.
    To eldest son, Francis Kenner, all money in hands of my son-in-law, William Seaton, but 40 pounds, the balance of the money said Seaton owes me (210 pounds) for the 250 acres of land (250 acres) which I sold to him. To daughter, Betty Seaton, 20 pounds. To daughter, Rebecca Clifton, 10 pounds, no more. To daughter, Mary Seaton, 10 pounds, no more. To son, George Turville Kenner, a tract of land and slaves. To grandson, Rodham Kenner

(son of George) a tract of land. To daughter, Peggy and husband, Stephen Prichard, a slave & 20 pounds. To grandson, Howson Kenner, (son of Francis) 20 pounds. To son, Rodham, tract of land that I now live on and 20 pounds curr. Grandson, George Seaton, 10 pounds, no more. To daughter, Catey Markham and her daughter Mary Ann, slaves and live stock. Gr. son, Samuel Eskridge, alias Kenner, son of dau. Susannah, 2 slaves and 100 pounds cash with which to educate him. Exrs: Mr. Joseph Blackwell and daughter Susannah. Wit: Original Young, William Pope. (p. 358)

HAMBUCKS, James
23 Nov. 1778. Inventory.
Apprs: John Morehead, Peter Laurance, John Southard. (p. 361)

STROTHERS, James, Sr.
28 Sept. 1778. Inventory.
Apprs: William Kinchloe, Harman Hitt, John Hathaway. (p. 361)

ELLIS, John
3 Dec. 1778. 22 Feb. 1779. Parish of Leeds, Fauquier County.
To daughter, Ann Ellis, household goods. To son, Jonathan Ellis, 8 hogs. Rest of estate to my 2 youngest sons, Owen and William Ellis. Exr: son Jonathan Ellis. Wit: Berry Neale, John Robertson, James Robertson. (p. 368)

MARTIN, Tilman
23 May 1778. 26 July 1779.
"Sick and Weak." To wife, Elizabeth Martin, live stock and land, which she may sell when she thinks proper and money to be used to purchase another place, which place is to be for my son, Tilman Martin, should he die it is to go to youngest son (unnamed). To daughter, Elinor Martin, mare colt, etc. Exrs: wife, son Elijah Darnall. Wit: Jeremiah Darnall, Thomas Parker, John Parker. (p. 377)

PRICE, Bennett
9 July 1774. 24 Oct. 1774. Parish of Hamilton. (p. 378)
To loving wife, Judith Price, lands. Daughters: Elizabeth, Ann, Judith. Exrs: wife, Martin Pickett, William Edmonds, Armistead Churchill. Wit: Martin Pickett, Joseph Blackwell, Jr., Samuel Blackwell, Jr., Ann Pickett.

GEORGE, Nicholas
24 June 1779. 27 Sept. 1779. (p. 380)
Wife, Margaret George, to have estate during her life, at her decease it is to be divided among following named children: Nicholas George (eldest son) to have slaves. Son William, slaves. To son, Joseph, livestock and slaves. Daughters, Elizabeth, Lydia and Wilmouth to receive slaves. Exrs: wife, sons Joseph and William George. Wit: John Nelson, Thomas Tidler (?).

BAILEY, John
8 Sept. 1778. 27 Sept. 1779.
To son, Wright Bailey, land and personal estate. Exrs: Charles Morehead, Thomas Morehead. Wit: Charles Turner, Mary Morehead. (p. 381)

BEACH, Peter
2 April 1777. 25 Oct. 1779.
To son, John Beach, a tract of land. To grandson, John Baker, a tract of land in Fincastle Co. (Va.). Daughters, Mary, Sarah, Lettice, Ann Beach to have 30 pounds cash, live stock and slaves. Exrs: Samuel Baker (son-in-law), William Butler. Wit: Peter Conway, William Butler. (p. 383)

SOUTHARD, Francis
20 Oct. 1779. 22 Nov. 1779.
To wife, Elizabeth Southard, a tract of land during her life, at her decease to son Levi. To son William, feather bed and furniture. To son, George, a mare. To daughter, Sarah Dodds, 3 sheep. To daughter, Jemina, feather bed & furniture. Exrs: wife and James Duff. (p. 384)

SCOTT, James
    2 Jan. 1779. 22 Nov. 1779. Of Parish of Leeds.
    To wife, Elizabeth Scott, whole of estate during widowhood; mentions land in Prince William County and on the Ohio river. Daughters: Sarah, Frances, Elizabeth and Nancy Scott. Sons: Alexander, James, Cuthbert and Thomas Scott. Exrs: wife, Cuthbert Bullitt, Cuthbert Harrison. Wit: James Stewart, Samuel Boyd, William Stewart. (p. 385)

SIAS, John
    6 Sept. 1773. 22 Sept. 1779.
    Wife to have full maintenance out of estate. Daughter, Mary Hamrick, to have 5 pounds curr. money. To Thomas Chapman, land and slaves. Exrs: Thomas Chapman, William Carr. Wit: James Marshall, James Guthrie, John Tebbs. (p. 386)

BARHAN, Peter
    6 Nov. 1779. 27 March 1780. (p. 387)
    To wife, Celia Barhan, whole estate during widowhood, should she remarry to have 1/3 of estate. To son, Peter Barhan, slaves and land in Fauquier Co. Children: Molly, Rawleigh Chinn, Elijah, Betsy and Sukey Barhan. Exrs: wife, Charles Chilton. Wit: John Norris, Joseph Taylor, John Coppedge.

FOOTE, Richard
    24 Feb. 1779. 24 April 1780. Of Stafford County.
    To brother, William Foote, whole of estate. Wit: William Lawerence, Lawerence Washington. (p. 389)

TOLLE, Roger
    2 Feb. 1778. 22 May 1780.
    Wife, Sarry Tolle. To sons, Roger and George, 5 pounds each. To granddaughter, Susannah (dau. of Jonathan), 5 pounds cash. Children: Jonathan, Ann Squires, Roger, James and Stephen. Exrs: wife, sons Roger and Stephen Tolle. Wit: Edward Turner, Mary Turner, Elizabeth Grogan. (p. 390)

ARNOLD, John
    7 Sept. 1771. 22 May 1780.
    To son Benjamin, 100 acres - where I now live. Wife to have stock and household goods. Admr: Benjamin Arnold. Wit: William Settle, Edward Settle, John Edwards. (p. 391)

PEAKES, John
    8 June 1779. 22 May 1780. Of Hamilton Parish.
    To wife, Mary Peake, all property to dispose of at her discretion. To daughters, Sally, Mary, Elizabeth Peake, slaves. To son, Thomas Peake, slaves. Exr: wife. Wit: John Carvell, Judith Carvell.

FEAGIN, Edward
    8 July 1778. 24 July 1780.
    To wife, Elizabeth Feagin, to have estate for life, at her decease to be divided among my nine children: John, Edward, William, Elizabeth, Sarah, Susannah, Cleary, Mary and Frances. Wit: Evan Griffith, James Thomson Clark, Charles Chadduck. (p. 398)

KIRK, William
    1 May 1779. 27 Nov. 1780.
    Sould he die without children, the estate to be sold and money sent to relatives in Scotland, John McIoar, James McIoar, Mary McIoar and Elizabeth McIoar, children of John McIoar and Sarah Kirke. To wife, Elizabeth Kirk, 1/2 personal estate and slaves. Exrs: David Allison, William Allison, Gavin Lawson (of Culpepper Co.). Wit: William Pickett, James Bell, John Peake, Jr., Charles Morehead, Presley Morehead, William Hinton. (p. 409)

ELLIOTT, Reuben
    29 July 1779. 27 Nov. 1780.
    Wife, Ruth Elliott, to have possession of estate to keep younger children.

William Cundiffe alias Elliott, 100 acres of land and wearing apparel. To son, Reuben Elliott, slaves and personal property. To son, Thomas Elliott, slaves and personal property. Children: Reuben, Thomas, Anne Roberson, Elizabeth, Mildred, Jemina and Molly Elliott. Exrs: wife, with her son, William Cundiffe - Elliott and John Obannon. Wit: John Hathaway, William Peake, John Barker, Daniel Morrison. (p. 410)

PRIEST, William
5 March 1781. 28 May 1781.
To wife, Eveles (?) Priest, and Samuel Priest, 5 pounds of curr. to be divided between them. To brother, John Priest, bed, bed stead, furniture, all woolen clothes, all linen clothes, except 7 yards of linen I leave to my loving mother, Sarry Priest. To "loving" brother, Thomas Priest, a slave. To sister, Sary Murry (?), chest, chairs, what pewter I have. To brother, George Priest, 34 bushels of corn. To brother, Richard Priest, a cow. To sister, Elizabeth Stark, 1 horse, all cash I have and 544 pounds of tobacco. Exrs: Thomas Priest (brother), James Stark. Wit: James Peters, James Darnall, James Stark. (p. 415)

ADAMS, John
14 Jan. 1780. 28 May 1781.
"Weak of body." To son John, all land in Maryland. To son, George, land on which I now live. To daughter, Elizabeth, 300 acres of land where she now lives. To dau. Susannah, 300 acres of land where James Hume now lives. To son, Josias, all land I purchased of Capt. Turner. To wife, Sarah Stacy, to have remainder for life or widowhood. Wit: Hezekiah Turner, John Hickman, John Chunn, Will Bailes (Bailes). (p. 416)

COMBS, John, Jr.
7 Oct. 1780. 28 May 1781. Nuncupative Will.
Estate to be divided between 2 sons and 4 daughters - Nimrod Combs, alias Luttrell; John Combs; Nannie Combs, alias Luttrell; Hetheland Combs, alias Luttrell; Betty Combs; Heland Combs, alias Luttrell; Sarah Combs. Proven by oath of Original Young and Evis Combs. (p. 416)

FOWKES, Gerrard
26 July 1781. Division of estate. (p. 419)

GRIGSBY, Samuel
11 May 1781. 22 Oct. 1781. Parish of Leeds.
To wife, Ann Grigsby, estate during her widowhood. Should she remarry estate to be sold and divided among the children. Mentions mother, Mrs. Dade, of Prince George Co., Va. Exrs: Henry Peyton, William Grigsby, James Grigsby. Wit: John Scott, John Fishback, Peter Tait. (p. 420)

PETERS, John
4 Oct. 1781. -----.
To wife (unnamed) to have dwelling house, land and slaves, during widowhood. To son, John Peters, land and slaves. To sons, Nimrod and James Peters, parcel of land in Stafford Co. that I purchased of James Peters - 413 acres and slaves. Nimrod to have 1/6 part of my land in Caintucky. Son, James Peters, part of land in Caintucky and slaves. To my two sons, Lewis and William, land on which I now live, after decease of my wife. Daughters, Nancy, Sarah, Betty, a slave each. Exrs: wife, John Ashby, John Peters, Joseph Combs, Cuthbert Combs. (p. 423)

BROWN, Charles
22 Oct. 1781. Inventory. (p. 422)

STEWART, James
26 May 1781. 22 Oct. 1781. Hamilton Parish.
To wife, the moiety of a tract of land that I purchased of Richard Grubbs, wheron my son John now lives, to have during her natural life, at her decease to son John. "Beloved" wife to have 2 cows, 2 ewes, 2 sows with pigs, feather bed, dishes and choice of horses. To son Allen, a Negro lad named

Solomon, feather bed, cow & calf. To son, William, 14 pounds in gold or silver. To son, James, 10 pounds in gold or silver. Son Charles has been provided for and he is not to possess any more of my estate. After my decease certain negroes are to be sold and all remainder of my estate, except what has been given or lent my wife, out of which above mentioned legacies to sons William and James are to be paid, remainder to daughters, Mary, Betty, Jane and Helen. All articles lent wife to be sold at her decease and divided between daughters. Exrs: wife, son James and James Hathaway. Wit: William Metcalfe, Betsy Metcalfe, Sarah Elliott. (Name of wife not given in will, but it was Jane Stewart.) (p. 424)

FOWKES, Elizabeth
20 June 1781. 22 Oct. 1781. (p. 426)
To son, George Fowkes, a tract of land and slaves, should he die land to go to son William Fowkes. Daughters, Mary and Enfiets (?) shall be in possession of dwelling house while they are single. All slaves to be divided among all children. Children: William, Mary, Chandler, Enfiets (?), George, Elizabeth Phillips. Wit: Willy Roy, William Wright, Joshua Butler, Joseph Morgan.

RECTOR, Henry
2 April 1781. 26 Nov. 1781.
Wife mentioned, but not named. To son, William Rector, land that Capt. William Smith now lives on. To son, John Rector, slaves, tract of land and part of moveable estate. To son, Enoch Rector, slave and 150 acres of land. Exrs: Benjamin Rector (brother), Frederick Rector. Wit: Harman Rector, Jr., Harman Rector, Sr., Henry Utterback. (p. 427)

SETTLE, William
5 Feb. 1782. 25 March 1782.
To wife, Sarah, estate during widowhood, afterwards to be divided between sons, Edward, Pope Williams, William Freeman. To daughter, Elizabeth Settle, 100 acres of land, household goods and slaves. To son, William Freeman, 100 acres of land. To son, Edward, 550 acres of land. Exrs: sons Edward and William Freeman. Wit: John Spillman, Nancy Settle, Henry Settle, Francis Sudduth, Benjamin Arnold. (p. 428)

JACKMAN, Thomas
15 March 1776. 25 March 1782.
To son, Thomas, 130 acres of land, he is to pay Betty Stone 50 shillings for it. To son, Richard, 130 acres of Pigmit Bridge tract, he is to pay my daughter, Sarah Neavill, 50 shillings for it. To son, Adam, old plantation, he is to pay Maragret Underwood 50 shillings for it. To son, William, 100 acres where he now lives. To son, Joseph -----. Daughters, Rebecca Smith and Hannah Smith, a slave each. Exrs: Thomas, Richard, Adam Jackman (sons). Wit: Thomas James, John Johnson, Henry Moffett, Jr. (p. 430)

NEWELL, Benjamin
2 Oct. 1780. 25 March 1782.
Legatees: Ann Wheatley, Leannah Wheatley, Sarah Wheatley (all of Fauquier Co.), each to have a gold ring of 20 shillings valuation. To beloved John Newell (son of bro. Richard), 400 pounds of curr. money. To sister Nancy Newell, balance of estate. Wit: Samuel Holiday, James Dobie. (p. 432)

HOLTON, Alexander
5 March 1782. 25 March 1782.
Wife, Elizabeth Holton. Exr: son William. Wit: John Monroe, Lewis Woodyard, Henry Ford. (p. 433)

MILLARD, William
4 Jan. 1782. 25 March 1782.
Land to wife (not named), should she remarry all estate to Thomas Cummings. Thomas Cummings to have all wearing apparel. Legatees: Ann Sudduth, wife of John Sudduth. Exrs: wife, James Thompson, Original Young. Wit: Richard Coram, Champ Coram, John Cummings. (p. 433)

SMITH, Mathew
   25 Nov. 1781. 25 March 1782.
   Wife, Martha Smith, to have use of estate during widowhood. To son, William Smith, a gun. To sons, Joseph and James, a horse each. Exrs: wife, James Smith (brother), Minor Winn. Wit: Thomas Smith, Joseph Smith, James Key. (p. 434)

COOK, Littleton
   28 Feb. 1782. 22 April 1782.
   To brother Giles Cook, horse and bridle and 1/2 of clothes. To brother, Thomas Cook, remainder of estate. Exrs: Richard Willis. Wit: Francis Whiting, Betty Whiting. (p. 437)

ROBINSON, Joseph
   21 May 1782. 22 July 1782.
   Wife, Martha, to have land and slaves during widowhood, at her decease estate to be equally divided among all children. Children: Maxmillian, John, William, Dorcas Murry, Hannah Kinchloe, Catherine Robinson, Peggy Robinson, Molly Robinson. To grandson, Maxmillian, 10 pounds curr. money. To gr. daughter, Hannah Robinson, 10 pounds curr. To gr. daughter, Lucy Robinson, 10 pounds curr. (The last 3 mentioned grandchildren were children of Berryman Robinson, dec'd). Exrs: wife and son John. Wit: John Barker, Joseph Robinson, Jesse Robinson, James Wright. (p. 445)

LUNCEFORD, George
   21 July 1781. Inventory.
   Apprs: Charles Morehead, Turner Morehead, Moses Bailey. (p. 446)

HULETT, Leroy
   28 Aug. 1782. Inventory.
   Wit: Thomas Payne, Josias Bayse, B. Piper.

BLAND, Mary
   3 Aug. 1782. 28 Oct. 1782. (p. 450)
   To son, Charles Bland, a tract of land I bought of William Sanford Pickett. To son, Jacky Bland (youngest son), a slave. To daughter, Betty Bland (youngest dau.), a slave. Eldest son, James Bland. Eldest daughter, Esther Bland, to have 1 shilling. To daughters, Peggy Mcoboy, Chloe Pitcher, Amelia Brady, a shilling each. Exrs: Charles Metcalfe, John Munney.

SEATON, William
   8 May 1782. -----.
   Each daughter at marriage to receive from their mother, household goods. Sons: James and William Seaton. Exrs: wife, Rodham Kenner, William Conway. Wit: George Marshall, Robert Kenner, George Turberville, David Wickliffe. (p. 452)

FIELDS, Daniel
   27 July 1777. 24 March 1783.
   To sons, George, Lewis, John and Fieldon Fields, slaves. Wife's dower to be divided among surviving children. Daughters: Ann, Hannah, Sarah, Elizabeth, Mary and Milly. Granddaughter, Charlotte Haddocks. Exrs: friend Daniel Fields, of Culpepper County. (p. 458)

FURR, Thomas
   20 July 1777. 25 March 1783.
   Thomas Furr alias Johnson. To loving wife, Elizabeth Furr, horse, saddle and furniture. To Benjamin Williams, horse, saddle and bridle. To Thomas Cummings (cousin) 10 pounds curr. To Thomas Fever (?), son of Moses, 10 pounds curr. Exrs: wife, Thomas Cummings. Wit: W. Waller, Ann Conway, William Smith, Ann McChosney. (p. 460)

BALL, William, Capt.
   10 Nov. 1772. Inventory. (p. 467)

JOHNSON, Jeffrey
    11 June 1782. 26 May 1783.
    Son, Alexander, to have tract of land. To wife, Sarah, land and rest of estate for life. Sons, Bailey, Alexander, James and Presley. Son Presley to have a tract of land. Daughters: Mary Cockrell, Elizabeth Morris, Sarah Johnson, Elizabeth Johnson. Exrs: sons Bailey and Alexander. Wit: Anderson Cockrell, Jesse Moffett, John Monroe. (p. 469)

ROPER, John
    6 April 1783. 23 June 1783. (p. 473)
    Sons, Richard and John to have land in Rappahannock Co., Sons John and William to have land where I now live. Daughters: Nancy, Sarah, Sukey, Violet, Letty, Winny, Sally, Elizabeth have received their share of estate.

MADDUX, Thomas
    15 Oct. 1782. 23 June 1783.
    To wife, Margaret, all personal estate, tract of land in Prince William Co., containing 260 acres. Daughter, Easter Sally Maddux, horse & saddle. Daughter, Fanny, to have furniture. Daughter, Darkes Jones, to have furniture. One shillings each to following named sons; Thomas, Mathew (or Martin), Lazarus, William, Nathaniel and Jethrofield. Exrs: wife and son Lazarus. (p. 476)

MURRY, James
    29 March 1783. 28 July 1783.
    Wife, Lydia, to have use of land during life. Land to son Ralph and John Seaton (son-in-law). Exrs: sons, Ralph, John, Reuben. Wit: John Butler, Nathan Cockran, Daniel French.

BRADFORD, Mary
    6 July 1775. July 1783.
    To daughter, Sarah Rose, saddle. Wearing apparel to be divided among three daughters. Granddau. Ann Fowler. Exrs: sons Alexander and Benjamin Bradford. (p. 480)

MAUZY, John
    20 Feb. 1764. 26 July 1764. (p. 83)
    To loving wife, Betty, 7 slaves and land where I now live, during widowhood. Daughter, Peggy, to have slaves. Should above heirs die then estate to go to daughter, Margaret. To dau. Molly, 226 acres of land in Culpepper Co.; 300 acres of land 15 miles from Winchester, slaves, my property for which I have sued Jonathan Perkins for in chancery, at my death suit is to be renewed. To daughter, Betty, 163 acres of land which I purchased of Robert Jackson in Frederick Co. and 198 acres in Hampshire Co. Mentions nephews, John, Henry and William Rousan. Exrs: wife, Henry Mauzy (brother), Peter Mauzy and William Rousan. Wit: Thomas Conway, John Edge, John Luttrell.

HARRILL, John
    25 Feb. 1764. Administrator Account. (p. 80)

GLASSCOCK, John
    8 March 1765. 22 April 1765.
    Wife, Mary Glasscock, to have 1/2 of my estate whether "Riall or Persoal." Daughter, Frances Glasscock, to have other 1/2 of estate. Exrs: wife Mary and Thomas Glasscock to be my "hole and Soul" executors in this my last Will and Testament. (p. 87)

FRAZIER, Daniel
    28 May 1765. 26 Aug. 1765.
    Legatee: "To Samuel Anderson, Joiner, my chest that is at Reuben Berry's, and all that is in it, after funeral expenses are paid. Remainder of estate to Catherine Thatcher, if she is living, if deceased to Charles Haynes' eldest son. Mary Bradford is to keep my mare until August next and then deliver to Catherine Thatcher." Exrs: Charles Haynes. Wit: Daniel Bradford, Joseph Morgan, Alexander Bradford. (p. 91)

PEARCE (Pierce), Peter
    6 Feb. 1768. 27 June 1768.
    To son, John, one slave. Daughters, Rosannah and Susannah Pearce. Wife, Lelia Pearce, to have land I purchased of William Waugh. Exrs: brothers John and Jacob Pearce. Wit: James Craig, Joseph Morgan, Elizabeth Maorgan. (p. 130)

LEES, Mary
    29 Oct. 1767. Inventory.
    Apprs: John Blackwell, Thomas Bronaugh, James Arnold. (p. 131)

RENNOLDS, John
    21 Jan. 1769. Inventory.
    Apprs: Thomas Marshall, John Keith, William Seaton. (p. 141)

OWENS, Jeremiah
    26 Nov. 1772. 23 Oct. 1773.
    Wife, Jane Owens. Young son, Jeremiah Owens, to have slaves. Other children mentioned, but not named. Wit: Evan Griffith, William Berry, John Kenton. (p. 261)

CHAMLAYNE, James
    26 Oct. 1775. Inventory.
    Apprs: Joseph Blackerby, John Metcalfe, George Sullivan. (p. 279)

## WILL BOOK NUMBER 2  1783-1796

FIELDING, Edwin
    11 Jan. 1781. 22 Sept. 1783.
    Wife, Nancy, to have 1/2 of Negroes, stock and household goods. Sister, Elizabeth Reaves, to have other half of estate. Exrs: wife and Joseph Taylor. Wit: John James, Jeremiah Morgan, Henry Bradford, Elizabeth Bradford. (p. 4)

MOREHEAD, Charles
    19 Jan. 1783. 27 Oct. 1783. Parish of Leeds. (p. 6)
    Son, Turner Morehead, to have tract of land and 50 pounds of Virginia curr. Daughter, Jenny Ransdell, to have tract of land and household goods. Daughter, Karenhappach Morehead, to have 80 pounds of Virginia curr. Sons, Armistead, James, Pressley, to have land. To daughter, Elizabeth Morehead, slaves, horse and saddle. Wife, Mary Morehead, to have slaves during her life time. To Ann Butler, for extraordinary service done, 5 pounds Virginia curr. Exrs: wife, Charles Chilton, sons Turner and Charles Morehead.

KELLY, John
    3 Sept. 1783.
    204 acres of land to be divided between Joseph Kelley and Joseph Henry, if Joseph Kelly does not return land to Joseph Henry's "eairs." Wit: Edmond Holmes, Thomas Kelly, Mikel Glass. (p. 8)

JONES, John
    28 Oct. 1783. Inventory.
    Apprs: Peter Grant, John Ashby, John Shumate. (p. 9)

BATTALEY, Ann
    12 May 1780. 24 Nov. 1783.
    To daughter, Hannah Battaley and son Fielding Battaley, all household goods, stock and all my part of my father's estate and 50 pounds that Col. Francis Tallaferrio left me in his will. Exrs: dau. Hannah Battaley, Maxmillian Berryman, Battaley Bryan. (p. 10)

GARNER, Daniel
    24 Nov. 1783. Inventory.
    Apprs: Aaron Fletcher, James Withers, Benjamin Garner. (p. 11)

WITHERS, James
9 Jan. 1784. 26 Jan. 1784.
To son, George Washington Withers (youngest son), 573 acres, slaves, furniture and gun. To eldest son, James, a slave. To daughter, Nancy Duncan, a slave. To son, John, 1 slave. To granddaughter, Betty McKay (dau. of Isaac & Betty), a slave. Wife, Jemina. Children: James, William, John, Hannah Pickett, Nancy Duncan, Betty Jennings. Exrs: Sons James and William, friend John Wigginton. Wit: William Harris, Sabbatiah Isarel, John Wigginton. (p. 12)

DODD, Nathaniel
9 May 1783. 24 May 1784.
To daughter, Mildred Pinkard, slave. To children of daughter Sarah Garner, 20 pounds of curr. To son, Allen Dodd, a slave. Daughter Hannah Hammit, to have 20 pounds of curr. Virginia money. Daughter Elizabeth to receive 20 pounds. (Elizabeth Williamson) To daughter, Mary Wheatley, 1 slave. A slave to each of following named sons: John, Benjamin and James. To wife, Sarah Dodd, part of estate during life. Exrs: wife, sons James and Nathaniel. Wit: Daniel Marr, Martha Allen, Paul Williams (Or Williamson). (p. 24)

GLASSCOCK, John
9 Dec. 1780. 28 June 1784.
Wife, mentioned, but not named. Son Thomas to have 100 pounds of tobacco - he has received land. To son, Hezekiah, a slave. To son, George, a horse. To daughter, Mary Rector, a pewter dish. To daughter, Margaret Turley, furniture & bed. Francis Jackson (son-in-law) to have what Mr. William Brent owes me. To son, John, 180 acres of land. Exrs: wife and son John. Wit: James Thompson, John Fishback, Philip Fishback. (p. 25)

EDMONDS, Elias
30 Oct. 1782. 28 June 1784.
All of estate to wife, Elizabeth Edmonds, at her decease to son Elias. Daughters, Ann Hubbard, Judith Buckner, Elizabeth Bruin, to have all moveable estate now in their possession. Exr: son Elias Edmonds. Wit: Jacob Holtzclaw, John Hendley, William Jenkins, John Barker. (p. 27)

MITCHELL, John
26 June 1784. Inventory.
Apprs: James Crockett, Frederick Burnett, John Kemper. (p. 32)

CONWAY, Thomas
25 Aug. 1784. 27 Sept. 1784.
To eldest son, William, slave. To son, Thomas, a tract of land on Town Run. To son, Peter, part of tract of land where I now live; remaining part to son Joseph. To son, Henry, tract of land in Shenandoah Co. To daughter, Susannah Crosby, 5 pounds currency. Grandson, James Conway (son of James), a slave. Grandson, George Crosby, a slave. To Sally Mauzy, a slave. Exrs: sons William, Thomas, Joseph. Wit: Peter Grant, John Smith, Ann Smith. (p. 39)

NEALE, Joseph
6 Nov. 1783. 24 May 1784.
To son, Benjamin, choice of a tract of land located by Squire Boon on the western waters and a rifle gun. Wife, Mary, to have 1/3 of the estate, to be divided among daughters at her decease. Daughters: Sarah, Ann, Mary, Judah, Joanna and unborn child. Exrs: wife, Mathew Neale (brother) and Frederick Burdette, John Burdette, William Suttle, John Bell. (p. 40)

NELSON, John, Sr.
9 Aug. 1784. 25 Oct. 1784. Of Elk Run.
Sons, John and Jesse, to have tract of land in Shenandoah Co. Children: Jesse, John and William, Lida Morehead, Nanny Fishback, Mary Rector, Margaret Nelson, Jemina Nelson, Lettice Nelson, Sarah Nelson. Exrs: wife, son William, friend Josias Fishback, Alexander Morehead. Wit: John Mathew, James Gillison, John Blackwell, Thomas Helm. (p. 46)

SHUMATE, John
19 May 1783.   25 Oct. 1784.
Mentions son, Thomas Shumate.  To Capt. Jonathan Gibson, a tract of land. To son, Bailey Shumate, 15 pounds of curr.  Sons, William, John, Joshua, Daniel, James and daughters, Lettice and Jemina, all property I gave them at the time of their marriage.  To wife, Judah Shumate, use of the estate. Exrs: wife, Thomas Helm, John Nelson.  Wit: Thomas Helm, William Conway, John Kerr.  (p. 47)

BROWN, Mary
22 Nov. 1782.   27 Oct. 1784.
Legatees: brothers and sisters: Elizabeth Priest, Marmaduke Brown, George Brown, Jonathan Brown, William Brown, Martin Brown, Frances Maddux, Sibby and Rebecca Brown.  The three last mentioned shall have 50% less than the others.  I give to sister Martha the deed of gift made to us by Sir Marmaduke Beckwith.  To sister Elizabeth Priest, a saddle.  To Peggy Brown, a silk bonnet.  Exrs: Marmaduke Brown, William Brown (bros.).  Wit: John Stark, Rodham Kenner, Peter Hodo.  (p. 50)

ROBINSON, Benjamin
11 Jan. 1785.   28 Feb. 1785.
Slaves are bequeathed to sons, Nathaniel, George, Dixon, Stephen, Elijah, James and John.  Daughters, Catherine Campbell, Elesha Robinson, Mary and Lydda Robinson, are bequeathed slaves.  To Ann Masters, 500 pounds of tobacco.  To wife (not named) slaves and land in Stafford County.  Exrs: sons Nathaniel, George and Dixon Robinson.  Wit: William White, William Nalle, Robert Gibson, Carr White.  (p. 52)

NUGENT, Ann
23 May 1785.   15 Sept. 1785.
To nephew, Lincefield Sharpe, slaves.  To brother, Edward Nugent, nephew William Ballard, niece Mary Ballard, 1000 pounds of tobacco and feather bed. Wit: Peter Grant, Thomas Nugent, Susannah Grant.  (p. 54)

KNOX, Robert
21 Sept. 1781.   29 Aug. 1783.   Charles Co., Md.
Taken from county court of Charles Co., Md.  To son, John Knox, land in Va. (500 acres), slaves.  To son, Robert Dade Knox, all land in Md.  To daughter, Janet Knox, land in Va., slaves.  As no provision has been made for unborn child -- to have 800 pounds sterling.  To wife, Rose Townsend, to have whatever is customary to give widow in the part of the world where my estate "lyes".  Exrs: wife Rose Townsend, Col. Robert Hooe (of Alexandria), Andrew Bailee, Alexander B. Martin.  Wit: G.R. Brown, Verlinda Martin, Andrew Bailee, Will Millar.  (p. 57)

THORNHILL, Bryant
13 Oct. 1785.   21 Oct. 1785.
Son, Charles Thornhill, to have property that came from his mother.  Daughters: Elizabeth and Parthenia.  Sons, James, William and Elijah.  Wife, Leannah Thornhill.  Exrs: William Hunton, Robert Sanders.  Wit: James Lawler, James Hunton.  (p. 75)

PEARL, William
24 May 1785.   28 July 1785.
Grandson, William Pearle (son of Samuel) to have tract of land after decease of grandmother, Martha Pearl.  Land to daughter, Elizabeth, during her life, at her decease to her son, Elijah.  To daughter, Margaret Fields (wife of John), 100 acres of land.  Slaves to daughters, Sarah Smares, Martha Evins, Mary Murray.  To grandchildren: William, John, Elizabeth and Anne Weadon, 10 pounds each.  To son, Samuel, 50 pounds curr. should he die to his son William.  To son, William, 1000 pounds of tobacco.  Son Richard ----.  To wife, all estate during widowhood -- children to receive bequest after her decease.  Daughter, Elizabeth Cundiffe alias Ellitt.  Exrs: wife, Samuel Pearle, Ralph Murry.  Wit: Reuben Strother, Daniel Brown, Benjamin Carpenter, Reuben Elliott, Benjamin Strother.  (p. 61)

NEALE, Ben
: 23 March 1779. 26 April 1785. Parish of Leeds.
"All Wareing Cloathes to be divided equally between two sons, Jesse and Moses, but if one dies then all to the longest liver." All rest of estate to beloved wife (not named). Exr: wife. Wit: Rebecca Hich, Christopher Hich, Clement Norman. (p. 76)

SMITH, Joseph
: 24 Oct. 1785. Account. (p. 77)

PARKER, Alexander
: 9 May 1785. 28 Nov. 1785.
To wife, Amy Parker, slaves and land at her decease to sons Richard and William Parker. Children: Richard, William, Elizabeth Scott and Lucy Parker. If unborn child be a son, name is to be Alexander, if a girl to be named Judy. Exrs: wife and brother Richard. Wit: Benjamin Neale, Catesby Woodford, Rawley Hogain. (p. 78)

LAURENCE, Edward
: 26 March 1783. 27 March 1786. (p. 82)
To son, John Laurence, slaves. To son, Peter, 5 slaves. Son Edward, to have 6 slaves. Daughter, Susannah Catlett, to have 5 shillings. Daughters, Sarah Priest, Winnifred Luttrell, Jean Wicks, to have slaves. Grandson, Rodham Tullos Laurence, 2 slaves & feather bed. To son, Richard, land and plantation where I now live (377 acres) and 14 slaves. Exr: son Richard Laurence. Wit: Original Young, Thomas Conway, Richard Priest, William Crosby.

MARTIN, Charles
: 12 Jan. 1785. 27 March 1786.
All estate to daughters, Catherine Baylie and Susan Allen. Daughters, Elizabeth Edwards, Mary Pore, Frances Wade and -- McCarty, to receive 1 shilling each. Exrs: Catherine Baylie, Susan Allen. Wit: William Carter, Joseph Bailey, Samuel Hazlerig, Margaret Mason. (p. 84)

McCORMICK, Stephen
: 3 Feb. 1786. 26 June 1786. Of Hamilton Parish.
Wife, Margaret McCormick, to have use of estate, at her decease it is to be divided between son John McCormick and daughter, Elizabeth Mountjoy Martin. To daughter, Ann Shumate, cow and calf. Exrs: wife, son and Gavin Lawson. Wit: Paul Williams, James Haydon, William Jones. (p. 89)

RAMSDELL, Wharton
: 27 Jan. 1786. 26 June 1786.
1000 acres to be sold and money divided among the following named children: William Ramsdell, Anne Morehead, Margaret Ramsdell, Sarah Ramsdell. Twenty pounds to be reserved for the education of grandsons, Charles Morehead Ramsdell and Wharton Ramsdell, also to have a tract of land in Jefferson County. To son-in-law, Cadwaller Slaughter, 2 slaves. To daughter, Ann Morehead, 5 slaves; dau. Margaret, 5 slaves; dau. Sarah, 4 slaves. Slaves bequeathed to sons, Edward, John and William. Son Thomas to have slaves and wearing apparel. Son Wharton Ramsdell, Jr. deceased. Exrs: Charles Chilton, Elias Edmonds, Thomas Ramsdell, Sr., William Ramsdell, Jr., Thomas Ramsdell, Sr. (p. 93)

SCOTT, John
: 9 Feb. 1783. 27 April 1785. Dettengen Parish, Prince William Co.
Estate to be divided between all children in America and Great Britain. Wife, Elizabeth, to have 1/2 of estate during widowhood. Mentions "Aunt Elizabeth Innes, of Great Britain." Exrs: wife, (should she remarry son Robert to take her place), friend Thomas Blackburn, William Alexander, Esquire. Wit: Cuthbert Bullitt, Alexander Scott, Thomas Fitzhugh. (p. 99)

HATHAWAY, John
: 13 April 1786. 25 April 1786.
To wife, Sarah Hathaway, land and slaves, after her decease estate to be di-

vided between children, Judy Kamper, Sarah Bartlett, Elizabeth Hathaway, John, Nancy, Susannah, Molly, Dolly, Peggy Lawson, Sarepta, Francis. Daughters, Juday and Sarah to have 2 pounds less than the others. Son, John Hathaway, to have land which Simon Kenton was to locate for me. Exrs: wife and son John. Wit: Josiah Fishback, Philip Fishback. (p. 104)

DARNALL, David
22 March 1785. 23 Oct. 1786.
To wife, Mary, all estate during her life. Son, John. Granddaughter, Molly Lees (or Leer). Grandson, John Shaver. Exrs: wife and son John. Wit: Eave Riley, Edward Riley, William Pickett. (p. 111)

WILLIAMS, George
13 Nov. 1786. 25 Dec. 1786.
Wife, Ann Williams, to have 1/2 of plantation during her life time. To son, Elijah, 1/2 of plantation. Grandsons: Richardson and George Williams (sons of John). To daughter, Elizabeth Butler, all estate she has received and 25 shillings. To grandson, Benjamin Butler, if living, 7 pounds, if not to surviving brother. Grandson, John Butler (son of John), 7 pounds curr. Daughter, Catherine Williams, to be supported during life. Sons, William, George, Elijah. Daughter, Margaret Freeman. Grandchildren: James, George and Ann Collins, children of dau. Ann Collins, dec'd. Exrs: sons George and William. Wit: James Routt, Augustine Jennings, Joseph Selman. (p. 112)

BLACKWELL, Joseph
26 April 1787. 25 June 1787.
Wife to have use of estate during life. Sons, Joseph, Samuel, John and George Steptoe. Daughter, Judith Keith. Son-in-law, Martin Pickett. Daughters: Ann, Lucy, Betty, Judah. Exrs: wife and four sons. Wit: Peter Grant, Peter Conway, James Thompson. (p. 116)

KEITH, Isham
13 March 1787. 24 Sept. 1787.
To wife, Charlotte Keith, 1/3 of estate during life. Son, John, to have all land in Fauquier Co. and land allowed me as a Continental officer. Daughters, Betty, Mary Isham Keith, Sarah Ashmore, Caty Gallashue Keith, Charlotte Ashmore Keith. Exrs: wife, brother Thomas Keith, Charles Martin. Wit: William Hunton, William White, George Roach. (p. 119)

HEALEY, John
2 April 1787. 22 Oct 1787.
Wife, Mary Healey, to have use of estate as long as she remains a widow, after that only what the law allows her. Exrs: John Dareing, John Morehead (friends). Wit: James Genn, Celie Genn, James Ball. (p. 122)

CHINN, Charles
13 May 1787. 25 Feb. 1788.
To son, Charles, silver watch, household goods. Sons: Rawleigh, John, William Ball, Nancy Chinn, to have household goods. Son Elijah to have 500 acres of land in County of Nelson, District of Kentucky. All residue of land in Kentucky to be divided between sons, Charles, John, Rawleigh, William and Joseph Chinn. Wife, Seth Chinn, to have land in Loudon and Fauquier Counties. Daughter, Lila Reno. Daughters, Penelope, Betty, Margaret, Betty and Sukey. Son, Christopher Chinn. Sons, Charles, Raleigh and John and friend Rawleigh Chinn, Sr. are named as executors. Wit: John French, Daniel French, Ralph Murry. (p. 125)

SETTLES, Gayton
9 July 1787. 25 Feb. 1788.
Wife Mary to have whole estate during life and at her decease it is to go to son William. Exrs: wife and son. Wit: John Askins, Edward Settles. (p. 127)

MACKIE, Thomas
19 May 1786. 28 April 1788.
Mrs. Elizabeth Scott, widow of my friend, James Scott, Esq., to be paid the

annuity left me by my friend, Rev. Mr. James Scott, from death of his widow, Sarah Scott, dec'd. until my death, also rest of my estate. Exrs: Mrs. Elizabeth Scott. Wit: Charles Chilton, William Stewart. (p. 133)

HAMILTON, William
17 Aug. 1784. 23 June 1788.
To brother, Henry Hamilton, all slaves and land. To sister, Rebecca Thrift, 10 pounds of currency; to her son, Hamilton, a watch. Legatees: William Waddle, Thomas Skinner, Thomas Keith, John Ridley. Exrs: Thomas Keith, Isham Keith. Wit: John Ridley, William Waddell. (p. 133)

WADDELLS, John
1 April 1788. 23 June 1788.
Estate to be divided between Mathew Waddell and all my children at decease of wife Elizabeth. To daughter, Teny Murphy, 1 shilling. Children: William, James, George, Margaret, Elizabeth, Polly, John, Frances. Exrs: wife and son William. Wit: Joseph Taylor, John Coppadge, James May. (p. 134)

BLAND, Thomas
1 April 1788. 22 Sept. 1788. (p. 136)
To son, Thomas, all land in Prince William Co. To son, James (youngest), land in Prince William Co. Daughters, Catherine and Mary Bland. Exrs: wife, Jane Bland, Thomas Bland, Benjamin Harrison. Wit: John Lansdown.

BARKER, William
27 May 1788. 27 Oct. 1788. Of Parish of Leeds.
Wife, Susannah Barker, to have estate as long as she remains a widow. Children: Charles, Nanny, Mary Parker, James and William. Children who are married have been provided for. Exrs: William Barker (son), Richard Parker. Wit: Hugh Bradley, Matt. Waddell, Jeremiah Morgan. (p. 138)

GRIGSBY, William
29 Dec. 1788. 25 June 1789.
Daughters: Fanny Rout, Winnifred, Eady. Granddaughter, Jane Rout. Sons, Lewis, Bayliss, Nathaniel, to have slaves. Exrs: son Lewis and Richard Rout. Wit: Hezekiah Turner, John White, John Catlett. (p. 146)

RECTORS, Harmon
23 Sept. 1782. 28 Sept. 1789.
To son, Harmon, 100 acres lying in the German Town and slaves. Household goods to be divided between three sons. Exrs: Capt. Tillman Weaver, John Martin. Wit: Charles Utterback, Henry Utterback, William Nelson (p. 147)

CRUMP, John
5 Feb. 1789. 23 Sept. 1789.
To son, George Crump, 5 shillings. Daughters, Elizabeth Utterback, Mary Waugh, Hannah Branan, Ann Lewis, to have 5 shillings each. Daughters, Sarah and Catherine to have feather beds. Son, John, to have all land where I now live unless "he takes up and marries a certain woman by name of Mary Westall." Land to go to son Daniel if son John marries Mary Westall. Exrs: brothers George and Benjamin Crump, William Eustace, Jr., John James. Wit: John James, John Shumate, Mason Shumate. (p. 148)

WITHERS, James
27 July 1789.
Allotment of Dower of Jemina Harris, late widow of James Withers, dec'd.

HALEY, Honor
27 Feb. 1787. 25 Jan. 1790.
To son, Michael Cavanaugh, all money. Legatees: Mary Johnston (dau. of Henry Peyton), Sarah Fishback (dau. of Josias Fishback), 1 guinea, John Morcy, 5 pounds curr. Exrs: Josias Fishback, Henry Peyton. Wit: George Leach, Jr., James Fishback. (p. 153)

EMBRY, Robert
26 Oct. 1784. 25 Jan. 1790.
Sons, Thomas and Robert to receive land. Grandson, Robert Embrey (son of Charles, dec'd.). Exrs: sons Thomas and Robert. Wit: Susannah Brown, John Brown. (p. 157)

BUTTON, Harmon
25 Dec. 1789. 25 Jan. 1790. (p. 158)
Lends to wife, Catherine, during her life. Son, Jacob Button, dau. Ann Hockman, Sarah Sinsee to have land that is now in their possession. Daughters: Susan, Rebecca and Catherine Button. Exrs: John Kemper, Sr. and Jacob Kemper, Sr. Wit: Charles Kemper, Robert Turnbull, Rand Smith.

NUGENT, Thomas
11 Sept. 1789. 22 Feb. 1790.
To nephew, Lincefield Sharpe, all land where I now live, slaves, cattle. Mentions children of brother Edward Nugent. Nephew Thomas Nugent to receive slaves. Brother, Edward Nugent, title to a tract of land. To niece, Mary Hampton's two daughters, Frances and Susannah. To Ann Nugent Sharpe (dau. of Lincefield Sharpe). Nephew, William Ballard. Exr: brother Edward Nugent. (p. 160)

GARNER, Benjamin
5 Sept. 1789. 26 April 1790.
Wife, Diannah Garner. Children mentioned, but not named. Exrs: wife, Vincent Garner (bro.), James Withers. Wit: James Withers, John Withers, James Garner. (p. 166)

EMBREY, Ann
9 Feb. 1790. April 1790. Nuncupative will.
To son, Robert Embrey, household goods, stock. To daughter, Elizabeth Taylor. Son, John Embrey. To daughter, Nancy Butler, my saddle. This will was proved by the oaths of William Snelling, Alexander Brown, Sarah Benjey. (p. 167)

THROCKMORTON, Frances
2 May 1790. 27 Sept. 1790.
Legatees: brother William Throckmorton, sisters Mary and Ann Throckmorton. Exrs: Morgan Tomkils (friend) of Glouchester Co. Wit: H. Brooks, Frances Brooks. (p. 174)

SANDERS, Robert
27 May 1790. 22 Sept. 1790.
To son, William a tract of land. Sons, James, Brittain, Gabriel, Thomas, Lewis, Larking Sanders. Exrs: James Sanders, William Hunton, James Hunton, Thomas Sanders. Wit: Charles Chilton, William Hunton, Jr., Elizabeth Sanders. (p. 175)

LEE, Richard
24 Sept. 1790. 25 Oct. 1790.
To sister, Priscilla, 200 pounds currency. To brother, Arthur, horse and bridle. Brothers: William, George, Kendall, Hancock and Arthur. Sisters: Betty Edwards, Judith Pierce. Exrs: brother George Lee, Thomas Edwards.

BURGESS, Garner
19 April 1790. Oct. 1790.
Wife: Anne Burgess. Children: Susannah, James, Peggy, John, Nancy, Mary Neal, Sarah Settle, Edward and John Burgess. Exrs: wife, son Edward, Matthew Neal. Wit: B. Shackleford, Matthew Neal, Isaac Arnold. (p. 180)

BROWNING, Caleb
14 Dec. 1787. July 1791. Inventory. (p. 201)

WITHERS, James
4 May 1791. July 1791.

Children: Thomas, John, Elizabeth, Hannah, Cain, Lucy, Centy, Enoch, William, Sithey, Sally and Patty. Exrs: wife Elizabeth and son John. (p. 202)

GIBSON, Jonathan
22 July 1788. 26 Sept. 1791.
Three youngest children: Joanathan Catlett, Susanna Grayson, Mary. Slaves bequeathed to sons, Thomas, John, Jonathan Catlett Gibson. To daughters, Ann Grayson Blackwell, Susanna Gibson and Mary Gibson, to have slaves. Granddaughter, Margaret Catlett Gibson and children of dau. Ann G. Blackwell, to have slaves, also niece Mary Adie, to have slave. Exrs: sons Thomas, John, Jonathan and Benjamin Harrison. Wit: John Mauzy, Mathew Harrison, Jr. (p. 204)

NELSON, John
22 March 1791. Dec. 1791.
Wife, Mary, to have use of estate during life. Land to be divided between the following legatees, two daughters of James Nelson, dec'd., Elizabeth Green and Catherine Horton. 1/5 part to Hannah James, wife of Thomas James. 1/5 part to Mary Nelson, widow of John Nelson, Jr., dec'd. 1/5 part to Thomas Nelson (son). 1/5 part to Joseph Nelson (son). Exrs: wife, William Phillips (of Stafford Co.), Garrett Gray, Jr. Wit: Original Young, John Green, Elizabeth James. (p. 210)

YOUNG, William
20 Dec. 1790. Feb. 1792. (p. 214)
Wife, Patience Young, to have use of estate during her life. To son, William, slave. To daughter, Mary Jeffries, slave. To daughters, Hannah Orsley (or Crosley), Sukey (Susannah Smith) 20 pounds of curr. Exrs: Joseph Jeffries, Thomas Fitzhugh. Wit: Menoah Stone, Edward Fegan, Benjamin Carpenter.

ASHBY, Robert
2 June 1790. 27 Feb. 1792. (p. 216)
Son, Benjamin, to have a tract of land on Shenandoah River, where he now lives, and slaves. Grandson, William Ashby (son of Benjamin) to have slaves. Lends to son Enoch and wife Sally, a tract of land, after the decease of Enoch land to go to sons of Enoch, Robert and Alexander. Daughter Ann Farrow, 10 pounds curr. To grandson, Bayliss Ashford, 1 feather bed. To gr. dau., Molly Faraguson, 1 feather bed. To daughter, Winnifred Peper, 1 cow, no more. Grandsons, Martin and Thomas Ashby (son of Nimrod), 1 slave. To daughter, Molly Athel, 1 gown, no more. Grandson, Benjamin Farrow, 1 slave. Exr: son John. Wit: William Withers, John Clark, John Fishback.

WRIGHT, John
1 June 1785. "7 Feb. 1792.
To son, James, land and slaves. To granddaughter, Betsy Wright (dau. of James Wright), slaves. Daughters, Mary and Rosamond, to have plantation where I now live. Wife, Elizabeth Wright. Sons, William and John Wright, to have 20 shillings each - the land I gave them they sold. Should Elizabeth Parlow ever apply to be given 15 pounds curr. Exrs: daughters, Mary and Rosamond. Wit: George Maddox, John Nelson, Francis Lathane. (p. 219)

COCKRELL, Anderson
7 Sept. 1791. 27 Sept. 1792.
Daughter, Rosanna Cockrell, 1 mare. Son, William, to have a horse. Estate to be kept together until youngest daughter, Sally Cockrell, arrives at the age of 18 years. Exrs: brother Jesse Moffett and son William. Wit: John Cooke, John Porter, Augustine Bannister. (p. 221)

FREEMAN, James
Youngest daughter, Sally, to have feather bed and household furniture with full benefits and profits of part of her grandfather, George Williams' estate, which was bequeathed to her mother - this to descend at mother's death. Wife, Margaret Freeman, to have 1/3 of estate during life. Grandson, Gollop Freeman (alias Duncan), household goods. Sons, Garrett and Nathaniel, personal estate and slaves. Daughter, Mary Hackley (wife of James) to have

30 shillings - she has received her share. Daughter, Elinor Silman (wife of Joseph), 10 pounds curr. Sons: William, James, Garrett, Nathaniel Freeman. Daughter, Elizabeth Fletcher (wife of John), to have money from sale of land. Exrs: wife, sons William and James. Wit: Samuel Wharton, Jr., William Williams, James Routt. (p. 226)

TOLLE, Stephen
    9 Oct. 1791. 25 June 1792. Nuncupative will.
    Wife Anne to have whole estate until son George comes of age. Mentions unborn child. Appoints George Tolle and Enoch Crosby to conduct affairs for wife. Wit: Samuel Pearle, George Tolle, Francis Murray. (p. 231)

WOODFORD, Catesby
    8 Sept. 1791. 24 Sept. 1792.
    Lends to wife, Mary, all of estate. Desires that sons be educated according to value of estate. Exrs: wife, son Mark (when he comes of age), friends George Buckner, Jr. and William Woodford. Wit: Thomas Montgomerie, Y. Johnson. (p. 242)

ROGER, George
    4 May 1792. 24 Sept. 1792.
    Wife, Betty Roger, to have use of estate. Sons: George and Edward. Daughters, Betty Newby and Mary Sanders. 1/5 part of estate to be used in support of daughter, Sally Mathew, and children. Mentions "trusty friend" Ambrose Barnett. Exrs: sons George and Edward. Wit: Samuel Steele, Henry Steele, Robert Gibson. (p. 244)

TAYLOR, Henry
    6 Sept. 1792. Inventory.

BULLITT, Joseph
    17 Nov. 1792. 24 Dec. 1792.
    Daughter, Susan Redd to have 5 slaves and her sons, Joseph Bullitt Redd and Permercis Redd, to have a slave each. Daughter, Mary Steatard to have 4 slaves, her son, Joseph Steatard to have 1 slave. Joseph Bullitt Redd, son of Priscilla, to have 3 slaves. Wife, Barsheba Norman, now Bullitt, use of 3 slaves, furniture and land. Exrs: Thomas Conway, Original Young, John Young. Wit: Peter Conway, Charles Coppadge, William Young. (p. 249)

KENNER, Rodham
    5 June 1793. 28 June 1793.
    Daughters, Lucy and Judith Kenner, to have 200 acres of land when they become of age. Son Lawerence to have rest of land and slaves. Son, Lawerence, to be given to his uncle, Rodham Kenner, if he is inclined to take him, when 10 years of age. Desire that he be placed in a seminary where he may be well ingrafted with the French language only. Exrs: Rodham Kenner, Samuel Blackwell, Judith Kenner. Wit: Samuel Blackwell, James Seaton, Jonathan Brown. (p. 252)

HEADLEY, James
    11 Dec. 1792. 28 June 1793.
    Wife, Lucy, to have all of estate during life or widowhood. Father and mother mentioned, but not named, also children. Exrs: Eppa Timberlake, William Day, John Cooke. Wit: John Cooke, James Ready, William Day. (p. 254)

MORGAN, Simon
    10 Nov. 1792. 25 Feb. 1793.
    Son, Joseph, to have 162 acres of land which I now live on, part of a tract of 486 acres. Son Charles to receive a tract of land. Son, Simon, tract of land. Son, Jeremiah, personal property. To daughter, Sukey Clark, cow & calf. Daughter, Caty Bradford. Daughter, Rosey Cockrin (wife of William), to have 1 shilling. Exrs: sons Simon and Joseph. Wit: Hugh Bradley, George Carter, William Carter. (Mention is made of late wife.) (p. 260)

SMITH, Joseph
    6 Jan. 1793. Feb. 1793. Of Parish of Leeds.
    Son William to have 200 acres of land, tract on which I now live. Daughters, Mary Burdette, Hannah Ball, to have slaves. To son, John, slaves, wearing apparel, 1 chest that was my father's. To sons, Rowley and Enoch, slaves. Daughter, Lucy Pepper, to have slaves. Grandson, Abner Smith, slaves, grandson to be taken care of by son, John Smith. To sister, Jean Owing, 10 pounds currency. Granddaughters: Ruth Smith and Willamina. Daughter, Jean Porter. Exrs: Sons, Rowley, John and John Porter. Wit: William Dulin, David Ball, Benjamin Ball, William Redding. (p. 263)

MANUEL, Francis
    6 Sept. 1792. Nov. 1793.
    Daughter, Abbe Manuel, to have all stock and furniture. Exrs: Daughter Abbe Manuel and her son, Zachariah Manuel. (p. 266)

JOHNSON, Smith
    16 Feb. 1793. Inventory.
    Apprs: John Dearing, Joseph Smith, John Morehead, Sr. (p. 270)

WEST, Ignatus
    16 Sept. 1791. 22 July 1793. Of Spottsylvania Co.
    Daughter Mary Hanor, to have 17 pounds and 2 shillings, placed in the hands of Mr. Harmon Hanor (her father-in-law). Daughter, Elizabeth Bolling. Other children mentioned, but not named. Exr: son Benjamin West. (p. 280)

MARTIN, Joseph, Sr.
    4 Nov. 1791. 1793.
    Youngest son, Benjamin Martin. Eldest son, John Martin, heirs of son Enoch, dec'd., all my sons and daughters to have equal share of estate. Exrs: wife, Katherine Martin, Charles Martin. Wit: John Fletcher. (Under the signature of Joseph Martin is written Hosea Martin) (p. 281)

FLETCHER, Thomas
    3 Nov. 1792. 22 July 1793.
    Son, John, to care for mother, brother and sisters. Exrs: Richard Fletcher, John Fletcher, Thomas Fletcher. Wit: John Dawson, Thomas Ball, Richard Fisher, William Pinchard. (p. 283)

DUNCAN, Joseph
    13 Feb. 1792. 23 Sept. 1793. (p. 284)
    Wife, Lydia, to have use of land and slaves during life. Children: Joseph, Myma Mauzy, Rose Withers, Hannah Porter, Houser Duncan, Mary Wright, Lydia Obannon. Exrs: Joseph and Houser (sons), John Obannon (son-in-law) and John Mauzy (son-in-law). Wit: John Kerr, Peter Kemper, James Parr.

GLASCOCK, James
    1 July 1793. 23 Sept. 1793.
    Wife, Agatha to hold estate during her life, "without making any waste." Wit: Charles Dulaney, Lucy Fishback, Elizabeth Cunningham.

ALLEN, Ursulla
    12 Aug. 1789. --- 1793.
    My father, James Withers, of Stafford Co., bequeathed to me 2 slaves - my late husband left these slaves by will and testament to his sons, William, James, Joseph Allen and his dau. Ann Bradford, to be given them at my decease, and doubt has arisen as to whether said husband had right to dispose of said Negroes. To daughter, Ann Bradford, all my wearing apparel. Grandsons: Baldwin Bradford and Armistead Minor. Sons, Thomas, Joseph, James Allen. Money to be paid widows of sons, John and William Allen. Exrs: Sons Thomas, James and Joseph Allen.

HURST, Rosanna
    17 Oct. 1793. 28 Oct. 1793.
    Son, Henry Hurst. One shilling each to following named daughters: Elizabeth

Thompson (wife of Jesse), Mildred Markwell (wife of William), Nancy Heffering (wife of Augustin), Delia Crum (wife of Joseph). Daughter Jane Hurst, to have personal property. Wit: John Ferguson, Gracey Quisenberry, Sally Thompson. (p. 303)

DUNCAN, John
4 April 1788. 23 Dec. 1795.
To son, John, to have 10 shillings. Son-in-law, Benjamin Grigsby, 5 shillings. All estate to be sold when son, Willis Duncan, "arrives to the age 20 years." Wife, Wilky Duncan. Children: Moses, Enoch, Willis, Milly, Lucinda. Exrs: Charles Duncan, Moses Duncan (sons). Wit: Charles Duncan, Cossom Day, Margaret Williams. (p. 312)

RILEY, John
21 Jan. 1791. 23 Dec. 1791.
Sons: Thomas, Hugh, Edward, John, George and Charles. To daughter, Catherine Darnall, 10 pounds curr. money. Daughters: Elizabeth Gear, Lettice Fenner, Mary Hill. Grandson, Charles Riley and gr. dau. Catherine Riley (father Charles Riley), Susan Riley (dau. of Edward Riley). Exrs: Edward, Thomas and Hugh Riley (sons). Wit: William Pickett, Francis Triplett, Reuben Bramlett, John Riley (son of Thomas).

MORGAN, Simon
24 June 1794. Inventory. (p. 323)

BALL, James
20 Feb. 1794. Sept. 1794.
Wife, Nancy, to have estate during life. Children: Peggy Stevinson, Judy Ball, Lucy Ball, Shoaltial Ball, Talliaferrio Ball, Elizabeth Ball, James Ball, John Ball, Nancy Ball and unborn child. Exrs: Benjamin Stephinson, John Singleton. (p. 328)

BARKER, John
25 Sept. 1794. 24 Oct. 1794. (p. 332)
Three oldest children, Elizabeth, Mary and Chloe, to have slaves when Chloe is eighteen. Other daughters, Ann, Milly and Sarah. Wife, Sarah Barker. Exrs: John Glasscock, George Adams. Wit: John Monroe, John Rawlins.

LYNN, John
18 Aug. 1794. Dec. 1794.
Sons, John and Lewis, to have tract of land where I now live. Son, Francis, to have 20 pounds curr., has received his share of estate. Children: Fielding, Thompson, Sukey Thomas, Gr. dau. Jane West. Exrs: sons Fielding and Thompson, Lewis Lynn. Wit: Charles Metcalf, James Lawson, Thomas Lawson. (p. 345)

WAITE, Jane
1 April 1794. 22 Dec. 1794.
Legatees: Mr. Richard Eustace Beale, Willy Roy and William Bronaugh (brother). Slaves to be liberated. Slaves, Bob and Lucy, to have 20 acres of land. Mrs. Margaret Beale to have my shag cream case, with 6 spoons, tongs and strainer. Exr: Capt. Thomas Gibson. Wit: John Fox, William Eustace, Jr., Lyons Luckett. (p. 346)

TRIPLETT, Francis
24 Sept. 1794. Jan. 1795.
Children: William, Hedgman, Robert, Betty, Benedicte, Anne and Frances. Amelia Triplett to have 20,000 acres of land on the north fork of Licking. Son, Robert, to have land in Kentucky. Daughters, Betty and Benedicte, to have a tract of land in Kentucky, County of Bourbon, containing 1400 acres. To wife, Benedicte, and daughters, Ann and Frances (youngest) to have 5000 acres of land in Kentucky, upon Cabin Creek. Moveable estate to be sold and money used to defray expenses to Kentucky. Exrs: sons William and Robert Triplett. (p. 347)

WITHERS, Thomas
    5 Nov. 1794. Dec. 1795.
    Sons: John, Enoch, Mathew Keen, Joseph, William and Benjamin. Daughters: Hannah Winn, Betty Winn, Nancy Jordan, Sally West, Susan Chinn. Granddaughter, Hannah Winn (dau. of Betty Winn), legacy to be in care of her father, Capt. Minor Winn. Mention is made that he is at law with brother, William Winn, about land. Also that he is trying to recover money from Isaac Hite (or Hitt), administrator of James Buchanan, dec'd. Exrs: sons William and Capt. Minor Winn. (p. 349)

ROGERS, John
    8 Aug. 1794. 22 Dec. 1794.
    Son, Henry and wife Sarah and their youngest son, John. Children: Stephen, John, Mary Rogers and Mary Mason. Exr: son Henry. Wit: Daniel Greenwood, James Dennis, Mathew Neal. (p. 354)

OLDAKER, Abraham
    10 Dec. 1794. 27 April 1795.
    Wife, Hester, to have use of estate during her life. Mention is made of 8 children, but they are not named. Exr: wife. Wit: Joseph Sheetzs, Benjamin Sheetzs, Benjamin Taylor. (p. 560)

McKENNEY, John
    24 Jan. 1795. 22 June 1795.
    Son, John, to have 200 acres of land, cattle, sheep, household goods. To son, Francis, 1 shilling. Wife, Mary, 1 shilling. Daughters: Mary Cain, Elizabeth McKenney, Alice McKenney, to have 1 shilling each. Granddaughter, Susannah McKenney (dau. of John), to have 1 slave. Exr: son John. Wit: Nimrod Utterback, Ezekiel Davis, David Evan, Daniel Carter. (p. 366)

SUDDUTH, William
    10 Nov. 1785. June 1795.
    Lends to wife, Alse, estate during her life, at her decease to be divided among all my children (not named). Mentions daughter, Mary Sudduth. Exrs: sons Francis and George Sudduth. Wit: Edward Settle, Benjamin Arnold, John Forrester. (p. 367)

DARNALL, Jeremiah
    10 April 1795. June 1795.
    Wife, Catherine Darnall. Children: Elizabeth Sinclair, Joseph, Ann Weaver, Mary Russell (to have 500 acres in Kentucky), Margaret Sinclair, Susannah Smith (20 shillings), Leannah Ashby, Caty Darnall, Rosamond Darnall. Granddaughter, Lucy Ashby. Exr: James Wright (friend). Wit: William Weaver, John Martin, Henry Kearns. (p. 368)

PRIEST, Thomas
    15 Feb. 1790. 28 Sept. 1795. (p. 378)
    Wife, Sarah, to have use of estate during her life time. Children: Peter and Mary Priest, other children mentioned, but not named. Exrs: wife and son Thomas. Wit: Richard Larrance, William Coppedge, Edward Larrance.

KIDWELL, Mary
    18 March 1795. Sept. 1795.
    Son, William Kidwell. George Thompson, Joshua Drummond and Nathaniel Snope (sons-in-law) to have remainder of estate. Exrs: Henry Peyton, Sr. and Henry Peyton, Jr. (p. 379)

BROOKS, Thomas
    20 Jan. 1792. Oct. 1795.
    Wife, Elizabeth, to have land during her widowhood. Sons: Thomas, William and John. Daughters: Elizabeth Brown, Nancy Fox, Sally Brown, Winny Northcutt, Mary and Dorcas Brooks. (p. 381)

BARBEE, Andrew
    28 Dec. 1790. 28 Dec. 1795.

Wife, Jane Barbee, to have land and slaves during life. Sons: Andrew and John. Daughters: Elizabeth, Mary Foley, Sarah Bradford. Grandsons: Abijah Withers, son of dau. Elizabeth Withers; Thomas and Andrew Russell Barbee (sons of Joseph). Exrs: sons Andrew and John Barbee. Wit: B.Shackleford, Thomas Harris, Aquilla Divis. (p. 387)

BELL, Frances
    14 Dec. 1795. 28 Dec. 1795.
    All estate to grandson, William Bell. Exrs: Elias Edmonds, William Edmonds, Jr., Eppa Timberlake (friends). Wit: John Edmonds, James Edmonds, Sarah Timberlake. (p. 389)

PETERS, John
    Oct. 1781-1784. Inventory.

## WILL BOOK NUMBER 3  1796-1803

GRIFFITH, Evan
    10 Sept. 1795. 25 April 1796.
    To son, John, wearing apparel. Son Willoughby to have land. Son Dennis to have plantation after decease of mother. Daughters, Amelia Owens, Rachel Creel, Peggy Griffith and Susannah Griffith, to have land in Kentucky. Wife, Sarah, to have land during wodowhood. Daughter, Sarianne, to have land and personal property. Exrs: wife and son Elijah. Wit: Benjamin Goldsmith, Rachel Flynn, William Flynn.

BROWN, Molly
    28 Feb. 1796. 2 March 1796.
    Legatees: George Brooke and heirs (George, Francis, Mathew and Anne Brooks); Kitty Powell, Elizabeth Diggs, Lucy Brooke, furniture and books. Will was proven by the oath of William Chilton that Molly Brown, wife of Robert Brown, Gentleman, made the above nuncupative will in the house of Thomas Digges and that she died sometime that night. (p. 3)

SEATON, William
    2 Oct. 1795.
    Division of property between Mary Brown, widow of William Seaton, dec'd. and his two sons, James and William Seaton. Mention is made of David Wickliffe as an heir. (p. 6)

GARNER, Vincent
    28 Aug. 1795. 27 June 1796.
    Son, John, land adjoining James Withers' line - formerly purchased of Jonas Garner. To son, Jonas, what land is now in his possession and 10 shillings. To heirs of daughter, Sarah Suttle (hus. William). Gr. son James Withers. Wife, Jemina, to have land during widowhood. Children: Vincent, William, Jesse, Elizabeth, Jemina Harris (hus. William). Wit: Enoch Withers, James Withers, Aaron Fletcher, John Kines.

REDMON, John
    25 July 1796. Inventory.
    Apprs: Willim Barker, Edward Burgess, Mark Shumate. (p. 23)

DUNCAN, John
    25 July 1796.
    Dower of Wilky Duncan, widow of John Duncan, dec'd. Moses Duncan, administrator of estate. Milly Duncan, heir of John Duncan, dec'd.

EMMONS, William
    5 Feb. 1795. 25 July 1796.
    All estate to wife during widowhood. Daughter, Agatha Emmons, to have personal property. After decease of wife all property to be sold and divided among all the children. Exrs: son Joseph and William Jones (son-in-law) Wit: Peter Grant, Thomas Keith, John Weeden. (p. 27)

WINN, Minor
   26 Feb. 1796. Inventory.

BILLINGSLEY, Clement
   24 Oct. 1796. Inventory.
   Apprs: Mathew Neale, Joseph Smith, L. Mallory. (p. 32)

RAMSDELL, Major Thomas
   Oct. 1796. Inventory.
   Apprs: Samuel Steele, George Rogers, Joseph Hale. (p. 33)

TALBUT, John
   12 April 1796. 24 Oct. 1796.
   Wife, Ann, to have slaves during lifetime. Daughter, Ann, to have slaves. Son John, to have slaves. A tract of land in Prince George Co., Md. to be sold and the money to be divided among wife and 4 children. Exrs: wife and son Benjamin. Wit: John Wrenn, Samuel Dennis, Isaac Wrenn. (p. 35)

KERR, John
   8 Nov. 1796. 26 Dec. 1796.
   Daughter, Margaret Bronaugh, 5 pounds curr. and other gifts. Daughter, Mary Peters, 1 Negro. Daughter, Betty Kerr, 2 Negroes. Sons, John Kerr, Jr. and William Kerr, each to have a slave. Wife, Sarah, to have use of estate during life. Children: Sarah Crosby Kerr, William Kerr, Dorcas Kerr, Lucy Kerr, Peggy Smith Kerr and Asenth Kerr. (Some of the above mentioned children were by a first wife). Exrs: wife, John Withers, John James. Wit: Benjamin Bronaugh, Garrett Freeman, James Fox. (p. 36)

MOREHEAD, Samuel
   17 Dec. 1796.
   Daughters, Lydia, Mary, Elizabeth and Peggy Morehead, to have slaves. Slaves to sons, Charles and Samuel Morehead. Grandson, Baylor Jennings, a slave. Wife, Wilmarth, all estate during her widowhood. Exrs: wife, Thomas Helm, Charles Morehead. Wit: Thomas Humston, John Morehead, Isaac Eustace. (p. 47)

GEORGE, Parnach
   24 Feb. 1797. Inventory.

FOLEY, James
   14 Oct. 1793. 24 April 1797.
   Wife, Elizabeth, all estate during widowhood. Children by wife Elizabeth - Susannah, Oglevie P., Oglivie Leah, Oglevie Lettice, Molly. Son Enoch. Other children: John James, Thomas William, Bryant, Sarah Watts, Enoch Foley. Exrs: wife and son Enoch. Exrs: Alexander Keith, Henry Harris, William Keith, Lettice Thornton. Wit: Obannon Keith, Henry Harris, Lettice Thornton, Catty Keith. (p. 55)

OBANNON, John
   21 Feb. 1797. 24 April 1797.
   Wife, Lydia, to have slaves and land during widowhood. To son, Joseph, 1/3 of all my land in Kentucky. Daughter, Elizabeth Smith. To son, James, 300 pounds of curr. Daughter, Jemina Johnston, slave. Son, Isham, a slave. To son, Elias, to have 1/3 of land in Kentucky. To son, William, residue of land in Fauquier County. To son, John, 1/3 of land in Kentucky. Exrs: wife, sons Joseph, James and John. Wit: William Metcalfe, Alexander Keith, Richard Parker. (p. 52)

CLARK, Benjamin
   27 Nov. 1794. 26 June 1797.
   Wife, Mary, to have estate during life and at her decease to be divided between children. Children: Thomas, Ann Crupper, Elizabeth Clark, Mary Clark. Grandchildren: children of dau. Cloe Crupper. Wit: Samuel Pearle, Henry Moore, Henry Downs. Exrs: wife and son Thomas. (p. 56)

SMOOTS, John
5 Sept. 1796. 26 June 1797.
To wife, Tomsen, land and household goods. Sons, Leonard, James, Clabour, Lewis, Enoch, to have 1 shilling each. Sons, Barton and William, to have 1 pence each. Daughters, Mary Betsy, Charity and Frances, to have 1 shilling each. Exr: wife. Wit: A. Davis, De Wood, William Wood. (p. 58)

DUNCAN, Lydia
2 Oct. 1795. 24 June 1797.
To sons, Joseph and Housen Duncan, Negroes. Daughters, Lydia Obannon (hus. John), Jemina Mauzy (hus. John), Hannah Porter (hus. Ebenezer), each to have slaves. Exrs: sons Joseph and Housen. Wit: Enoch Withers, Moses Duncan, John Kerr. (p. 66)

CAVE, Thomas
26 July 1797. 25 Sept. 1797.
Estate to be equally divided among 4 children: Rhody, John, Sarah and Samuel Cave. They are to receive their share at age of 17 years. Wit: Joseph Dickman, Philip Cooksey. (p. 67)

HARRISON, Benjamin
2 Jan. 1798. 22 Jan. 1798.
To daughter, Margaret Short Wagner, 10 pounds curr. To David Harrison, 10 pounds and my wearing apparel. Slave Samuel to be emancipated. All rest of estate to be given grandson, Benjamin Harrison Wagner. Exrs: Col. Peter Wagner, Benjamin Bitts, of Dumfries. Wit: Philip Spille, James Lloyd, Charles Waller. (p. 90)

LAWSON, John
Probated 22 Jan. 1798.
Capt. Hancock Lee has a warrant for 840 acres which I wish to be located for the benefit of my creditors. Edward Digges to inherit land after the decease of my wife (not named). Wit: Willy Roy, Edward Digges, Jr. (p. 92)

PICKETT, William
10 Jan. 1798. 26 Feb. 1798.
To wife, Martha, bedstead, 1 pair of fire dogs. Son, William, 1 mare & colt, furniture and household goods. Son, James, 1 feather bed and furniture. Daughter, Ann Pickett, feather bed & furniture, choice of slaves in lieu of Daniel. Daughter, Sukey Brady, 1 horse and property in her possession. Children: John, Sanford, William, James, Patty Fishback, Sukey Brady, Molly Jackson, Sally Metcalfe, Ann Pickett, Subrey Smith. Exrs: sons James and William. Wit: William Metcalfe, Joseph Smith. (p. 102)

SMITH, William
15 Oct. 1789. 26 Feb. 1796. Hamilton Parish.
Son William and dau. Mary Soddust (?) to have slaves. Son Andrew to have slaves and stock. Exrs: son Andrew and James Withers (cousin). Wit: Thomas Withers, John Withers, Hannah Smith.

HARRISON, Benjamin
30 Jan. 1798. Renunciation. (p. 109)
Mary Harrison, wife of Benjamin, will not accept any provision made for her by her late husband. Wit: Ennis Comb, Thomas Gibson, Joseph George.

MATHEWS, John
24 Feb. 1798. 28 July 1798.
Schoolmaster. To Mary, dau. of Josias Fishback, a tract of land containing 500 acres, being in the County of Lincoln in State of Kentucky. To William Blackwell (son of Col. John Blackwell) a horse & bridle. After payment of funeral expenses money is to be divided between Sarah Battaile Fitzhugh, Dudley Fitzhugh (dau. of George Fitzhugh of Turkey Run). Exrs: Col. John Blackwell, of Tinpot, William Fitzhugh, of Prospect Hill, and George Fitzhugh, of Turkey Run. (p. 128)

JOHNSON, Isaac
    9 June 1798. 23 July 1798.
    Wife, Lydia, to have 2 slaves and lease of land where I now live. After decease of wife brother Baldwin Johnson shall possess all estate. Exrs: John Smith and his son Thomas. Wit: Isaac Neigh, Ann Neigh, Dosha Crim, William Griffin.

ROUSAN, William
    19 July 1792. 25 July 1798.
    Wife Priscilla to have land during her life, at her decease to be divided between 3 children - Henry, Margaret Combs, Nancy Peters. Sons, John, William (wife Lydia), Henry (wife Sarah). Grandson, William Rousan (son of William), a Negro. Daughter Margaret Comb (wife of Ennis), a Negro. Dau. Susannah Payne and husband, Benjamin Payne, to have possession of a Negro. Daughter Nancy and husband, John Peters, to have a Negro woman. Gr. dau. Betsy Kerr, to have slave after decease of wife. Exrs: wife, son Henry, Ennice Combs. (p. 130)

PICKETT, William Sandford
    28 Jan. 1799. Inventory. (p. 146)

SINKLAR, William
    24 Jan. 1798. ----. (p. 137)
    After decease of wife land is to be sold and divided among the children: James, John, Isaac, Archibald, William, Middleton, Horatio, Elizabeth Jones, Nancy and Mary Fogan (hus. Edward). Exrs: wife (Lydia), sons James and John. Wit: William Metcalfe, Charles Barnett, George Payne, Joshua Kennard.

DAVIS, Charles
    16 May 1796. 24 Sept. 1798.
    Wife Lydia to have estate during life and widowhood. Daughters, Lucy Wheat and Lydia Davis. Sons: Griffith, Charles, William, Levi, Richard and John. Two granddaughters - Elizabeth Davis, Elizabeth Davis - personal property. Exrs: Sons, Griffith, Charles, William. Wit: James H. Beckman, Gerrard Keating, Jemina Keating. (p. 140)

SANFORD, Richard
    2 Sept. 1798. 22 Oct. 1798.
    Wife Betty to have estate during widowhood. Sons: Robert, John, William, Bennett. Exrs: wife, Robert Sanford (son), James Hunton, Richard Baker. Wit: Hannah Hunton, Bernard Duffy, Owen Thomas, Thomas Hunton. (p. 145)

KEMPER, John
    2 Feb. 1796. 25 Feb. 1799.
    Wife, Ann, to have land where she now lives, during widowhood. Son, Peter, horse & bridle and land in Culpepper Co. Son, Moses, to have horse. Dau. Susannah Hardistrees, 5 pounds curr. Son, John, 100 acres of land in Culpepper Co. Sons, Charles, Joseph and Elias, each to have a horse and bridle. Daughters: Catey, Elizabeth, Susannah, Mary, Anney Kemper. Son Tilman Kemper. Estate to be divided equally among children. Exrs: sons, Peter, John, Charles, Joseph. Wit: Jacob Kemper, Sr., Jacob Kemper, Jr. (p. 153)

THOMAS, William
    14 Nov. 1798. 22 April 1799.
    All estate to wife, Allenner, except that bequeathed the following children: Daniel, Eramus, John, William (last 2 are the youngest). Daughters, Rebecca and Precious, to have slaves and furniture. Exrs: wife, sons Daniel and William. Wit: Reuben Strother, Richard Turner, James Channel. (p. 176)

MALLORY, Clement P.
    -- 1800. Inventory. (p. 222)

WINKFIELD, Honor
    24 Nov. 1798. 22 April 1799.
    To Ben, a Negro slave, belonging to James Gillison, Sr., whom I claim as

my husband, all my estate. Exrs: John Gillison, Lewis Shumate. Wit: Elizabeth Shumate, Betty Shumate, Jane Shumate. (p. 177)

BUCHANAN, Michael
    15 Jan. 1799. 24 June 1799. (p. 181)
    Brother, John Buchanan and Aquilla Janny, of Berkeley Co., are appointed executors, they are to give 1000 acres of land that I purchased in the Northwest Territory of Dr. Selden, to my nieces, Mary and Hannah Buchanan (daus. of bro. Thomas, dec'd.), of Pa. Aquilla Janny to have 100 acres and $200 for his kindness. Wit: Hezekiah Glascock, William McEndress (?).

RECTOR, Henry
    8 Jan. 1799. June 1799.
    Son, Elijah, to have 35 pounds curr. Daughter, Caty, 12 pounds curr.; her dau. Polly to have personal property. Son Spencer and his children - Edward, John, Henry, Mary Ann, Pencey (or Percy). Wit: Joseph Lloyd, Hezekiah Glascock, William Finch. (p. 182)

PORTER, Thomas
    10 May 1799. 24 June 1799.
    Son, Eli, to have 150 acres of land. Daughter, Betty Porter. Children who are married: Hannah Jackman, Sarah Scott, John Porter, William, Thomas, Charles and Edwin Porter. Wearing clothes to be divided among my servants, Jack, Will and Sam. Exrs: sons, William, Thomas. (p. 184)

BROWN, Jonathan
    19 May 1799. 22 July 1799.
    To wife, Mary Brown, whole of estate for her use and disposal forever. Wit: Samuel Chilton, William Brown, James Seaton, Betty Kenner. (p. 188)

ROOKHARD, Thomas
    8 Aug. 1788. July 1799. (p. 189)
    "Wife to have estate during widowhood, unless she makes waest with any part of estate then she foffetts the above gift." Daughter Nancy and her son, Robert Carter Rookhard. Dau. Lydia Aden to have 1 shilling. Grandchildren, Hiram and Elizabeth Rookhard, to have 1/2 of estate. Exrs: wife Sarah and George Calvert. Wit: James Weeks, George Walker, Richard Cochran.

BARBEE, Joseph
    27 Jan. 1800. Sale of Estate. (p. 225)

THORNBURY, John
    3 Nov. 1795. 23 Sept. 1799.
    Wife, Elizabeth Thornbury. Sons, Henry, Samuel and Francis, to have plantation where they now live. Daughters, Peggy Myers and Mary Wigginton. Children: Henry, Daniel, Samuel, Francis, William, Thomas, Peggy, Mary, Zachariah and Elizabeth. "Have a patent in 1700 acres of land in Kentucky." Exrs: sons Samuel, Francis and William. Wit: Henry Dade Hooes, Moses Moss, Thomas Green. (p. 196)

STEWART, James
    An Account of estate of James Stewart, dec'd. James Stewart, Jr., Exr. Apprs: Charles Marshall, Thomas Diggs, Willy Roy, B. Duffy. (p. 212)

LUCKETT, Thomas
    6 Jan. 1800. 21 Jan. 1800.
    Sons, John, Douglas, Thomas, William, to have 3 pounds and 2 shillings each, that was left them by their aunt Elizabeth. Son Richard to have 17 pounds curr. Daughters, Cloe Tongue, Elenor Cox, Nancy and Mary. Exrs: son Ignatus, James Cox, Joshua Tongue. Wit: Daniel Orear, John Peters, Samuel Cave. (p. 219)

GIBSON, Jonathan
    27 Jan. 1800. (p. 227)

PORTER, Thomas
24 Feb. 1800. Sale of estate.
Exrs: William, Thomas and Edwin Porter. (p. 239)

EDMONDS, John, Jr.
1 Sept. 1798. 18 Sept. 1798. Nuncupative.
(Died Tuesday, 8 Aug. 1798.) Proved by the oath of William Edmonds. Land to be equally divided among William, George, John, Elias and Peggy. Property intended for Nancy, wife of William Blackwell, to be left in trust for her. William Blackwell to have nothing. (p. 244)

BRADFORD, Daniel
16 Jan. 1800. 25 April 1800. Hamilton Parish.
Slaves to sons, John, William and Charles. Sons, Enoch and Fielding, a tract of land in Kentucky, where they now live. Son, Simon, 250 acres in Fauquier Co. and tract of land in Kentucky. Daughters, Mary Allen, Violetta Bradford, Sarah and Katy, land. Exrs: wife (not named), sons, William and Simon. Wit: Benjamin Edwards, John Estham (or Eastham). (p. 246)

BRENT, William
13 Feb. 1793. 23 June 1800.
To wife, Hannah Brent, estate for life, 11 slaves and household goods. After decease of wife the estate to go to sons, Christopher Neale Brent and George Brent. Children: Thomas, William, Alexander, Christopher Neale, George, Ann, Mary Waddy Brent and Elizabeth Mary Brent. Exrs: wife, Thomas Brent, William Brent, David Blackwell. (p. 258)

BUSSEY, Cornelias
13 Feb. 1800. 23 Sept. 1800.
To wife, Jane Bussey, all estate during life. Mentions children but does not name, except daughter, Peggy Bragg (hus. Dozzer Bragg). Wit: William Adams, Walter Adams, Richard Well. (p. 263)

HACKLEY, Lott
4 March 1798. 25 June 1798.
Wife, Jael (or Joel) to have estate, wife to decide whether slaves are to be free, if they are kept they are to be divided among brothers and sisters at decease of wife. Mention is made of brother Francis Hackley, sister Lucy Johnson, Mary Underwood, Samuel Reed (bro.-in-law) and Mildred Stigler (wife of James Stigler). Exrs: wife, James Stigler, Thomas Keith. Wit: Peter Grant, Thomas Peyton, Daniel Hickson. (p. 264)

CUNDIFF, Isaac
4 July 1796. 22 Sept. 1800.
Wife, Lettes Cundiff, to have estate during her life time. Children: James, Betty Laws, Sally Feagins, Lucy Roberson, Mimey Furr. Exrs: wife, John Laws (son-in-law). Wit: Benjamin Carpenter, Margaret Barten, Joseph Jefferson, Jr., John Feagan, William Furr. (p. 265)

CHILTON, Charles, Dr.
27 Oct. 1800. Admrs: Joseph Blackwell, Thomas Chilton. (p. 272)

BOWERS, Peter
15 Oct. 1800. 22 Dec. 1800. (p. 277)
Son, Michael, to receive 5 pounds curr. Gr. daughter, Susan Bowers (dau. of Michael), slave. Son, William, to have land, slave and surveying instruments. Daughter, Molly, to have 5 pounds curr. and her children to have land and slave. Granddaughter, Betsy Glendenning. Daughter, Rachel, to receive 60 pounds curr. Daughter, Rosannah, to have slaves and land, to have support through life. Daughter Peggy's children to have 5 pounds curr. Daughter Betsy to live with daughter Molly. Exrs: James Wright, Williams Bowers, Peter Connay. Wit: Joseph King, Elizabeth King, Henry King.

GIBSON, Abraham
27 Oct. 1800. ------.

Wife, Ann Gibson, to have estate during life and widowhood. Children: Mary Barnes, Nancy Yates, Jane Strother, Elizabeth Davis, Jacob, Frances Yates (formerly Frances Holtzclaw, lately intermarried with Lewis Yates), Sarah Lambert. Exrs: Ann Gibson, Lewis Yates. Wit: Hugh Chinn, William Yates, Joseph Cross. (p. 292)

EUSTACE, William
7 Dec. 1800. 23 Feb. 1801.
Wife Ann to have slaves and estate during life. Son, Hancock, to have land where I now live, all furniture except what I have given his mother. Son, William, to have 2 slaves. John Gibson (or Gilson), grandson. Daughter Mary and son William. Wit: Thomas Blackwell, Samuel Blackwell, William Jones. (p. 293)

PINKARD, William
25 April 1798. 23 Feb. 1801.
All estate to wife, Mildred, and to be disposed of at her decease among the children as she thinks proper. Wit: Cornelius Bussey, Richard Well. (p. 294)

HANSON, Ann
6 April 1800. 3 Oct. 1800.
(Ann Hanson was formerly from Charles Co., Md.) Son, Sam Claggett, to have land I bought of my son, Gustavus Brown Horner, 300 acres, in another tract 114 acres. I give Samuel the above property as an act of justice as he has sustained much loss by my two marriages. Grandson, William Edward Horner (son of William). Mentions former husband, Robert Horner. Sons, William and John Horner. Susanne W. Harris, granddaughter of late husband, Samuel Hanson, is needy, to be given 50 pounds curr., but money not to be under control of her husband. Gold sleeve buttons to Ann Hanson, daughter of Col. Samuel Hanson of Georgetown. Granddaughters: Frances, Elizabeth and Catherine Horner. Exrs: Samuel Claggett, Gustavus Brown Horner, William Horner. Wit: Ann Ireland Brown, G. R. Brown, Gustavus Brown, Jr. (p. 299)

McNEEL, John
4 June 1784. 22 June 1801.
Legatees: Sarah Ball (wife of David), 170 acres of land - "she and her ayars." Wit: Anne Ball, Benjamin Ball, William D. Darnall. (p. 305)

NICKOLS, Thomas
27 March 1801. 27 July 1801. Of Parish of Leeds.
Wife, Mary to have entire estate. Son of brother James Nickols, by name of Nathan, to have 1 shilling. Exrs: wife and Charles Adams. Wit: Gregory Glasscock, Carly Adams, Nancy Adams. (p. 317)

CRAIG, James
2 July 1792. 22 June 1801.
Slaves to be liberated. Samuel Holiday to have 400 pounds of curr. Jane Stewart (widow of James) to have 5 pounds in case she survives me, if she does not the same amount to her daughter, Betty. Jane Smith, widow of Alexander Smith, 5 pounds currency. Mrs. Williams, mother-in-law of Cossun Day, to have 5 pounds curr. Bequest to children of John and Margaret Doby, their son James excepted. Legatees: Joseph Craig (brother), James Doby and wife, Ann. Exrs: Gavin Lawson (of Stafford Co.) and William Allanson (of Fauquier Co.), each to receive 50 pounds curr. Wit: Edward Pendleton, Daniel Morgan, William Lawson, Daniel Wheatley. (p. 303)

DULIN, William
18 June 1801. 27 July 1801. (p. 319)
To son, William Dulin, 5 pounds currency. Daughter, Elizabeth Welch, 40 pounds currency. Son, John, to have 25 pounds curr. Son, Edward, to have 50 pounds curr. Son, Philip, to have 50 pounds curr. Son, Charles, to have 3 pounds of curr. Son, George, to have 7 slaves. Daughter, -- Glascock Clemence. Grandson, George Dulin (son of William). Grandson, William Elzey Dulin. Elizabeth Haddox Dulin, feather bed. Exrs: wife (Clemence) and son George. Wit: James W. Fishback, Gregory Glasscock, David W. Morris.

JONES, William
    25 July 1793. 22 Dec. 1800. (p. 320)
    Wife, Mary, to have estate during widowhood. Daughters, Sarah and Hannah. Daughters, Cary and Lucretia, to receive as much as first children when they married. Exrs: sons James and William. Wit: Septimus Norris, John Norris.

HANSBOROUGH, Gabriel
    8 Dec. 1799. 28 July 1800.
    Wife, Molly Hansborough. Mentions two sons, James and Peter. Exrs: Peter Conway, Nathaniel Graves, John Peters.

MASSIE, Thomas
    20 Oct. 1801. 28 Dec. 1801. (p. 339)
    Wife, Dolly Massie. Daughter, Mary Triplett. Children: Ase, Thomas, Samuel, Josias, Benjamin Morehead, John. Son Robert Massie, Dollie and Nimrod Massie, to have slaves made over to them by John Morehead. Son, Asa, to have 100 acres of land in Kentucky. Exrs: wife, son Ase, Joseph Chilton. Wit: Joseph Chilton, Edward Shacklett, John Cooke, Joseph Smith.

LEWIS, James
    21 Jan. 1802. 26 Jan. 1802.
    Estate lately received from James Lewis (uncle) of Spottsylvania Co. to go to wife, Jane. All estate that comes from father to go to brother, William Lewis. Wit: George Pickett, Charles Marshall, James Walker. (p. 347)

SKINKER, Thomas
    1 March 1801. 26 April 1802.
    Legatees: Ephiram Abell, John Hickerson, Samuel Skinler (son of bro. William) to have land in Stafford Co., William Skinker (son of bro. Samuel). William Skinker (nephew). (p. 354)

HINSON, Robert
    29 March 1802. 26 April 1802.
    Elizabeth Whitton to receive $20 per month. Daughter, Ann Dialls (or Dealls), all children not named. Exrs: James Hinson, Tapley Hinson (sons) Wit: John Blackwell, John Bronaugh, Thomas Blackwell. (p. 355)

BROOKS, Humphreys
    7 April 1802. 24 May 1802.
    Wife, Milly, to have use of plantation during widowhood, slaves and silver. Sons, Francis and Mathew Whiting Brooks. Daughters: Ann Brooks, Catherine Powell, Lucy Igram, Elizabeth Digges. Exrs: Mathew Whiting Brooks (son) and Burr Powell (son-in-law).

NORRIS, William
    15 Dec. 1801. 26 April 1802.
    Estate to be divided into twelve equal parts. Sons: John, Joseph, Samuel and William. Daus: Elizabeth, Hannah, Ellin, Sarah, Mary, Catherine, Nancy Bailey. Grandchildren: children of daughter, Susannah Robinson. Exrs: sons, John and Joseph Norris. Wit: William Barker, Charles Barker, Presley Hampleton. (p. 357)

JAMES, John
    8 Sept. 1801. 25 April 1802.
    Wife, Elizabeth James. Children: Mary, Margaret, Aldridge and David. Exrs: sons Aldridge and David, James Wright. Wit: Peter Conway, Britain Lewis, John Shumate, Sr. (p. 387)

HUME, Andrew
    20 March 1802. 24 May 1802. (p. 382)
    Children: Robert, Andrew, John, George and Hannah Hume. Exrs: sons Andrew and George. Wit: James Wood, Zaccheus Quisenberry, Henry Warden.

SPENNY, William
    11 May 1802. 24 May 1802.

Estate to brother, Benjamin Spenny. Exr: brother Benjamin Spenny (or Sperry). Wit: Nathaniel Rector, Charles Pickett, Eppa Timberlake. (p. 382)

McFARLAND, John
Legatees: John McFarland (nephew) and children of Robert McFarland (bro.) Extrx: wife Jane McFarland. Wit: James Batson, Jesse McVeigh, M. Lacy. (p. 346)

KERNES, William
18 Dec. 1799. 27 Sept. 1802.
Daughters, Elizabeth Stadler and Ann Kernes. Sons: John, Daniel, William, John M. and Benjamin Horton Kernes. Exr: son John Kernes. Wit: James Wright, Benjamin Horton, Augustine Horton, Samuel Elliott. (p. 397)

TOMPKINS, John
25 June 1802. 22 Nov. 1802.
At present at the home of Mr. Samuel Steeles, in Fauquier Co. Wife to receive $2,000 (not named). Mention is made of brother, Fontanatus Tompkin and other brothers and sisters. Exrs: Christopher Tompkins and Henry Tompkins (bros.). Wit: George Rogers and Ann Garner. (p. 403)

WINN, John
18 Aug. 1801. 24 Jan. 1803.
Wife, Mary Winn. Children: Mary, John Smallwood, Thomas Roley, Zachary Cox, John Noble, Elizabeth Lombard, Sarah Ann, Hester V. Grandson, Daniel Gellerson. Exrs: wife and son Thomas. Wit: Walter Oliver, Enoch Jameson, James Cox. (p. 419)

HAMPTON, Joseph
15 Oct. 1802. 28 Feb. 1803.
Wife, Molly Hampton. Children: John, Lawson, Jeremiah, Susannah, Joseph, Francis and Alfred. Exrs: wife, Richard Nutt, Thomas Weeks. Wit: Burr Powell, Elizabeth Batson, Winny Nutt, Minny Hampton. (p. 423)

PEYTON, Yelverton
Probated 28 Feb. 1803.
Son: Yelverton Peyton. Wife: Margaret C. Peyton (formerly Scott). Mentions brother, Richard Henry Peyton. The will was proven by the oaths of Chandler Peyton, John Scott, Charles Marshall. (p. 424)

CHADWELL, John
27 Nov. 1799. 23 ---- 1803.
Wife, Elizabeth Chadwell. Estate to be divided among my first children. Exrs: wife, William Guttridge. Wit: Alexander Monroe, Thomas White, Elijah Gutridge. (p. 431)

COX, Abraham
1 Feb. 1803. 25 July 1803.
Wife: Elizabeth Cox. Daughters: Mary Winn, Ann, Elizabeth Cox (dau.-in-law). Sons: Thomas, William, Zachariah Cox. Exrs: wife, Zachariah Cox (son), James Cox (gr. son). (p. 436)

SMITH, Enoch
6 Oct. 1803. 25 July 1803.
Wife: Elizabeth Smith. Sons: John (eldest), Elijah, Hedgman, Isham, Elias. Daughter, Lucinda. Unborn child. Exrs: wife, John Smith (son), John Obannon, William Obannon. Wit: James Elias and William Obannon. (p. 437)

HEFLIN, William
21 April 1803. 25 July 1803.
Wife mentioned, not named. Son: William Heflin. Daughters: Darkey, Polly, and Anna. Exrs: Elijah Arnold, William Heflin, Jr. Wit: Chapman Grant, Mitchell Bird. (p. 439)

JOHNSTON, Moses, Sr.
    16 June 1803. 25 July 1803. Of Parish of Leeds.
    Wife: Duanna Johnston. Sons: Moses, Daniel, David, Nimrod, John. Daughters: Molly, Susannah Waddle, Margaret McMecklin, Charlotte Johnston. Exrs: Am---- Bailey, Simon Cornwell. Wit: James Ellis, Joseph Ellis, Isham Obannon. (p. 440)

HITT, Peter
    17 Aug. 1802. 25 Oct. 1802.
    Wife: Hannah Hitt. Children: Presley, Harrison, Alexander, Mary, Susannah, Thaddeus, Nancy, Fanny, Elizabeth and unborn child. Unless wife remarries estate not to be divided until her decease. Exrs: son Pressley and Gabriel Green (of Culpepper Co.). (p. 440)

WOOD, Dickerson
    23 Jan. 1803. 25 July 1803.
    Wife: Mary Wood. Sons: Dickerson, William, Elijah, James. Mentions a daughter, but does not name. Wit: Lewis Jones, Enoch Smoot. (p. 441)

SEATON, John
    Probated 24 Oct. 1803.
    Wife: Alice Seaton. Mention is made of estate left by father, James Seaton. Children: James, Francis, Lydia, George, John and William. Exr: Reuben Murray.

ASH, Francis
    17 Feb. 1800. 24 Oct. 1803. (p. 466)
    Wife: Nancy Ash. Children: Sarah, Elizabeth, Thornton, Susannah, Maria, Lucy, Kitty, Harriett, John Richard and Juliet. Exrs: Thomas Adams, William Ash (brother). Wit: Cornelius King, Orphy King, John A. Bolling.

KEARTON, Anthony
    18 May 1803. 24 Oct. 1803.
    Wife: Fanny Kearton. Legatees: brothers, John and Thomas Kearton and sister Elizabeth. Exrs: Richard Baker, Thaddeus Norris, Charles Marshall. (Executors refuse to act.) (p. 467)

WAKE, Robert
    6 July 1803. Sept. 1803.
    Legatees: brother, William and mother. Extrx: Mary Wake (mother). (p. 468)

BURKE, William
    17 May 1803. 26 Dec. 1803.
    Wife, Susannah, to have lease of land in Fairfax Co. Children: Jane, Sarah, John, George, Elizabeth, Polly, William, Susan and Ann Burke. Wit: Jesse Tharp, Henry Benard. (p. 481)

WITHERS, William
    21 Nov. 1803. 23 Jan. 1804.
    To son, James Withers, a tract of land in Culpepper Co. Son, Spencer Withers. Daughters, Susan, Elizabeth Withers (wife of John Withers). Daughter, Molly Withers (wife of William Withers). Daughter, Alese Withers (wife of John Ball). Daughter, Agatha, wife of Martin Porter. Son, Jesse Withers, to have land willed to testator by his father. Sons, Lewis and Elijah Withers. Granddaughter, Betty Withers (dau. of William). Exrs: sons, James, Jesse and Lewis Withers. Wit: Enoch Withers, Mathew Withers, Jennette Withers. (p. 492)

JAMES, Benjamin
    27 Sept. 1803. 23 Jan. 1804.
    Wife: Elizabeth James. Sons: Benjamin, Thomas and John. Exrs: wife, son Benjamin and cousin Joseph James.

CURTICE, John
    8 Feb. 1802. 24 Jan. 1804.

Legatees: Susannah Stigler (or Steggers), "my companion," to have all of estate, after her decease it is to be equally divided between the following: John Stigler, alias Curtice; Lewis Stigler, alias Curtice; Elijah Steigler, alias Curtice. "Only sons Susannah Stigler has had by me." Daughters: Elizabeth and Lucy Stiglers. Exrs: William Hampton, William Hunton. (p. 495)

MAUZY, Henry
31 Dec. 1799. 27 Feb. 1804.
Wife: Elizabeth Mauzy. Children: John, Nancy Bayse, Henry, Peter, William, Priscilla Roper, George, Ethel Newman, Susannah Kemper, Thomas, Richard, Michael and Joseph. Exrs: wife, Thomas, Richard and Michael and Joseph. James Peters (son-in-law) and his ten children that he had by daughter Betty Mauzy.

PICKETT, Martin
4 May 1803. 25 April 1804.
Daughters, Lucy Marshall (hus. Charles), Letty Johnson, Milly Clarkson, Judah Slaughter (hus. Stanton), Betsy, Nancy Brooke (hus. Francis). Sons: George Blackwell Pickett and Steptoe Pickett. Brothers: John and William Pickett. All land in Kentucky bequeathed to five daughters. Exrs: son George Pickett, Gen. John Blackwell, Stanton Slaughter. (A long will) (p. 519)

CHUNN, John Thomas
31 Jan. 1804. 28 May 1804.
Wife, not named. Legatees: children of sister Henrietta Turner; children of sister, Charity Edwards; Zach Vowells; children of dec'd. nephew, Henry Vowels; children of sister, Elizabeth Dyson; children of dec'd. sister, Winnifred Dyson; nephew, John Thomas Chunn; children of dec'd. brother, Zach Chunn; nephew Charles Chunn; friend, Charles Marshall. Exrs: wife, Zach Vowel (nephew), Andrew Chunn, Zephanie Turner. Wit: Charles Marshall, Nimrod Ashby. (p. 527)

MALLORY, Clement
1800. Inventory. (p. 222)

BARBEE, Jonathan
27 Jan. 1800. Sale of estate. (p. 225)

ALLISON, William
24 May 1793. 28 April 1800.
To daughter, Mary Semour Hall Allison, at present wife of Robert Rose, to have a tract of land equal to 500 acres that came to me by her worthy mother, now deceased, and another large tract of land of about 1000 acres. Daughter's present husband, Robert Rose, is not entitled to any of legacy. Exr: David Allison (brother) (p. 249)

YOUNG, James
4 June 1795. 25 Feb. 1799.
To grandson, James Neale, to have 6 Negroes during life and at his decease they are to be divided between his sons, Richard and William. To daughter, ---- Jones, 5 shillings. Philip Fishback, to have 32 pounds curr. To grandson, James Dale, to have wearing apparel. Mentions 2 daughters, --- Neale and -- Dale and their children. Exrs: Francis Whiting, James Neale, W. Fitzhugh, W. Fitzhugh. (p. 255)

MOXLEY, Jeremiah
9 Oct. 1803. 27 Feb. 1804.
Wife: Hannah Moxley. Daughter, Sebella Moxley, dau. Hannah Moxley (mentions her grandfather Morris). Sons: James and Solomon. Exr: Sanders Morris.

WILLS FROM MISCELLANEOUS COURT ORDERS - Fauquier Co.

WAUGH, Mary
27 March 1749. 14 Dec. 1756. Stafford Co.

To son, William Mountjoy, large Bible, table, 40 acres of land. To son, Peter, 300 acres of land in Prince William Co., where Francis Watts now lives. To daughter, Elizabeth Conway, 150 acres of land, after her decease to her son, John Markham, should he die without heirs, then to grandson, Peter Conway. Mentions grandson, Thomas Conway. To daughter, Mary Donphan, personal estate. Wit: Michael Bryan, Winifred Ryan, Raleigh Traverse, John Mauzy, Jr.

MAUZY, Peter
12 Feb. 1750. 11 June 1751.
To son Michael, to have part of land where I now live, after decease of loving wife, Elizabeth Mauzy. Son, Peter Mauzy. Son, John, to have land in Prince William Co. Daughters, Mary Mauzy and Elizabeth Mauzy. Appoints the following friends to bind out sons until they are 21 years of age: William Mountjoy, Alexander Donphan, John Mauzy, Jr. Extrx: wife. Wit: Adam Stephen, John Mauzy, John Petcher (?). Stafford County.

ALLEN, William
16 Aug. 1739. 12 May 1741.
Of Stafford Co., Overwharton Parish. Mentions land left by Margaret Janaway, dec'd., unto her grandchildren, William and Margaret Lunsford (brother and sister). Wife: Margaret Allen. Legatees: John Crump; Sarah Walton (dau.) to have slaves; gr. son, William Walton (son of William); gr. dau. Ann Walton (father, William Walton). Daughter, Elizabeth Walter (hus. George) and son, William Walter. Daughter, Margaret, to have land in Prince William Co. Daughter, Dinah James (hus. John) to have slaves and land in Prince William Co., on Elk Run. Daughter, Hannah Withers, and son, James Withers, to have slaves. Wife and son William to have plantation where I now live. Grandson, John Allen. Exrs: wife and son William. Wit: Richard Young, John Tibbs, Darly Murphy.

CRUMP, John
27 Oct. 1744. 23 June 1746.
Of Hamilton Parish, Prince William Co., Va. Daughters: Elizabeth Blackwell, Susannah Hewlett, Hannah Crump. Sons, George and John, to each have 10 shillings. Son, Joseph, to have a tract of land in Northumberland Co. and 8 Negroes. Estate to be divided when Benjamin arrives at the age of 21 years. Wit: Lazarus Taylor and William Coale.

SINKLERS, Samuel
24 Jan. 1752. 6 Feb. 1752.
Of Hanover Co., Va. Sons, Samuel, John, Thomas, William and George, ---- land and slaves. Mention is made of a tract of land where Daniel Taylor now lives as one of the tenants. Money for the education of grandson, John Simpson. Daughter, Sarah Sinkler, to have 100 pounds of curr. on day of marriage. Exrs: wife Dinah, sons Samuel and Thomas Sinkler. Wit: T. Turner, William Cope and Mary Simpson.

MARRIAGE BONDS

| | | |
|---|---|---|
| Abell, Ephiram | Stringfellow, Betsy | 14 Jan. 1784 |
| Adams, Charles | Furr, Nancy | 8 Jan. 1788 |
| Adams, Gavin | Miller, Susannah | 4 March 1790 |
| Adams, George | Turner, Anna | 8 June 1769 |
| Adams, John | McCormack, Betsy | 25 July 1785 |
| Alexander, Ellis | Phillips, Drusilla | 21 Oct 1791 |
| Alford, William | Suttle, Fanny | 14 Jan 1786 |
| Allen, ---- | Heflin, Sally | 22 March 1787 |
| Allen, Azariah | Leach, Sarah | 24 Dec. 1794 |
| Allen, Henry | Nelson, Betty | 27 June 1772 |
| Allen, Henry | McKonkey, Catherine | 14 Dec. 1781 |
| Allen, John | Snelling, Hannah | 13 July 1786 |
| Allen, William | Bradford, Mary | 8 Dec. 1764 |
| Allen, William | Pepper, Hannah | 4 Aug. 1781 |
| Ambler, David | Monroe, Molly | 24 July 1793 |
| Ambler, William | Colvin, Sarah | 30 Oct. 1790 |
| Anderson, Cornelius | Riddle, Kitty | 6 Sept. 1790 |
| Anderson, Joseph | Freeman, Charlotte | 11 Dec. 1790 |
| Anderson, Theophiles | Lear (Sear), Molly | 27 Oct. 1788 |
| Anderson, Thomas | Anderson, Sally | 22 Dec. 1799 |
| Aramsmith, William | McBee, Susan | 14 Sept. 1789 |
| Ardeb, Aaron | Mahoney, Eliza | 4 Oct 1796 |
| Arnold, Isaac | Porter, Mary | 23 Oct. 1771 |
| Arnold, Samuel | Wright, Elizabeth | 5 Sept. 1771 |
| Arnold, Samuel | Hitch, Rebecca | 21 Sept. 1798 |
| Asbury, George | Taylor, Mary | 14 March 1780 |
| Ash, Francis | Adams, Ann | 20 Dec. 1774 |
| Ash, Uriel | Churchill, Milly | 4 March 1783 |
| Ashby, Benjamin | Ash, Jane | 2 Aug. 1781 |
| Ashby, John | Huffman, Catherine | 27 Oct. 1783 |
| Ashby, John | Smith, Sarah | 5 Aug. 1799 |
| Ashby, Nathaniel | Mauzy, Peggy | 3 Dec. 1777 |
| Ashby, Robert | Combs, Catherine | 28 April 1783 |
| Ashby, Robert | Walters, Ann | 26 Feb. 1793 |
| Ashby, William | Tibbs, Mary | 24 April 1767 |
| Ashly, Nimrod | Wright, Frances | 30 Nov. 1759 |
| Ashton, Lawerence | McBee, Susan | 14 Sept. 1789 |
| Athey, Joshua | Hitch, Elizabeth | 17 April 1780 |
| Atwell, Francis | McDonald, Mary | 25 Oct. 1768 |
| Atwood, John | Robinson, Lucy | 1 June 1790 (or 1794) |
| Auberry, Thomas | Fletcher, Ann | 13 Dec. 1764 |
| Austin, John | Burgess, Elizabeth | 20 Jan. 1783 |
| Austin, John | Browning, Elizabeth | 23 Oct. 1788 |
| | | |
| Bailey, George | Bragg, Phoebe | 13 April 1781 |
| Bailey, Green | Bragg, Mary | 13 Oct. 1788 |
| Bailey, James | Ball, Sarah | 6 March 1786 |
| Bailey, John | Barnes, Betsy | 2 Jan. 1793 |
| Bailey, Joseph | Newby, Hannah | 9 Aug. 1777 |
| Bailey, Samuel | Anderson (?), Agga | 8 Aug. 1795 |
| Bailey, Simon | Lunce, Hester | 4 Dec. 1781 |
| Bailey, Stephen | Lunceford, ---- | 19 April 1781 |
| Bailey, Thomas | White, Elizabeth | 28 Feb. 1786 |
| Bailey, Thomas | Campbell, Sarah | 8 Jan. 1787 |
| Bailey, William | Minter, Betty | 20 March 1789 |
| Bailey, William | Mays, Nancy | 22 Dec. 1796 |
| Bailey, William | Eaton, Abigail | 21 April 1798 |
| Bale, James | Claypool, Anne | 20 Jan. 1799 |
| Bales, John | Redd, Barbary | 8 April 1788 |
| Balis, Henry | Edmonds, Sophia | 25 Feb. 1787 |
| Balis (Baylis), William | Turner, Elizabeth | 22 May 1780 |
| Ball, Benjamin | Cook, Nancy | 28 Oct. 1794 |

| | | |
|---|---|---|
| Ball, William | Keas (Keys), Ann | 9 Feb. 1788 |
| Ball, William | Creek, Peggy | 12 Dec. 1794 |
| Ballard, John | Brown, Mary | 20 Oct. 1785 |
| Ballenger, Edward | Routt, Hannah | 29 Nov. 1799 |
| Barbee, Edward | Woodward, Caty | 20 Dec. 1797 |
| Barbee, John | Dyson, Mary | 24 June 1782 |
| Barbee, Joseph | Withers, Ann | 2 Feb. 1768 |
| Barbee, Joseph | Laurance, Elizabeth | 28 April 1783 |
| Barbee, William | Hickerson, Ann | 23 Jan. 1785 |
| Barker, Charles | Drake, Jean | 14 May 1789 |
| Barker, John | Glascock, Sarah | 21 Dec. 1789 |
| Barnes, John | Shumate, Judith | 2 Oct. 1796 |
| Barnett, Achilles | James, Ann | 11 Oct. 1788 |
| Barnett, Ambrose | Neavill, Judith | 18 July 1766 |
| Barnett, James | Spinney, Mary | 28 Nov. 1796 |
| Barnett, Joseph | Hitt, Mary | 2 Jan. 1789 |
| Barnett, William | Smith, Catherine | 22 Nov. 1790 |
| Barnough, John | Curtis, Elizabeth | 1 Aug. 1792 |
| Barry, Greenberry | Davis, Frances L. | 7 Aug. 1787 |
| Barry, Willis | Oldacres, Hannah | 26 Feb. 1793 |
| Bartlett, James | Phillips, Sarah | 12 Aug. 1790 |
| Bartlett, John | Bartlett, Ann | 20 April (?) 1780 |
| Bartlett, Thomas | Carroll, Sarah | 2 Jan. 1777 |
| Barton, William | Heflin, Peggy | 8 June 1799 |
| Bates, Robert | Johnson, Betsy | 20 June 1785 |
| Batterson, Robert | Walker, Ann | 3 Nov. 1796 |
| Baxter, John | Briant, Amelia | 26 Nov. 1772 |
| Bayley, William | Newby, Nancy | 11 Feb. 1782 |
| Bayse, Isaac | Bashaw, Frances | 7 Jan. 1786 |
| Bayse, Josiah | Sinclair, Sarah | 22 May 1775 |
| Bayse, Richard | Taylor, Nancy | 14 Dec. 1781 |
| Beadle (Bedle), John | Evan, Margaret | 3 March 1795 |
| Beatty, John | Shipp, Nancy | 23 March 1785 |
| Bennett, Sanford | Cremon, Anne | 14 Jan. 1787 |
| Benson, Charles | Benson, Franky | 15 May 1781 |
| Benson, Robert | Stringfellow, Ann | 14 Oct. 1788 |
| Benson, Zachariah | Parklow, Sarah | 11 May 1785 |
| Berry, Elijah | Fegan, Susannah | 9 May 1777 |
| Berry, George | Conway, Sarah | 17 May 1777 |
| Berry, Thomas | Hampton, Ann | 15 Feb. 1798 |
| Berry, William | Fegan, Clara | 7 May 1777 |
| Berryman, Benjamin | Bryant, Anna | 1 April 1775 |
| Berryman, Francis | Barr, Elizabeth | 8 March 1788 |
| Billingsley, James | Moreland, Nancy | 16 Nov. 1791 |
| Bishop, Daniel | Leake, Ann | 25 June 1787 |
| Bishop, James | Lake, Cloe | 11 Dec. 1789 |
| Blackaby, George | Palmer, Elizabeth | 22 Jan. 1800 |
| Blackerby, Jeduthon | Chamberlayne, Mary | 13 May 1780 |
| Blackman, William | Bashaw, Betsy | 11 Sept. 1785 |
| Blackwell, James | Blackwell, Ann | 3 March 1766 |
| Blackwell, Joseph | Gibson, Ann Grayson | 14 Aug. 1787 |
| Blackwell, Samuel | Gillison, Peggy | 1 Dec. 1780 |
| Blackwell, Samuel | Bragg, Mary | 27 Dec. 1788 |
| Blackwell, Thomas | Grant, Judith | 26 Sept. 1781 |
| Bland, James | Randall, Hannah | 1 Dec. 1788 |
| Bogers (Rogers), Rodham | Runnells, Ann | 1 Feb. 1798 |
| Boley, Elijah | Barracks, Asey | Aug. 1792 |
| Borain (Borein), Peter | Edmonds, Elizabeth | 27 Jan. 1781 |
| Bowen, James | Bower (?), Rachel | 17 Dec. 1781 |
| Bowling, Thomas | Brown, Peggy | 20 June 1797 |
| Bowman, George | Duncan, Priscilla | 19 Nov. 1789 |
| Boyce, Richard | Helm, Sarah | 19 June 1765 |
| Boyd, John | Wright, Milly | 20 Nov. 1785 |
| Boyd, Samuel | Brooke, Molly | 13 Aug. 1777 |
| Bradford, Austin | Hard, Elizabeth | 14 Sept. 1787 |

| | | |
|---|---|---|
| Bradford, Benjamin | Allen, Ann | 30 Dec. 1764 |
| Bradford, William | Steele, Molly | 20 Dec. 1786 |
| Bradley, Hugh | Bashaw, Celia | 4 Aug. 1781 |
| Bragg, David | Crawley, Margaret | 17 Nov. 1786 |
| Bragg, Dozier | Bussey, Peggy | 10 Dec. 1790 |
| Bramlett, Henry | Gough, Gladah | 30 Dec. 1785 |
| Bramlett, William | Laurance, Ann | 26 Dec. 1793 |
| Brangham, Thomas | Wilson, Elizabeth | 10 March 1787 |
| Branthan, Richard | Crump, Frances | 26 Jan. 1781 |
| Bray, John | McKinsey, Elizabeth | 6 Aug. 1795 |
| Bredwell, Teba | Matthew, Polly | 30 --- 1797 |
| Brian, James | Linn, Mary | 23 May 1780 |
| Brimm, Thomas | Johnson, Sally | 30 July 1795 |
| Brink, Alexander | Sullivan, Elizabeth | 4 Feb. 1788 |
| Broadbent, James | Bailey, Sarah | 26 Feb. 1789 |
| Broadhurst, Joseph | Fanbin, Sally | 1 Oct. 1788 |
| Broadhurst, William | Howell (?), Franky | 31 Dec. 1787 |
| Bronaugh, Thomas | Kendall, Lucretia | 23 Feb. 1790 |
| Bronaugh, William | Hall (Hale), Jane | 26 Dec. 1789 |
| Brooke, George | Marshall, Judy | 20 April 1785 |
| Brooke, William | Anner, Eleanor | 23 Nov. 1793 |
| Brown, Francis | Smith, Elizabeth | 23 Sept. 1783 |
| Brown, John | Stringfellow, Dolly | 3 Dec. 1781 |
| Brown, John | Hunton, Polly | 17 March 1796 |
| Brown, Robert | Boyd, Molly | 29 May 1786 |
| Brown, Thomas | Winterton, Sally | 11 Dec. 1781 |
| Brown, Thomas | Ash, Ann | 20 Oct. 1785 |
| Brown, Thomas | Sanders, Molly | 29 Dec. 1788 |
| Brown, Thomas | Simmons, Katy | 9 March 1793 |
| Brown, William | Parker, Mary | 19 March 1785 |
| Brumm (Brimm), John | Simmons, Catherine | --- No date --- |
| Bryan, Battaley | Berryman, Elizabeth | 20 May 1777 |
| Buckley, William Lawerence | Shipps, Mary | 14 Feb. 1785 |
| Burdette, Joseph | Smith, Milly | 23 Oct. 1794 |
| Burdette, William | Chirley, Mary | 17 Dec. 1788 |
| Burgess, Edward | Porter, Frances | 29 Nov. 1787 |
| Burras, William | Dews (Deros), Eliz. | 26 Oct. 1797 |
| Burton, James | Singer, Nancy | 1 April 1789 |
| Butler, William | James, Margaret | 17 Dec. 1770 |
| Butler, William | Shadwell, Eliza | 15 Sept. 1793 |
| Button (Bulton), Jacob | Kamper, Sarah | 5 Aug. 1782 |
| Byrn, Thomas | Leach, Elizabeth | 29 Dec. 1785 |
| Callahan, James | Phillips, Elizabeth | 24 Sept. 1787 |
| Calmes, Marquis, Jr. | Heale, Priscilla | 18 Feb. 1782 |
| Calvin, Henry | Williams, Catherine | 21 Dec. 1787 |
| Calvin, William | George, Ann | 26 Dec. 1788 |
| Camack, Henry | Ellis, Molly | 25 May 1790 |
| Campbell, Owen | Settle, Betty | 15 June 1772 |
| Camragg, David | Wood, Mary | 29 Dec. 1795 |
| Camron, Angus | Haley, Ann | 30 Oct. 1794 |
| Cannon, John | Brazier, Sarah Harrison | 30 Sept. 1782 |
| Canor (?), Mathew | Hinson, Ann | 25 May 1781 |
| Carpenter, Benjamin | McFarlin, Elizabeth | 20 July 1788 |
| Carroll, Sanford | Bartlett, Betty | 13 Feb. 1771 |
| Carter, Dale | Robinson, Molly | 23 Nov. 1785 |
| Carter, Isaac | Newstead, Lydia | 1 Aug. 1793 |
| Carter, James | Dermont, Sarah | 3 Jan. 1787 |
| Carter, James | Scoggins, Elizabeth | 30 Aug. 1799 |
| Carter, John | Wood, Mary | 4 Dec. 1780 |
| Carter, William | Chester (?), Mary | 5 March 1789 |
| Carthron, John | Boswell, Molly | 12 Feb. 1776 |
| Carvell, James | Jeffries, Lettice | 24 March 1788 |
| Catlett, John | Routt, Rachel | 22 Jan. 1777 |
| Chaddick, Charles | Hainey, Winnifred | 2 Jan. 1774 |

| | | |
|---|---|---|
| Chadwell, John | Gutridge, Elizabeth | 6 July 1795 |
| Chandler, William | Martin, Caty | 13 April 1799 |
| Chewnor, John | Hawkins, Sally | 28 Jan. 1795 |
| Childs, James | McKonkey, Milly | 16 May 1781 |
| Chilton, Charles | Blackwell, Bettie | 18 Dec. 1760 |
| Chilton, Joseph | Smith, Ann | 2 April 1795 |
| Chinn, Chichester | Withers, Susannah | 9 Jan. 1789 |
| Chinn, Hugh | Ash, Peggy | 15 Dec. 1789 |
| Chinn, Thomas | Moore, Ann H. | 25 Dec. 1789 |
| Chrisman, George | Rector, Sally | 25 Feb. 1796 |
| Christian, Martin | Hayes, Betsy | 23 March 1797 |
| Christy, Charles | Smith, Nancy | 23 Dec. 1786 |
| Clarke, George | Hudnall, Alice | 29 June 1772 |
| Clarke, John | Ransdell, Mary | 5 Jan. 1789 |
| Clayton, John | Hurill (?), Elizabeth | 7 June 1764 |
| Clayton, Philip | Churchill, Ann | 6 May 1799 |
| Clayton, William | Chinn, Elizabeth | 20 Feb. 1788 |
| Cockran, Nathan | Keys, Margaret | 2 Dec. 1789 |
| Collins, Joseph | McClanahan, Jane | 15 Jan. 1796 |
| Compton, Richard | Barbee, Anna | 4 March 1799 |
| Conner, James | Parson, Matilda | 24 Oct. 1796 |
| Conner, William | Greening, Franky | 9 Aug. 1788 |
| Conway, Joseph | Turner, Sarah | 7 July 1788 |
| Cooke, John | Fielding, Nancy | 31 Jan. 1783 |
| Cooper, Vincent | Cooper, Mary | 26 Jan. 1785 |
| Coppage, John | Raley, Peggy | 25 Oct. 1786 |
| Coppage, William | Really, Sarah | 17 Sept. 1783 |
| Coppedge, William | Triplett, Mary | July 1795 |
| Corbin, John | Tapps, Molly | 16 Jan. 1799 |
| Corder, Bulis | Stone, Parsiall | 18 Feb. 1788 |
| Corder, John | Utterback, Caty | 18 Oct. 1800 |
| Cornet, Richard | Bowmer, Polly | 24 Sept. 1793 |
| Cornwell, Jacob | Hayes, Molly | 7 Sept. 1790 |
| Cornwell, Peyton | Elliott, Molly | 14 Jan. 1799 |
| Courtney, James | Embrey, Sarah | 25 Dec. 1794 |
| Courtney, William | Smith, Anna | 10 Jan. 1786 |
| Covert, Asa | Hudson, Sarah | 19 Dec. 1799 |
| Covert, Martin | Obannon, Susannah | 22 Oct. 1790 |
| Crafford, George | Humes, Mary | 12 April 1797 |
| Cranch, John | Groves, Mary | 26 Feb. 1795 |
| Crawford, William | Holder, Susannah | 7 Oct. 1789 |
| Crisman, George | Rector, Sally | 25 Feb. 1796 |
| Crosby, George | Glasscock, Sally | 7 Sept. 1797 |
| Crosby, George | Peters, Elizabeth | 8 Feb. 1799 |
| Crosson, John | Lewis, Acken | 2 July 1788 |
| Crupper, John | Thomas, Ann | 20 Dec. 1788 |
| Cummings, Daniel | Sullivan, Sarah | 28 Sept. 1785 |
| Cummings, Levi | Keys, Naomi | 18 Jan. 1797 |
| Cummins, George | Fullers, Sally | 11 Sept. 1799 |
| Cummins, William | Cornelias, Peggy | 16 June 1793 |
| Cunningham, Timothy | Fishback, Sarah | 25 Aug. 1789 |
| Curtis, Chester | Giles, Pensela | 5 Sept. 1793 |
| | | |
| Daniel, John | Hardin, Nancy | 8 Jan. 1795 |
| Darnall, David | Carlin, Milly (Molly) | 24 Dec. 1799 |
| Darnall, Joseph | Ball, Sarah | 22 March 1790 |
| Darnall, Joshua | Mauzy, Jemina | 21 Dec. 1798 |
| Darnall, Raleigh | Brown, Winnifred | 5 May 1788 |
| Darnall, William | Monroe, Elizabeth | 18 Dec. 1787 |
| Davis, Eli | Bannister, Frances | 13 Feb. 1782 |
| Davis, George | Grinnan, Elizabeth | 17 Dec. 1770 |
| Davis, James | Monday, Millah | 30 May 1793 |
| Davis, Levi | Kearns, Lydia | 14 March 1786 |
| Davis, Thomas | Withers, Lucinda | 23 Sept. 1795 |
| Dawson, William | Jenkins, Susannah | 26 Aug. 1799 |

| | | |
|---|---|---|
| Day, George | Dennis, Susannah | 24 Sept. 1790 |
| Day, John | Hudnall, Nancy | 23 Aug. 1790 |
| Day, William | Corder, Nelly | 26 Sept. 1785 |
| Dean, John | Pragh, Elizabeth | 6 May 1780 |
| Dearing, Conrad | Black, Nancy | 31 Aug. 1791 |
| De Bell, Lewis | Priest, Elizabeth | 3 Oct. 1799 |
| De Bell, William | Talbert, Ann | 26 March 1799 |
| Dells, John | Maddux, Mary | 14 April 1782 |
| Dennally (Donnelly), Thomas | Carter, Ann | 17 May 1790 |
| Dennis, Isaac | Walker, Sally | 24 May 1793 |
| Dennison, Henry | Dixon, Jenny | 21 March 1787 |
| Dennison, John | Norman, Sally | 5 March 1795 |
| Dermont, William | Williams, Mary | 21 Feb. 1787 |
| Devers, William | Johnson, Elizabeth | 22 Dec. 1789 |
| Dobin, James | Whitley, Ann | 26 Nov. 1781 |
| Dodd, Daniel | Settle, Hannah | 13 Sept. 1800 |
| Donaldson, Daniel | Morehead, Cary | 30 Oct. 1786 |
| Donaldson, Stephens | Boswell, Susannah | 17 June 1782 |
| Dowdall, Browner | Humes, Alecy | 21 Jan. 1788 |
| Dowdall, Thomas | Wickliffe, Bettie | 13 Feb. 1781 |
| Dowell, Nehemiah | Dearen, Bettie | 28 March 1793 |
| Drake, Dennis | James, Phebe | 26 Feb. 1793 |
| Drummond, Aaron | Oldacres, Nancy | 3 Nov. 1796 |
| Drummond, Joshua | Kidwell, Mary | 8 March 1786 |
| Drummond, William | Williams, Winny | 21 March 1772 |
| Duff, John | Whiting, Mary | 7 Jan. 1788 |
| Dulin, Edward | Rhodes, Elizabeth | 28 Jan. 1788 |
| Dulin, John | Glascock, Fanny | 24 March 1771 |
| Dulin, Lewis | Shud, Ann | 8 Sept. 1789 |
| Duncan, Archibald | Williams, Hannah | 27 Aug. 1792 |
| Duncan, Benjamin | Foley, Lettice | 13 Sept. 1800 |
| Duncan, Charles | Kish, Peggy | 27 Nov. 1786 |
| Duncan, Christopher | Hilburn, Elizabeth | 15 Feb. 1788 |
| Duncan, Jesse | Duncan, Rose | 1 March 1786 |
| Duncan, Joseph | Fletcher, Sarah | 18 Feb. 1766 |
| Duncan, Joseph | Freeman, Hannah | 21 Aug. 1771 |
| Duncan, Joseph | Jennings, Hannah | 26 Sept. 1785 |
| Duncan, Leroy | Williams, Aggy | 24 April 1799 |
| Duncan, Nimrod | Martin, Hannah | 11 Jan. 1786 |
| Duncan, William | Duncan, Lydia | 16 May 1780 |
| Dye, Martin | Hinson, Hanley | 3 Feb. 1786 |
| | | |
| Eady, Benjamin | Gillison, Margaret Gibson | 16 March 1787 |
| Eaton, Samuel | McBee, Fanny | 8 Feb. 1791 |
| Edge, Forrester | McCormack, Ann | 14 May 1799 |
| Edge, John, Jr. | Cummins, Mary | 3 Jan. 1781 |
| Edmonds, Elias | Edmonds, Frances | 11 Jan. 1786 |
| Edmonds, William | Foote, Hester | 12 Jan. 1799 |
| Edwards, George W. | Rust, Mary | 10 March 1798 |
| Edwards, Martin | Garner, Celia | 17 March 1783 |
| Edwards, William | Blackwell, Celia | 16 March 1764 |
| Einsor, George | Stephens, Docia | 25 Dec. 1785 |
| Elliott, William | Burger, Eleanor | 22 Sept. 1763 |
| Ellis, Reuben | Anderson (?), Nancy | 23 Sept. 1805 |
| Ellis, William | Clendenning, Nancy | 22 Dec. 1789 |
| Embry, Jesse | Hickerson, Mary | 4 April 1785 |
| Embry, William | Duncan, Franklin | 22 Dec. 1785 |
| Emmons, James | Stigler, Caty | 14 Oct. 1788 |
| Eustace, Isaac | James, Susannah | 14 Dec. 1777 |
| Eustace, William | Gillison, Mary | 21 Jan. 1789 |
| Evans, John | Wright, Sary | May 1800 |
| Evans, Samuel | Mathew, Elpha (?) | 20 March 1793 |
| Evinston, Francis | Corder, Minna | 18 Feb. 1794 |
| | | |
| Fannin, John | Riley, Lettice | 26 July 1789 |

| | | |
|---|---|---|
| Fant, Armistead | Duff, Ann | 17 July 1798 |
| Farguson, William | Amiss, Dolly | 25 Jan. 1783 |
| Fegan, Daniel | Harrison, Lydia | 19 July 1791 |
| Fegan, Edward | Sinkler, Polly | 22 June 1789 |
| Ferguson, Lewis | Pepper, Molly | 27 Jan. 1783 |
| Ferguson, William | Pepper, Ann | 28 Aug. 1789 |
| Feunce, William | Collins, Lilly | 22 Oct. 1788 |
| Fewell, Benjamin | Henry, Tabitha | 24 June 1795 |
| Fewell, James | Lowe, Mary | 3 Dec. 1794 |
| Fields, Henry | Wheatley, Mary | 16 Feb. 1799 |
| Fields, Reuben | Jones, Frances | 1 June 1785 |
| Fields, Thomas | Lawerence, Lydia | 3 Dec. 1793 |
| Fishback, Jacob | Morgan, Phebe | 18 Feb. 1771 |
| Fisher, Samuel | Pickard, Mary | 20 Dec. 1785 |
| Fitzhugh, Thomas | Moffitt, Charlotte | 17 Feb. 1780 |
| Fleming, Archibald | Watkins, Elizabeth | 17 Jan. 1799 |
| Fletcher, Benjamin | McKinney, Mary | 23 Sept. 1797 |
| Fletcher, John | Freeman, Elizabeth | 30 May 1780 |
| Fletcher, Richard | Ratcliffe, Elizabeth | 17 Sept. 1788 |
| Flinn, William | Stinson, Ann | 19 Jan. 1799 |
| Floweree (Flowers), William | Smith, Ann | 15 Aug. 1799 |
| Flowerell (Flowers), John | Grigsby, Edith | 28 March 1793 |
| Floyd, Henry | Crosby, Franky | 20 July 1783 |
| Foard, Thomas | Payne, Molly | 14 Dec. 1799 |
| Fogg, Nathaniel | Giles, Elizabeth | --------- |
| Foley, James | Ogleby, Elizabeth | 1 Aug. 1785 |
| Foley, James | Bradford, Mary | 1 March 1789 |
| Foley, John | Ashby, Milly | 24 April 1767 |
| Foley, John | Wheatley | 27 Aug. 1787 |
| Foote, William | Foster, Elizabeth | 26 Aug. 1780 |
| Ford, George | Calvert (Colvert), Charity | 15 Jan. 1789 |
| Ford, Henry | Payne, Nancy | 16 Dec. 1790 |
| Foster, Andrew | Crouch, Jane | 28 Aug. 1789 |
| Foster, George | Conway, Sarah | 25 Aug. 1786 |
| Foster, Robert | Leake, Milly | 25 Dec. 1786 |
| Foster, William | Bowers, Violet | 5 Nov. 1795 |
| Fowkes, Chandler | Harrison, Mary | 19 Dec. 1759 |
| Fox, Charles | Lathane, Elizabeth | 27 July 1799 |
| Frances, Joseph | Holmes, Sebrasta | 18 Sept. 1797 |
| Freeman, Harris | --------------- | 21 Aug. 1771 |
| Freeman, James | Sharpe, Elizabeth | 28 Aug. 1771 |
| Freeman, James | William, Margaret | 26 March 1782 |
| Freeman, William | Settle, Sally | 15 June 1777 |
| Froggett, Andrew | Smith, Moein | 25 Aug. 1788 |
| Frye, Abraham | Morgan, Polly | 2 April 1797 |
| Fulton, James | Downing, Winnifred | 14 Jan. 1799 |
| Furr, John | Furr, Nancy | 22 Jan. 1795 |
| | | |
| Gabriel, George | Neale, Mary | 18 Oct. 1788 |
| Gant, Ambrose | Vaughn, Sarah | 26 May 1786 |
| Garner, Joseph | Oar (Orr ?), Sally | Dec. 1790 |
| Garner, Smith | Bale, Jane | 22 June 1796 |
| Garner, Vincent | Withers, Susannah | 20 April 1799 |
| Garrett, James | Harley, Phebe | ----------- |
| Garrett, James | McKay, Ann | 13 March 1785 |
| Garrett, Nimrod | McCoy, Elizabeth | 23 Feb. 1790 |
| George, Aaron | Robinson, Lydia | 24 Oct. 1785 |
| George, Abner | Thorndyke, Elizabeth | 18 March 1799 |
| George, Joseph | Shumate, Lydia | 1 June 1786 |
| George, Reuben | Wilson, Nancy | 21 Nov. 1795 |
| German (Gorman), Michael | Masters, Ann | 6 Nov. 1790 |
| Gibson, Alexander | Jeffries, Lucy | 28 April 1789 |
| Gibson, John, Jr. | Eustace, Ann | 24 March 1783 |
| Gibson, Moses | Wrenn, ----- | 7 April 1795 |
| Gibson, Robert | Newby, Sinah | 7 Dec. 1790 |

| | | |
|---|---|---|
| Gibson, Thomas | Beale, Charlotte | 8 May 1782 |
| Gibson, William | Settle, Hannah | 31 March 1777 |
| Gilbert, Felix | Grant, Ann | 19 Oct. 1761 |
| Gillison, John | Alexander, Sarah | 13 Sept. 1782 |
| Gillison, John | Blackwell, Ann Lee | 10 Sept. 1799 |
| Gladstone, Arthur | Hitt, Susannah | 18 Dec. 1786 |
| Glascock, Downing | Strother, Sukey | 30 Oct. 1800 |
| Glascock, John | Glascock, Susannah | 1 Jan. 1799 |
| Glascock, Peter | Glascock, Anna | 24 Nov. 1783 |
| Glasscock, Archibald | Kinchloe, Hannah | 9 Oct. 1787 |
| Glasscock, John | Hathaway, --- | 1 Dec. 1788 |
| Glasscock, Michael | Rector, Catherine | 2 Dec. 1788 |
| Glasscock, William | Green, Ann | 20 Jan. 1789 |
| Glendenning (Clendenning), Geo. | Duncan, Milly | 31 Jan. 1786 |
| Godley, John | Sparks, Elizabeth | 10 March 1796 |
| Goe, Robert | Cox, Allinda | 2 Aug. 1785 |
| Goff, William | Weaver, Frances | 8 Jan. 1790 |
| Golden, Joseph | Henry, Sally | 16 March 1791 |
| Gore, Jonah | Hayes, Parthenia | 16 May 1797 |
| Gough, Bailey | Hensley, Dudley | 7 Oct. 1799 |
| Goulding, Vincent | Burdette, Nancy | 10 March 1790 |
| Graham, George | Blackwell, Alice | 14 June 1785 |
| Grant, George | Shackleford, Mary | 12 March 1772 |
| Grant, Joseph | Taylor, Elizabeth | 25 Oct. 1796 |
| Grant, Robin | Smith, Sarah | 22 Nov. 1790 |
| Grant, William | Clark, Nancy | 16 March 1797 |
| Graves, Duncan | Farrow, Dolly | 6 Sept. 1781 |
| Graves, Thomas | Williams, Amelia | 9 Feb. 1787 |
| Gray, Nathaniel | Ransdell, Sally | 26 Sept. 1786 |
| Gray, Nathaniel | Ransdell, Betsy | 18 March 1789 |
| Gray, Thomas | Payne, Patty | 30 Jan. 1792 |
| Grayer, George | Riley, Elizabeth | 1 Dec. 1788 |
| Green, Gabriel | Grant, Sarah Ann | 23 Sept. 1783 |
| Green, George | Barnes, Dinah | 23 May 1799 |
| Green, James | Jones, Elizabeth | 28 Jan. 1782 |
| Green, James | Triplett, Celia | 18 Feb. 1787 |
| Green, John | Collins, Betsy | 12 May 1785 |
| Green, Moses | Blackwell, Mary | 13 Feb. 1764 |
| Green, Robert | Edmonds, Frances | 15 Aug. 1787 |
| Green, William | Blackwell, Lucy | 13 May 1775 |
| Green, William | Crockett, Mary Ann | 18 Dec. 1786 |
| Greenwood, Henry | Dye, Sarah | 23 July 1799 |
| Griffin, George | Glascock, Molly | 24 Dec. 1787 |
| Grigsby, Aaron | Moffitt, Milly | 28 Jan. 1785 |
| Grigsby, Benjamin | Duncan, Elizabeth | 23 Dec. 1786 |
| Grigsby, Benjamin | Browning, Alice | 24 --- 1790 |
| Grigsby, Samuel | Cornwell, Franky | 4 Sept. 1786 |
| Grigsby, Taliaferrio | Keith, Elizabeth | 15 Feb. 1785 |
| Grigsby, William | Bullitt, Elizabeth | 8 Feb. 1771 |
| Grimsley, Nimrod | Roberts, Amelia | 17 Dec. 1787 |
| Groves, John | Crump, Sarah | 7 May 1790 |
| Gutridge, Allen | Deal, Lucy | 15 Dec. 1790 |
| Gutridge, Peter | Chadwell, Lucy | 11 Nov. 1794 |
| Gutridge, Reuben | Payne, Susannah | 7 Jan. 1794 |
| | | |
| Hackley, James | Freeman, Mary | 14 June 1771 |
| Haddux, Abraham | Hefflin, Ann | 26 Jan. 1795 |
| Hagan, John | Mauzy, Molly | 31 Oct. 1781 |
| Hailey, Anthony | Dennison, Mary | 20 Sept. 1785 |
| Hailey, John | Jett, Peggy | 19 Sept. 1785 |
| Hailey, William | Jett, Nancy | 23 Dec. 1786 |
| Hailey, William | Jett, Susan | 16 Sept. 1790 |
| Hall, John | Monroe, Sarah | 13 May 1791 |
| Hall, William | Kennard, Frances | 29 May 1789 |
| Hammons, John | Hefferling, Susannah | 20 July 1788 |

| | | |
|---|---|---|
| Hampton, George | Ballard, Mary Nugent | 14 Nov. 1782 |
| Hampton, Joseph | Hathaway, Margaret | 9 April 1787 |
| Hampton, Thomas | Morehead, Lucy | 2 Sept. 1794 |
| Hampton, William | Hinton, Fanny | 14 Dec. 1773 |
| Hamrick, Gilson | Thomas, Sally | 9 Nov. 1785 |
| Hancock, William | Grigsby, Susannah | 27 Oct. 1788 |
| Hand, John | Robinson, Jenny Argle | --- No date --- |
| Haney, Thomas | Chappelle, Margaret | 26 Dec. 1789 |
| Hansborough, John | Shehogan, Sarah | 3 March 1789 |
| Hansborough, Peter | Harrison, Ann | 23 Oct. 1790 |
| Hansborough, William | Watts, Sarah | 27 April 1766 |
| Hardin, Benjamin | Routt, Nancy | 16 March 1785 |
| Harley, Joseph | Hummins (Cummins), Sally | 26 Oct. 1797 |
| Harper, Isaac | Constable, Jemima | 15 April 1787 |
| Harrill, ---- | Shanks, Katy | 31 Dec. 1787 |
| Harrington, John | Shank, Susannah | 26 April 1791 |
| Harris, Arthur | Toff, Elizabeth | 3 Sept. 1785 |
| Harris, Elisha | McCormack, Margaret | 21 Nov. 1780 |
| Harris, George | Harris, Catherine | 16 June 1773 |
| Harris, Henry | Williams, Joanna | 15 Oct. 1787 |
| Harris, Samuel | Duncan, Nancy | 23 Aug. 1789 |
| Harrison, Burr | Pickett, Lucy | 24 Aug. 1789 |
| Harrison, William | Humston, Jane | 23 Feb. 1767 |
| Hatfield, Stewart | Fidler, Rebecca | 6 Sept. 1788 |
| Hathaway, James | Nevill, Joanna | 25 March 1771 |
| Haugh, James | Barratt, Nancy | 25 Nov. 1795 |
| Hawkins, Benjamin | Bowers, Ann | 29 Oct. 1764 |
| Hawkins, Jesse | Jones, Polly | 8 March 1797 |
| Hayes, Jacob | Rector, Betty | 21 Dec. 1785 |
| Hayne, Jonathan | Whitacre, Martha | 5 Feb. 1795 |
| Head, Cornelius | Hilkins, Margaret | 14 Jan. 1790 |
| Head, Richard | Newport, Sarah | 5 Jan. 1771 |
| Headley, James | Jeffries, Lucy | 14 June 1783 |
| Headley, Robert | Boley, Elizabeth | 9 March 1797 |
| Heaton, James | Harris, Martha | 2 Dec. 1797 |
| Heaton, Thomas | Taylor, Susannah | 11 March 1789 |
| Hefflin, William | Collins, Lilly | 27 Oct. 1789 |
| Heiner [Hainer], George | Whitley, Selah | 18 May 1799 |
| Helm, William | Neaville, Lettice | 23 Feb. 1764 |
| Helm, William | Pickett, Agatha | 3 March 1789 |
| Henderson, Pierce Bayley | Duncan, Milly | 17 Dec. 1789 |
| Herndon, George | Stephen, Elizabeth | 1 Sept. 1790 |
| Hickman, John | Thompson, Ann | 20 June 1790 |
| Hickman, John | Thompson, Ann | 1 July 1790 |
| Hickman, William | Rakestraw, Nancy | 9 April 1796 |
| Higgison, Walter | Elley, Esther | 23 Nov. 1793 |
| Hill, James | Leach, Sarah | 19 Feb. 1788 |
| Hinson, Dennis | Doty, Elizabeth | 23 March 1796 |
| Hinson, George | Little, Susannah | 17 Sept. 1771 |
| Hinson, James | Cushenberry (Quisenberry), Ann | 18 Jan. 1786 |
| Hinson, Jesse | Sullivan, Mary | 19 April 1787 |
| Hinson, Jesse | Crawford, Eliz. | 28 Nov. 1787 |
| Hitch, John | Elgin, Casandra | 27 Feb. 1787 |
| Hitch, Wise | Williams, Nancy | 24 Sept. 1797 |
| Hitt, John | Holtzclaw, Franky | 25 Nov. 1793 |
| Hitt, Peter | Hitt, Lucy | 23 Aug. 1796 |
| Hogan, Rawleigh | Conway, Peggy | 21 May 1786 |
| Holder, Dorris | Shumate, Anna | 11 July 1786 |
| Holly, Rolly | Calvin, Mary | 20 Dec. 1788 |
| Holtzclaw, Amos | Hopwood, Sally | 7 Oct. 1799 |
| Holtzclaw, Archibald | Hitt, Miriam | 3 Jan. 1786 |
| Holtzclaw, Nathaniel | Gibson, Isa | 8 April 1782 |
| Homes, Edwin | Starke, Sarah Ann | 23 April 1764 |
| Homes, James | Hume, Agatha | 11 Jan. 1786 |
| Hoomes, Nathaniel | Jones, Betty | 17 Oct. 1799 |

| | | |
|---|---|---|
| Hopp, Thomas | Bird, Mary | 21 Aug. 1796 |
| Hopper, John | McMeekin, --- | 12 Feb. 1782 |
| Hopper, William | Williams, Litty | 9 Feb. 1788 |
| Hord, James | Hord, Sarah | 11 March 1786 |
| Hord, Peter | Wheatley, Honor | 28 May 1771 |
| Horner, Gustavus Brown | Scott, Frances | 13 April 1785 |
| Horner, William | Edmond, Mary | 19 Oct. 1790 |
| Horton, Charles | Cooper, Elizabeth | 29 Dec. 1788 |
| Horton, Craven | Newhouse, Polly | 8 Feb. 1799 |
| Horton, Elijah | Nelson, Catherine | 12 Feb. 1781 |
| Hotten, William | Cook, Betty | 3 Nov. 1795 |
| Howell, Benjamin | Harper, Sally | 23 Nov. 1795 |
| Hubbard, Epaphroditus | Edmonson, Ann McCarthy | 20 Oct. 1785 |
| Hubbard, Ephiram | Edmonds, Ann | 27 Dec. 1773 |
| Hudnall, Joseph | Taylor, Mary | 30 Nov. 1759 |
| Hudnall, William | Cockrell, Roannah | 20 Feb. 1793 |
| Huffman, William | Guy, Ann | 29 April 1789 |
| Hughes, Abraham | Marshall, Sarah | 20 Feb. 1780 |
| Humes, Charles | James, Hannah | 26 Dec. 1764 |
| Humphrie, John | McConchie, Dorothy | 21 April 1790 |
| Humston, Edward | Quarles, Susannah | 13 Jan. 1768 |
| Hurley, Daniel | Riley, Nancy | 23 Dec. 1791 |
| | | |
| Ingram, Thomas | Brooks, Lucy | 21 Nov. 1799 |
| Ireland, James | Burgess, Jane | 16 April 1771 |
| | | |
| Jackman, Richard | Neavill, Mary | 2 May 1766 |
| Jackson, Daniel | Tolls, Anne | 3 July 1793 |
| Jackson, Dempsey | Pickett, Molly | 29 Dec. 1787 |
| Jackson, Ephiram | Norman, Tabitha | 9 Sept. 1799 |
| Jackson, Samuel | Grinnan, Vashti | 11 Aug. 1771 |
| Jackson, Samuel | Jackson, Peggy | 9 Feb. 1799 |
| Jacob, William | Roswell, Mary | 18 June 1789 |
| James, Benjamin | -----, Elizabeth | 14 May 1799 |
| James, Isaac | Parker, Sarah | 3 Jan. 1787 |
| James, John | Wright, Elizabeth | 27 June 1785 |
| James, John | Wood, Louisa | 8 Jan. 1787 |
| James, Joseph | James, Mary | 3 June 1777 |
| James, Thomas | White, Hannah | 11 Dec. 1787 |
| Jeffries, Anderson | Goodin, Mary | 18 Aug. 1788 |
| Jeffries, Briant | Dulin, Mary | 19 Jan. 1799 |
| Jeffries, Ephiram | Norman, Tabitha | 9 Sept. 1799 |
| Jeffries, Henry | Chamberlain, Margaret | 18 Aug. 1788 |
| Jeffries, John | Coodnick, Alice | 27 March 1786 |
| Jeffries, Joseph | Young, Mary | 12 Sept. 1785 |
| Jeffries, Thomas | Hume, Frances | 24 Sept. 1795 |
| Jenkins, John | Shaver, Rebecca | 2 June 1792 |
| Jenkins, Thomas | Robinson, Katy | 1 Nov. 1786 |
| Jennings, Alexander | Bronbaugh, Nancy | 19 May 1799 |
| Jennings, Lewis | Bradford, Lucinda | 4 Oct. 1786 |
| Jennings, William | Withers, Elizabeth | 24 Dec. 1764 |
| Jermert, Joshua | Wright, Mary | 8 Feb. 1797 |
| Jett, James | Grant, Aggy | 29 Dec. 1795 |
| John, Benjamin | Stevenson (?), Patty | 13 March 1798 |
| Johnson, Archibald | Obanon, Jemina | 30 Nov. 1786 |
| Johnson, Bushby | Welch, Margaret | 1 Sept. 1791 |
| Johnson, Charles | Barber, Nancy | 14 Nov. 1797 |
| Johnson, David | Odor, Sarah | 21 March 1789 |
| Johnson, John | Crockell, Sally | 5 Jan. 1797 |
| Johnson, Minor | Johnson, Hannah | 23 Feb. 1790 |
| Johnson, Nimrod | Adams, Polly | 24 Feb. 1790 |
| Johnson, Tennis | Settle, Rose | 8 Aug. 1788 |
| Johnson, Thomas | Miller, Molly | 3 Sept. 1795 |
| Johnson, Wilfred | Peyton, Mary | 21 Aug. 178 |
| Jones, Edward | Hathaway, Eliz. | 21 June 1790 |

| | | |
|---|---|---|
| Jones, Isaiah | Thomas, Susannah | 3 Dec. 1795 |
| Jones, James | Bradford, Mary | 21 Dec. 1786 |
| Jones, John | Tibbetts, Elizabeth | 30 Dec. 1786 |
| Jones, John | Weeks, Peggy | 28 Sept. 1794 |
| Jones, John | Murphy, Jane | 18 --- 1797 |
| Jones, John Warner | Tullos, Mary | 29 Sept. 1788 |
| Jones, Joseph | Brooks, Molly | 2 Jan. 1794 |
| Jones, Levi | Smoot, Franky | 31 Jan. 1799 |
| Mones, Moses | Hamilton, Sarah | 4 Feb. 1786 |
| Jones, Richard | Guy, Sarah | 19 April 1786 |
| Jones, Robert | Florence, Hannah | --- No date --- |
| Jones, Robert | Ashby, Dolly | 23 June 1789 |
| Jones, William | Eustace, Ann | 14 Dec. 1780 |
| | | |
| Kampe, Peter | Fisher, Susannah | 18 Oct. 1788 |
| Kamper, Frederick | Jeffries, Molly | 24 Oct. 1773 |
| Keith, Thomas | Blackwell, Judith | 23 May 1775 |
| Kemper, David | Kemper, Nancy | ----- |
| Kemper, John | Fisher, Martha | 2 May 1787 |
| Kemper, Lewis | Bayse, Hannah | 26 Jan. 1789 |
| Kemper, Martin | Kemper, Rosanna | 3 July 1799 |
| Kemper, Thomas | Kemper, Anna | 21 Aug. 1799 |
| Kendall, Jesse | Easthane, Catherine | 16 Jan. 1781 |
| Kenner, Robert | Clark, Dolly | 11 Feb. 1785 |
| Kenner, Rodham | Barker, Jemina | 26 Nov. 1787 |
| Kenny, Andrew | Horton, Nancy | 23 Dec. 1789 |
| Kerns, Jacob | Robey (Roley), Betsy | 17 Jan. 1799 |
| Kerns, Thomas | Russell, Mary | 26 Aug. 1786 |
| Key, Price | Queens, Sally | 25 March 1787 |
| Key, Thomas | Foley, Sarah | 29 June 1793 |
| Kibble (Kebbie), William | Kebble, Mary | 17 Dec. 1799 |
| Kidwell, Thomas | Pearson, Elizabeth | 5 April 1788 |
| Kinchloe, James | Hardewicke, Elizabeth | 7 Dec. 1790 |
| King, George | Johnston, Elizabeth | 12 July 1795 |
| King, John | Bethel, Ann | 23 Nov. 1790 |
| King, Joshua | Kennady, Rachel | 24 Nov. 1780 |
| Kirby, James | Campbell, Nancy | 7 Aug. 1790 |
| Kirkpatrick, William | Fegan, Mary | 23 Nov. 1786 |
| Kittson, John | Brown, Mary | 5 Dec. 1787 |
| Knight, John | Boscarver, Susanna | 4 July 1787 |
| Knowlong Knowland), John | Arnold, Jemina | 12 Oct. 1785 |
| | | |
| Lacy, Moses | Pratt, Henrietta | 3 March 1787 |
| Lacy, Nathaniel | Grant, Mary | 11 Sept. 1793 |
| Lake, Vincent | Drummond, Frances | 16 Jan. 1793 |
| Lamkin, James | Barker, Sarah | 24 Sept. 1786 |
| Lanketer, Alexander | Vanderbilt, Chloe | 22 Feb. 1794 |
| Larrance, John | Obannon, Joyce | 13 March 1786 |
| Lawerence, Edward | Priest, Nancy | 29 Jan. 1786 |
| Lawerence, Mason | Obannon, Nancy | 24 March 1788 |
| Lawerence, Rodham | Lawerence, Eliz. | 9 Jan. 1786 |
| Leach, George | Craig, Ann | 16 July 1785 |
| Leach, George | Bigbie, ---- | 27 Dec. 1785 |
| Leach, J ---- | Hall, Molly | 4 Oct. 1796 |
| Leach, Marshall | Davidson, Ann | 28 Aug. 1793 |
| Leach, Valentine | Furrow, Molly | 23 June 1785 |
| Leake, Bazie | Anderson, Mary | 22 Jan. 1795 |
| Lear (Sear), William | Bailey, Hannah | 8 Aug. 1786 |
| Lee, Hancock | Hancock, Lena Ann | 23 Aug. 1788 |
| Lee, James | Lee, Mary | 2 Feb. 1787 |
| Lewis, Britain | Crump, Ann | 3 March 1788 |
| Lewis, Jacob | Lewis, Lovey | 10 June 1793 |
| Linn, Alexander | Kamper, Hannah | 28 Oct. 1782 |
| Linn, Joseph | Brooke, Sarah | 8 Dec. 1789 |
| Lion, John | Holtzclaw, Susannah | 18 June 1787 |

| | | |
|---|---|---|
| Little, Jordan | Crafford, Lucy | 15 Feb. 1786 |
| Lloyd, George Emory | Brown, Ann | 3 July 1787 |
| Lloyd, Joseph | Brown, Frances | 4 Oct. 1797 |
| Logan, Henry | Herring, Catherine | 27 June 1789 |
| Logan, John | Gibson, Alse | 11 Dec. 1797 |
| Love, William | McClanahan, Lettice | 24 Dec. 1795 |
| Lowe, Jesse | Kemper, Fanny | 29 Nov. 1798 |
| Lowe, John | Adams, Franky | 2 March 1789 |
| Lowry, Daniel | Emory, Ann | 26 April 1786 |
| Lowry, William | Grant, Elizabeth | 22 Jan. 1799 |
| Lunsford, John | Fowkes, Elizabeth | 8 Jan. 1787 |
| Lunsford, Rodham | Ball, Clementine | 18 Dec. 1786 |
| Lunsford, Roldy | Crees, Judith | 26 Dec. 1796 |
| Luttrell, John | Smith, Hannah | 2 April 1791 |
| Luttrell, Nelson | Tharpe, Fanny | 1 Sept. 1802 |
| Lynn, Francis | Wheatley, Sarah | 22 Jan. 1799 |
| | | |
| Mackarel, James | Morgan, Sally | 26 April 1790 |
| Maddux, George | Neale, Judith | 21 Jan. 1795 |
| Maddux, Jesse | Blackerby, --- | 8 June 1782 |
| Maddux, Nathaniel | Tennison, Ann | 9 March 1786 |
| Mahoney, Benjamin | Harris, Elizabeth | 21 Dec. 1785 |
| Mahoney, Misten (Martin) | Smith, Jemime | 23 Dec. 1795 |
| Majors, Alexander | Howell, Letty | 24 Dec. 1787 |
| Mallory, James | Dowell, Elizabeth | 6 Sept. 1792 |
| Mallory, Philip | Harrison, Jane | 24 Nov. 1783 |
| Mallory, William | Harrison, Lucy | 12 Jan. 1785 |
| Markham, James | Kenner, Catherine | 20 Nov. 1770 |
| Markham, William | Smith, Mary | 28 July 1789 |
| Marshall, Charles | Pickett, Lucy | 11 Sept. 1787 |
| Marshall, John | Benn, Rachel | 22 Jan. 1790 |
| Marshall, Simon | ----, Caty | 22 Oct. 1794 |
| Marshall, Thomas, Jr. | Adams, Susannah | 11 Sept. 1783 |
| Martin, Charles | Fishback, Franky | 9 Aug. 1790 |
| Martin, Charles | Stigler, Martha | 1 Sept. 1791 |
| Martin, George | McCormack, Eliz. | 24 Oct. 1785 |
| Martin, James | Hughes, Agatha | 17 April 1789 |
| Martin, Nimrod | Hopwood, Fanny | 22 Dec. 1787 |
| Mason, Colbert | Rogers, Margaret | 25 March 1786 |
| Mason, Jesse | Embry, Nancy | 12 Feb. 1788 |
| Mason, Thomas | Singleton, Caty | 15 May 1790 |
| Massey, Thomas | Morehead, Molly | 23 Dec. 1772 |
| Mather, Benjamin | Snyder, Mary | 18 May 1795 |
| Mathers, Robert | Rogers, Sally | 10 Jan. 1787 |
| Mathews, Simon | Stamps, Molly | 26 Dec. 1788 |
| Mauzy, Henry | Morgan, Elizabeth | 23 July 1764 |
| Mauzy, Peter | Shumate, Sarah | 4 Dec. 1799 |
| Maybin, David | Kenner, Catherine | 15 Dec. 1785 |
| Mayes, Henry | Palmer, Mary | 26 Dec. 1796 |
| Metalfe, Asa | Weeks, Elizabeth | 24 July 1796 |
| Metcalfe, Charles | Blackerby, Elizabeth | 18 Jan. 1781 |
| Metcalfe, Elias | Pickett, Sally | 29 Dec. 1788 |
| Metcalfe, John | Shackleford, Milly | 1 May 1782 |
| McBee, John | Randall, Margaret | 22 Dec. 1790 |
| McBee, Benjamin | Randall, Hannah | 28 Jan. 1789 |
| McCaron, Daniel | Dodd, Mary | 29 Oct. 1789 |
| McCarty (?), Cornelius | Hardwicke, Sukey | 12 Dec. 1787 |
| McClanahan, David | Frye, Elizabeth | 3 June 1786 |
| McClanahan, Gerrard | Rust, Sally | 5 May 1796 |
| McClanahan, John | Elliott, Sally | 5 Nov. 1795 |
| McClanahan, William | Tolling, Elizabeth | 23 Nov. 1789 |
| McCloud, Martin | Fowkes, Nancy | 15 Nov. 1790 |
| McConchi, Robert | King, Mary Ann | 25 Dec. 1790 |
| McCoy, Daniel | Kemper, Agnes | 10 Feb. 1790 |
| McCoy, Joseph | Williams, Mary | 15 March 1787 |

| | | |
|---|---|---|
| McDaniel, John | Horton, Finton | 19 June 1786 |
| McDaniel, John | Oliman (Climan), Ann | 15 Dec. 1788 |
| McDonald, Archibald | Lowry, Mary | 21 March 1790 |
| McDonald, Jared | Marshall, Nancy | 25 Jan. 1795 |
| McEntree, William | Glascock, Phebe | 28 Jan. 1799 |
| McGraw, Isaiah | Morris, Anne | 19 Oct. 1797 |
| McKenny, Mathew | Milton, Mary | 31 Dec. 1796 |
| McMeeker, Archibald | Johnson, Margaret | 27 Feb. 1800 |
| McNeal, William | Kearne, Elizabeth | 24 Aug. 1790 |
| Meoll [Mcall], Samuel | Luttrell, Elizabeth | 26 Dec. 1788 |
| Middleton, Studley | Wickliffe, Nancy | 29 Oct. 1788 |
| Miller, Henry | Neale, Lettice | 10 Feb. 1791 |
| Miller, John | Hitt, Nancy | 16 Dec. 1789 |
| Minor, George | Heale, Mildred | 22 Jan. 1788 |
| Mitchell, John | Rosser, Mary | 21 Dec. 1771 |
| Mitchell, Joshua | Stiggens, Elizabeth | 22 Dec. 1788 |
| Moffett, William | Stone, Ann | 3 Feb. 1760 |
| Monday, Charles | Fishback, Polly | 13 Dec. 1793 |
| Monroe, James | Willis, Sally | 25 Jan. 1787 |
| Moon, McLanahan | Metcalfe, Eliz. | 21 Nov. 1786 |
| Moore, Francis | Foote, Frances | 2 April 1764 |
| Moore, Samuel | McFeavor, Elizabeth | 22 Nov. 1768 |
| Moore, Samuel | Payne, Lucy | 1 May 1782 |
| Moore, Samuel | Hill, Sarah (widow) | 11 Nov. 1799 |
| Morehead, Charles | Slaughter, Margaret | 30 Oct. 1786 |
| Morehead, George | Hampton, Sally | 5 Jan. 1791 |
| Morgan, Benjamin | Kenner, Elizabeth | 31 Oct. 1782 |
| Morgan, C. | Glascock, Margaret | 15 Jan. 1790 |
| Morgan, Charles | Robinson, Mary | 1 Jan. 1781 |
| Morgan, Francis | Read, Mary | 20 Nov. 1773 |
| Morgan, John | Thomas, Anne | 12 Oct. 1782 |
| Morgan, Joseph | Bradford, Elizabeth | 26 Nov. 1773 |
| Morgan, Spencer | Kenner, Susannah | 14 Oct. 1780 |
| Moring, John | Fishback, Sarah | 12 June 1790 |
| Morris, David | McDonald, Lydia | 23 Dec. 1793 |
| Morrison, John | Berditt, Peggy | 24 Sept. 1793 |
| Moss, Daniel | Hathaway, Sarefta | 3 March 1795 |
| Moss, Tealy | Glascock, Jenny | 13 Sept. 1786 |
| Moss, William | Glascock, Lydia | 13 Sept. 1786 |
| Mott, William | Welch, Mary | 22 Aug. 1785 |
| Mourse, George | Green, Mary | 26 Sept. 1786 |
| Murphew, John | Waddell, Jane | 24 Sept. 1781 |
| Murphy, David | Roe, Lydia | 27 Dec. 1797 |
| Murphy, Leander | Duncan, Rose | 11 Feb. 1789 |
| Murphy, William | Bowen, Sally | 16 Lec. 1790 |
| Murray, Enoch | Crosby, Frances | 7 Aug. 1787 |
| Murry, Benjamin | Grant, Elizabeth | 14 March 1787 |
| Murry, Reuben | Chinn, Catherine | 24 Sept. 1795 |
| Myers, Michael | Thornberry, Margaret | 2 April 1774 |
| | | |
| Nalls, William | Blithe, Mary | 28 Dec. 1796 |
| Nash, William | Bradford, Mary | 23 Feb. 1764 |
| Nay, Joseph | Mahoney, Frances | 10 Jan. 1789 |
| Neale, James | Pinckard, Sarah | 18 Dec. 1788 |
| Neale, Thomas | Rozier, Elizabeth | 14 April 1790 |
| Neavil, Joseph | Ellett, Mary | 20 Dec. 1777 |
| Neavil, Thomas | Stewart, Mary | 31 July 1772 |
| Nelson, James | Obannon, Betty | 11 Feb. 1765 |
| Nelson, John | Hogain, Bathasheba | 10 Dec. 1780 |
| Nelson, John | Withers, Seathley | 14 Sept. 1796 |
| Nelson, Joseph | Obannon, Catherine | 23 Dec. 1771 |
| Nelson, Joseph | Bradford, Jane | 16 April 1790 |
| Nelson, Thomas | Grigsby, Rachel | 24 Oct. 1768 |
| Newland, William | Turner, Nancy | 7 Oct. 1799 |
| Norman, George | Utterback, Elizabeth | 22 Jan. 1799 |

| Groom | Bride | Date |
|---|---|---|
| Norris, John | Jones, Mary | 25 March 1782 |
| Norris, Septimus | Brown, Margaret | 5 Nov. 1795 |
| Northcutt, Benjamin | Brooks, Winny | 19 Dec. 1788 |
| Northcutt, John | Henry, Nancy | 1 Jan. 1789 |
| Nutt, Richard | Hathaway, Eliza | 26 Nov. 1788 |
| Obannon, Andrew | Smith, Mary (widow) | 10 Oct. 1777 |
| Obannon, Benjamin | Ash, Eleanor | 13 Nov. 1780 |
| Obannon, Joseph | Grigsby, Elizabeth | 2 Sept. 1782 |
| Obannon, Thomas | Barker, Hannah | 21 Jan. 1783 |
| Oliver, Josias | Morehead, Mary | 28 Aug. 1789 |
| Oliver, Samuel | Brown, Elizabeth | 24 April 1787 |
| Oneal, Thomas | Murray, Esther | 24 April 1787 |
| Orear, Jesse | Bolton, Malinda | 20 Dec. 1783 |
| Owens, Aaron | Hathaway, Dorothy | 1 Oct. 1794 |
| Owens, Bethel | Owens, Elizabeth | 17 Dec. 1787 |
| Owens, Mason | Flourence, Sarah | 13 Nov. 1796 |
| Owens, Thomas | Austin, Nancy | 30 Dec. 1786 |
| Owens, William | Owens, Nancy | 27 Nov. 1786 |
| Paine, William | Johnston, Nelly | 27 May 1795 |
| Parker, Abraham | McKay, Priscilla | 18 Feb. 1789 |
| Parker, Joseph | Duncan, Betty | 11 Jan. 1781 |
| Parker, Martin | Shumate, Mary | 24 Dec. 1787 |
| Parker, Thomas | Marshall, Alice | 23 Nov. 1793 |
| Parmer, Isaac | Tomson, Milly | 15 Nov. 1792 |
| Parsons, William | Holtzclaw, Eliz. | 4 Jan. 1797 |
| Patterson, James | Constable, Nancy | 3 Nov. 1790 |
| Paulie, Issachar | Bryan, Rachel | 15 Nov. 1783 |
| Payne, Augustine | Young, Caty | 14 Jan. 1789 |
| Payne, Benjamin | Rosseau, Susannah | 2 Jan. 1781 |
| Payne, Coldton | Smoot, Charity | 20 Oct. 1790 |
| Payne, Merryman | Johnson, Frances | 17 March 1789 |
| Payne, William, Jr. | Payne, Molly | 17 March 1789 |
| Peach, John | Neale, Nancy | 4 Jan. 1800 |
| Pearle, Samuel | Kerr, Dorcas | 25 Aug. 1773 |
| Pearle, Samuel | Strother, Nancy | 15 June 1790 |
| Pearle, Samuel | Darnale, Delia | 26 March 1798 |
| Pearle, William | Thompson, Ann | 1 July 1790 |
| Pendleton, Robert | Haddrick, Charlotte | 30 Dec. 1792 |
| Penny, James | Dulin, Lydia | 30 May 1789 |
| Pepper, Elijah | Obannon, Sally | 20 Feb. 1793 |
| Pepper, Jeremiah | Billingsby, Ellander | 6 July 1797 |
| Pepper, Jesse | Lamkin, Betty | 2 Feb. 1796 |
| Peters, James | Ashby, Winnifred | 17 Jan. 1764 |
| Peters, James | Starke, Sally | 8 Feb. 1796 |
| Peters, John | Rousann, Ann | 20 Oct. 1783 |
| Pettet, Nathaniel | Owen, Rebecca | 19 Dec. 1781 |
| Pettet, Samuel | Bragg, Elizabeth | 10 Dec. 1783 |
| Pettet, Thomas | Owen, Bethelon | 16 April 1785 |
| Petty, Marshall | Bowmer, Jemina | 15 Dec. 1794 |
| Peyton, Cuthbert | Brough, Catherine | 26 May 1782 |
| Peyton, Valentine | Hale, Sally | 21 Dec. 1789 |
| Phillips, Fielding | Linton, Nancy | 5 Feb. 1790 |
| Phillips, William | Fowkes, Elizabeth | 7 June 1774 |
| Pickett, John | Chamberlain, Eliz. | 20 Nov. 1790 |
| Pickett, Martin | Blackwell, Ann | 31 May 1764 |
| Pickett, William Sanford | Smith, Martha | 26 Sept. 1795 |
| Pierce, John | Hume, Patience | 4 June 1793 |
| Pilcher, Steven | Fishback, Sarah | 9 Jan. 1793 |
| Pilcher, William | Fishback, Lilly Tibbs | 26 April 1797 |
| Pollard, Abner | Clark, Harriet | 18 Jan. 1798 |
| Pope, Benjamin | Young, Mary | 15 Jan. 1766 |
| Popkins, Jehu | Perry, Sally | 6 Nov. 1787 |
| Porter, Charles | Benson, Ann | 11 March 1786 |

| | | |
|---|---|---|
| Porter, Christopher | Baker, Elizabeth | 17 March 1789 |
| Porter, Edwin | Mauzy, Polly | 25 Sept. 1797 |
| Porter, Eli | Hale, Martha | 5 Jan. 1800 |
| Porter, Eppa | Porter, Elizabeth | 17 Oct. 1799 |
| Porter, John | Smith, Jean | 7 June 1785 |
| Porter, Martin | Withers, Aggy | 16 March 1789 |
| Porter, Samuel | ------, Polly | 22 Aug. 1796 |
| Porter, Thomas | Porter, Susannah | 31 Dec. 1782 |
| Powan (Rowan), William | Griffin, Mary | 26 Dec. 1796 |
| Powell, Henry | Strothers, Sally | 9 April 1787 |
| Powers, Patrick | Snyder, Caty | 12 Oct. 1790 |
| Powers, Thomas | Fields, Elizabeth | 12 Sept. 1793 |
| Prage, John | Kirke, Elizabeth | 20 July 1781 |
| Prainer, Philip | Wolf, Catherine | 8 Dec. 1796 |
| Pratt, Zephania | Cooke, Ann | 22 April 1782 |
| Price, Richard | James, Peggy | 3 Aug. 1776 |
| Price, Samuel | Clemans, Mary | 23 March 1793 |
| Priest, Mason | Lawerence, Sally | 20 Jan. 1786 |
| | | |
| R ---, Richard | Morehead, Polly | 31 Dec. 1775 |
| Race, William | Seaton, Jenny | 12 May 1796 |
| Ralls, Charles | Brown, Hannah | 24 Aug. 1780 |
| Ralls, Joel | Bird, Lena | 23 June 1796 |
| Ransdell, Thomas | Ransdell, Mary | 8 Nov. 1786 |
| Ransdell, Wharton | Morehead, Mary | 16 Jan. 1781 |
| Read, Theophielus | Duncan, Peggy | 16 Nov. 1797 |
| Read, Thomas | Fishback, Milly | 25 April 1785 |
| Rector, Lewis | Green, Elizabeth | 22 Dec. 1794 |
| Rector, Moses | Green, Elizabeth | 25 Feb. 1788 |
| Rector, Spencer | Tiffin, Mary | 3 Oct. 1785 |
| Redd, Allen | Bullitt, Elizabeth | 28 July 1777 |
| Redding, Reuben | Robert, Elizabeth | 26 Jan. 1789 |
| Renas (or Renoe), Zeky | Chinn, Mary | 26 July 1775 |
| Renoe, George | Baylis, Jean | 20 Feb. 1785 |
| Resen, Thomas | Kennady, Sarah | 2 Dec. 1800 |
| Rhodes, Hezekiah | Putman, Elizabeth | 20 Jan. 1765 |
| Rhodes, Jacob | Green, Frances | 5 Oct. 1792 |
| Rhodes, John | Doubtman, Nancy | 10 Nov. 1768 |
| Rickard, William | Blackwell, Ann | 21 Feb. 1786 |
| Rice, Bailey | Morehead, Eliz. | 19 June 1789 |
| Rickett, James | Smith, Nancy | 5 June 1800 |
| Ridley, John | Bailey, Elizabeth | 24 April 1781 |
| Rings (Ringo), Burtis | Rector, Hannah | 22 Feb. 1790 |
| Rixby, Richard, Jr. | Morehead, Eliz. | 18 Nov. 1764 |
| Roach, George | White, Sarah | 25 Aug. 1789 |
| Roach, John | McClanahan, Patty | 24 Aug. 1785 |
| Robert, John | Holly, Sally | 22 June 1789 |
| Robertson, Benjamin | James, Margaret Bruce | 31 Oct. 1783 |
| Robertson, John | Benson, Elizabeth | 8 Sept. 1787 |
| Robinson, David | Wilson, Sally | 5 April 1790 |
| Robinson, Dixon | Pinkstone, Anna | 2 Feb. 1793 |
| Robinson, Elijah | Norris, Susannah | 3 Oct. 1785 |
| Robinson, George | Foster, Ann | 25 Aug. 1789 |
| Robinson, James | Robinson, Molly | 23 Jan. 1790 |
| Robinson, Maxmillian | Elliott, Jemina | 27 Jan. 1795 |
| Robinson, William | Lee, Susannah | 13 March 1790 |
| Robinson, William | Garner, Nancy | 28 March 1796 |
| Roe, Original | Kenner, Sarah | 16 June 1788 |
| Roe, Steven | Clendenning, Peggy | 23 Oct. 1799 |
| Roe, William | Glascock, Teally | 20 Dec. 1792 |
| Roger, Henry | Jett, Sally | 23 March 1789 |
| Roose, Aaron | Phillips, Ruth | 25 March 1786 |
| Roose, Nicholas | Hichlhorn, Eve | 12 Dec. 1799 |
| Rossen, John | Clendenning, Nelly | 22 Feb. 1781 |
| Rossey, Thomas | Fishback, Lydia | 24 Dec. 1798 |

| | | |
|---|---|---|
| Rouins, James | Finch, Polly | 31 Oct. 1799 |
| Routt, Peter | Crosby, Ann | 6 June 1765 |
| Routte, Daniel | Stegler (Stigler), Martha | 6 Sept. 1788 |
| Roy, Willy | Fowkes, Sarah | 26 Dec. 1772 |
| Runnells, John | Phillips, Caty | 30 Oct. 1794 |
| Rusley, George | Jeffries, Mary | 29 April 1797 |
| Russell, Daniel | Matthew, Rachel | 15 Aug. 1792 |
| Russell, William | Darnall, Mary | 18 Oct. 1771 |
| Russell, William | Curtis, Mary | 12 Jan. 1787 |
| Rust, John | Atkinson, Elenn | 20 Jan. 1771 |
| Rust, John | McClanahan, Molly | 28 Dec. 1796 |
| Rust, Peter | Taylor, Eliza | 3 Dec. 1799 |
| | | |
| Sanders, Thomas | Rogers, Molly | 1 June 1785 |
| Saunders, William | Jeffries, Agnes | 15 Jan. 1790 |
| Scantland, Fielding | Spiller (?), Sophia | 23 April 1786 |
| Scott, Charles | Stanton, Lucinda | 8 Oct. 1798 |
| Scott, William | Sullivan, Mary Ann | ---- 1790 |
| Seaton, George | Seaton, Sarah | 23 May 1786 |
| Seaton, John | Murry, Alice | 21 Oct. 1768 |
| Seaton, William | Kenner, Mary | 6 Feb. 1764 |
| Selman (Silman), Zack | Lawerence, Janney | 7 Aug. 1790 |
| Settle, Edward | Morgan, Rosanna | 28 Sept. 1772 |
| Settle, Strother | Ash, Dorothy | 10 June 1782 |
| Settle, William | Gavner, Sally | 13 June 1786 |
| Settle, William | Hunton, Melinda | 11 May 1787 |
| Sharpe, Spencer | Arnold, Nancy | 15 April 1793 |
| Shaver, John | Neale, Mary | 17 Feb. 1789 |
| Shaw, Charles | Jett, Catherine | 19 Jan. 1790 |
| Shaw, John | Cleveland, Fanny | 10 July 1785 |
| Shesterson, George | Baker, Lettice | 17 April 1792 |
| Shipp, Elijah | Price, Rebecca | 10 Jan. 1792 |
| Shipp, Joseph | Etcheson, Letty | 2 Oct. 1785 |
| Shipp, Laban | Turner, Rebecca | 10 Feb. 1786 |
| Shirley, James | McMeekin, Mary | 9 Oct. 1781 |
| Short, John | Leach, Nancy | 25 Dec. 1794 |
| Shultz, Joseph | Thompson, Sally | 15 Dec. 1794 |
| Shumate, Benjamin | Gregory, Winny | 31 March 1790 |
| Shumate, Hohn | Preston, Sarah | 28 Jan. 1788 |
| Shumate, John | Crump, Susannah | 2 Sept. 1775 |
| Shumate, William | Morman, Frances | 26 Feb. 1787 |
| Shurlock, James | Norman, Judy | 20 Sept. 1785 |
| Slaughter, Cadwalder | Fowkes, Mary | 4 Aug. 1786 |
| Slaughter, Henry | Taylor, Remey | 26 Sept. 1786 |
| Slaughter, Jess | Hampton, Elizabeth | 22 July 1772 |
| Slaughter, Joseph | Harper, Rachel | 5 Feb. 1787 |
| Slaughter, Matthew | Thomas, Ann | 18 Dec. 1798 |
| Slaughter, Samuel | Lampkin, Peggy | 14 Dec. 1798 |
| Slaughter, Samuel | Jenkins, Peggy | 15 Dec. 1798 |
| Smarr, Andrew | Murray, Lydia | 8 Dec. 1791 |
| Smedley, William | Simpson, Lydia | 17 April 1791 |
| Smith, Augustine | Darnall, Susannah | 30 Dec. 1780 |
| Smith, Augustine | Chilton, Nancy | 13 Dec. 1798 |
| Smith, Berryman | Martin, Elizabeth | 31 Aug. 1785 |
| Smith, Caleb | Smith, Mary Waugh | 18 Dec. 1794 |
| Smith, Delaney | Wright, Mary | 26 Sept. 1785 |
| Smith, James | Pickett, Sebba | 16 June 1796 |
| Smith, James | Bencer, Clacy | 16 Dec. 1798 |
| Smith, John | Berryman, Mary | 22 April 1777 |
| Smith, John | Spicer, Rebecca | 24 Dec. 1787 |
| Smith, John | Allen, Margaret | 24 Oct. 1788 |
| Smith, John | Williams, Betty | 14 April 1789 |
| Smith, John | Dodd, Elizabeth | 19 Dec. 1796 |
| Smith, Lewis | Davis, Ruth | 21 April 1798 |
| Smith, Matthew | Winn, Martha | 25 April 1771 |

| | | |
|---|---|---|
| Smith, Scarlett | Jackson, Lydia | 19 March 1788 |
| Smith, Thomas | Adams, Elizabeth | 26 June 1769 |
| Smith, William | Ashly, Ann | 18 April 1782 |
| Smith, William | McQueen, Elizabeth | 23 July 1789 |
| Smoot, Claiborne | Payne, Mary | 4 Feb. 1790 |
| Smoot, Edward | Hitch, Susannah | 11 June 1788 |
| Smoot, John | Hitch (Hetch), Peggy | 16 Dec. 1789 |
| Smoot, Lewis | Marvet (Marvel), Eliz. | 8 Feb. 1799 |
| Snape, Nathaniel | Kidwell, Fanny | 20 Dec. 1789 |
| Snyder, Nimrod | Hall, Catherine | 28 Nov. 1795 |
| Sparks, James | Dawson, Margaret | 15 Dec. 1785 |
| Spellman, John | Freeman, Elizabeth | 1 Jan. 1797 |
| Spettler (?), Phillip, Jr. | Hume, Elizabeth | 9 Sept. 1782 |
| Spring, Nicholas | Butcher, Catherine | 20 Aug. 1771 |
| Stanford, James | Burroughs, Judith | 23 Feb. 1790 |
| Stanton, William | Blackwell, Lucy | 24 Sept. 1773 |
| Stark, James | Duncan, Elizabeth | 18 Dec. 1799 |
| Stark, William | Smith, Ann | 17 Jan. 1793 |
| Stephenson, Samuel | Hogan, Barbara | 10 Aug. 1786 |
| Stevens, Allen | Jones, Elizabeth | 21 Feb. 1795 |
| Stevens, James | Chadwell, Cinthia | 23 Dec. 1792 |
| Stevenson, Benjamin | Ball, Peggy | 13 Feb. 1793 |
| Stevenson, William | Hickman, Sarah | 24 Dec. 1787 |
| Stevenson, William | Cahoon, Prudence | 15 Oct. 1792 |
| Stevson (Stenson), James | Ball, Judith | 14 Jan. 1800 |
| Stewart, Allen | Grinnan, Sarah | 28 May 1785 |
| Stewart, William | Grigsby, Susannah | 25 March 1770 |
| Stigler, Price | McCanahan, Jane | 3 April 1796 |
| Stone, Nimrod | Russell, Sarah | 18 Dec. 1786 |
| Stout, Isaac | Reed, Winny | 23 Jan. 1800 |
| Stribling, Thomas | Ayers, Elizabeth | --- No date --- |
| Striker, Henry | Michael, Caty | |
| Stringfellow, George | Jennings, Milly | 18 Jan. 1795 |
| Stringfellow, Harry | Brannin, Mary | 30 Jan. 1793 |
| Stukle, George | Michael, Jenny | 21 Nov. 1789 |
| Suddith, John | Williams, Nancy | 25 Dec. 1798 |
| Suddith, Levi | Bowers, Margaret | 25 Nov. 1792 |
| Sullivan, Sylvester | McCabe, Hanson | 3 June 1796 |
| Sullivan, William | Jones, Ann | 20 Feb. 1790 |
| Suthard (Southard), Benjamin | Payne, Ann | 30 Dec. 1785 |
| Sutton, John | Lawler, Polly | 1 Aug. 1798 |
| Taylor, Benjamin | Weaver, Catherine | 30 Nov. 1789 |
| Taylor, James | Triplett, Helen | 2 April 1794 |
| Taylor, Jesse | Embry, Sarah | 5 Dec. 1795 |
| Taylor, John | Buckner, Catherine Talliaferrio | 22 Nov. 1790 |
| Taylor, John | Doleas, Polly | 24 Oct. 1796 |
| Taylor, Raleigh | Waddell, Elizabeth | 10 Sept. 1792 |
| Taylor, Thomas | Gore, Caty | 26 Nov. 1794 |
| Taylor, William | Drummond, Susannah | 5 Sept. 1778 |
| Thayer, William | Jones, Hannah | 16 Jan. 1789 |
| Thomas, Benjamin | Glascock, Catherine | 14 Feb. 1788 |
| Thomas, Daniel | Moss, Mary | 22 Dec. 1795 |
| Thomas, Elisha | Glascock, Alice | 24 May 1788 |
| Thomas, James | Stevenson, Peggy | 29 Feb. 1788 |
| Thomas, William | Weeden, Polly | 9 May 1791 |
| Thompson, Aaron | Elliott, Sary | 7 Dec. 1791 |
| Thornton, Thomas | Hampton, Elizabeth | 16 Dec. 1795 |
| Threlkyeld, William | Spiller, Chloe | 5 Feb. 1787 |
| Tinsal, John | Button, Sarah | 10 Dec. 1785 |
| Tippett (Triplett), William | Hill, Sarah | 14 Jan. 1765 |
| Tolles, Jonathan | Henderson, Elizabeth | 23 July 1798 |
| Tolles, Micajah | Babson, Polly | 21 Dec. 1796 |
| Tolles, Reuben | Tarlton, Sarah | 15 May 1796 |

| | | |
|---|---|---|
| Tolles, Reuben | Tarlton, Sarah | 13 March 1798 |
| Tolles, Stephen | Crosby, Ann | 5 Nov. (?) 1788 |
| Tolles, William | Benam (Benum), Diana | 19 Oct. 1790 |
| Tolls, John | Debell, Elizabeth | 7 Nov. 1799 |
| Tolton, James | West, Jane | 4 May 1796 |
| Tomlin, William | Rogers, Kissy | 23 March 1789 |
| Tracy, Philip | Frie, Susan | 23 Jan. 1800 |
| Tracy, William | Grigsby, Winny | 29 April 1789 |
| Triplett, John | Morehead, Susan | 9 May 1791 |
| Triplett, Lawerence | Triplett, Benedicte | 24 April 1786 |
| Triplett, Reuben | French, Margaret | 8 July 1790 |
| Triplett, William | Morehead, Eliz. | 12 Dec. 1785 |
| Triplett, William | Rector, Darius | 9 Jan. 1800 |
| Trueman, John | Embrey, Leanna | 2 Jan. 1795 |
| Tullos, Rodham | Finnie, Ann | 21 Aug. 1764 |
| Turley, John | Squire, Susannah | 18 March 1783 |
| Turner, Alexander | Rollins, Peggy | 17 May 1786 |
| Turner, James | Debell, Ann | 6 Dec. 1792 |
| Turner, John | Bailey, Jenny | 12 June 1782 |
| Turner, John | James, Franky | 31 Dec. 1798 |
| Turner, Thomas | Randolph, Elizabeth | 1 Sept. 1798 |
| Tyler, Benjamin | Foote, Mary | 9 April 1764 |
| | | |
| Underwood, Anthony | Douglas, Sarah | 11 Dec. 1798 |
| Underwood, John | Teagle, Susan | 3 April 1789 |
| Utterback, Benjamin | Snelling, Elizabeth | 15 Nov. 1780 |
| Utterback, Charles | Nelson, Jemina | 7 Sept. 1789 |
| | | |
| Vorris, Thaddeus | Brown, Elizabeth | 5 Dec. 1794 |
| Vowls, John | Battaly, Hannah | 26 Feb. 1781 |
| | | |
| Waddell, Mathew | Waddell, Elizabeth | 21 May 1789 |
| Waddell, William | White, Ann | 31 Oct. 1786 |
| Wake, John | Grigsby, Mary | 24 Aug. 1766 |
| Waller, Charles | Crosby, Mary | 9 March 1772 |
| Walpole, Edward | Chinn, Ann | 19 June 1772 |
| Warden, Elisha | Dearing, Fanny | 27 March 1798 |
| Warden, Henry | Ford, Ann | 12 Jan. 1790 |
| Warden, John | Elliott, Ann | Jan. 1795 |
| Waters, Thomas | Ashby, Ann | 18 Oct. 1796 |
| Watts, Francis | Foley, Sarah | 16 Oct. 1777 |
| Waugh, Tyler | Crump, Mary | 23 Aug. 1773 |
| Weaver, Jacob | Nouman, Molly | 8 -- 1792 |
| Webb, Isaac | Riley, Betsy | 28 March 1793 |
| Weedon, Nathaniel | Smith, Mary | 18 Sept. 1782 |
| Welch, John | White, Elizabeth | 26 Dec. 1796 |
| Welch, Sylvester | Glascock, Am. | 14 March 1798 |
| Welch, Thomas | Turty, Nancy | 29 March 1797 |
| Welch, William | Congrove, Lydia | 29 Sept. 1788 |
| Welch, William | Moore, Margaret | 3 Feb. 1795 |
| Wells (Wills), John | Smith, Susannah | 19 Feb. 1787 |
| West, Benjamin | Wrenn, Elizabeth | 10 Sept. 1788 |
| West, Charles | Withers, Sally | 20 June 1785 |
| Wey, Amos | Fletcher, Lydia | 27 July 1795 |
| Wey, Henry | Crupper, Molly | 15 Feb. 1790 |
| Wey, John | Atterburn, Polly | 20 Oct. 1795 |
| Whalon, Patrick | Leach, Susannah | 28 July 1775 |
| Wharton, Long | Dillard, Molly | 22 Sept. 1792 |
| Wharton, Samuel | Bowman, Rebecca | 1 Dec. 1783 |
| Wheatley, George | Darnall, Diana | 10 Feb. 1760 |
| Whitacre, Caleph | Whitacre, Keziah | 1 May 1793 |
| White, Goring | Duncan, Leanna | 19 Jan. 1789 |
| White, John | Bailey, Ann | 7 Jan. 1783 |
| White, John | Dairs, Mary | 19 Feb. 1798 |
| White, Thomas | Finch, Elizabeth | 16 Oct. 1798 |

| | | |
|---|---|---|
| White, William | McDonald, Lydia | 1 Jan. 1798 |
| Whitecotton, Harris | Shumate, Margaret | 4 May 1790 |
| Wickliffe, David | Seaton, Margaret | 28 Oct. 1782 |
| Wickliffe, Robert | Hardin, Mary | 18 June 1759 |
| Wicks, Thomas | Jacobs, Moring | 6 Feb. 1795 |
| Wigginton, Benjamin | Thornberry, Mary | 1 Oct. 1783 |
| Wilkins, Thomas | Weeks, Peggy | 20 Feb. 1800 |
| Wilkinson, John | Moffett, Lucretia | 21 Dec. 1782 |
| Wilkinson, Joshua | Thompson, Ann | 3 Oct. 1798 |
| Williams, George | Sharp, Ann | 28 Oct. 1782 |
| Williams, John Pope | Minter, Hannah | 19 June 1773 |
| Williams, Paul | Wheatley, Sarah | 22 June 1786 |
| Williams, Richard | Hudnall, Molly | 27 Dec. 1790 |
| Williams, William | Settle, Elizabeth | 31 Dec. 1767 |
| Williangham, William | Corder, Eve | 10 Oct. 1793 |
| Willingham, John | Borden, Sarah | 23 Dec. 1792 |
| Willoughby, David | Griffin, Margaret | 2 Nov. 1797 |
| Willoughby, Elijah | Leachman, Susannah | 18 Oct. 1787 |
| Willoughby, John | Leachman, Mary | 28 Oct. 1787 |
| Wilson, Alexander | Oliver, Mary | 8 Dec. 1786 |
| Winn, James | Withers, Hannah | 3 March 1767 |
| Winn, Minor | Withers, Betty | 17 Oct. 1766 |
| Withers, Benjamin | Robinson, Nancy | 24 Feb. 1783 |
| Withers, Enoch | Chinn, Jenny | 18 May 1786 |
| Withers, James | Pickett, Sarah | 19 Nov. 1773 |
| Withers, James | Jennings, Cloe | 4 Nov. 1775 |
| Withers, James | Mauzy, Betsy | 6 Sept. 1798 |
| Withers, Jesse | Porter, Catherine | 6 Aug. 1789 |
| Withers, John | Wood, Elizabeth | 23 Dec. 1795 |
| Withers, John | Rose, Susannah | 6 Sept. 1796 |
| Withers, William | Rosser, Hannah | 18 March 1769 |
| Withers, William | Barber, Elizabeth | 17 March 1777 |
| Withers, William | Ashby, Patty | 28 March 1786 |
| Wolfe, Jacob | Mason, Mary | 4 Jan. 1798 |
| Wood, Dickinson | Withers, Hannah | 24 Dec. 1793 |
| Wood, James | Evans, Elizabeth | 3 Sept. 1786 |
| Wood, John | Maddux, Margaret | 26 April 1792 |
| Wood, Mark | Bashaw (?), Mary | 12 July 1787 |
| Wood, Thomas | Buckman, Sarah | 27 Aug. 1759 |
| Wrenn, Daniel | Bishop, Elizabeth | 11 Feb. 1796 |
| Wrenn, Jeremiah | McDonald, Eleanor | 7 Feb. 1798 |
| Wrenn, Thomas | Turley, Nancy | 14 March 1798 |
| Wright, David | Martin, Nancy | 28 Jan. 1790 |
| Wright, Elijah | Brannin, Polly | 17 Jan. 1794 |
| Wright, James | Duncan, Mary | 8 Dec. 1763 |
| Wright, John | Mason, Ann | 5 Nov. 1790 |
| | | |
| Young, James | Peters, Sally | 22 Sept. 1795 |
| Young, John | Singleton, Elizabeth | 9 Feb. 1788 |
| Young, Nimrod | Settle, Elizabeth | 25 Feb. 1789 |
| Youngblood, William | Carter, Elinor | ---- 1786 |

CEMETERY INSCRIPTIONS
Warrenton, Fauquier County, Va.

Adams, Sarah, wife of John T. Adams, died 1850.
Adams, Virginia, daughter of Dr. John and Mary Adams. 1842-1897. (Sower lot.)
Allen, Edmund, 1810-1884.
Allen, Margaret E., wife of Edmund Allen. 1814-1883.
Andrew, Alice, daughter of M. B. Goyston. 1813-1874.
Armitage, Mary Ann, wife of Robert Mandeville Hamilton, born Accomac Co., Va. 1797-1891.

Barker (Barler), Edward, born in England, 1865, died 1921.
Barker, Lillie Maddux. 1863-1928.
Barry, Julia. 1843-1910.
Barry, Robert. 1839-1912.
Bartenstein, Edward. 1858-1913.
Bartenstein, Elizabeth, died 1878, aged 56 years.
Bartenstein, Ferdinane, born in Germany. 1816-1864.
Bartenstein, Miss L. A., died 1887, aged 23 years.
Bartenstein, Sarah Fitzhugh, Oct. 1849 - 1921.
Bartlett, John. 1813-1882.
Bartlett, Martha Ann, 1842-1879.
Bartlett, Mary Ann. 1919-1876.
Baylor, Anne Bridges, relict of John Walker Baylor, born in Clark Co., Va., daughter of George Fitzhugh, of Fauquier Co., Va. 1784-1866.
Baylor, Fanny Courtneay. 1824-1842.
Beckham, John G. and wife Mary, children, Mary and Alexander - no dates.
Becksler, William. 1841-1910.
Bendall, Virginia Stone, wife of R. T. 1840-1927.
Bendall, Virginius Oldner, son of R. T. and Virginia. 1863-1900.
Bentles, Annie E., died 1818, aged 25 years
Blackburn, John. 1840-1927.
Blackwell, Eleanor Foote, dau. of John D. and Frances. 1875-1912.
Blackwell, Frances Grayson Smith, wife of John Davenport Blackwell. 1848-1924.
Blackwell, John Davenport, A. M. D. D. 1822-1887.
Boorman, Elizabeth Duvall, wife of Robert, died 1921.
Brooke, Annie Amelia, dau. of James V. and Mary E. Brooke, died 1876, aged 18 years.
Brooke, Francis Calvin. 1858-1911.
Brooke, James V. 1824-1888.
Brooke, Richard Harris (?). 1847-1920.
Brooke, Virginia, dau. of Reuben and Ann S. H. Brooke, died 1884. (See Payne)
Brooke, Virginia Dandridge, dau. of H. L. and Virginia Brooke. Died Sept. 1846.
Brown, Anabelle. 1846-1924.
Brown, F. Turner. 1829-1907.
Brown, Florence H., wife of William. 1869-1912.
Brown, Hannah. 1823-
Brown, Lillie Maddux. 1920-1923.
Brown, W. Judson. 1834-1902.
Brown, William. 1866-1929.
Browning, Henry R. 1837-1900.
Browning, Maria, wife of Henry H. 1846-1904.
Bullock, Lilly, wife of Capt. W. E., born in England, died in Shelton, Washington, 1935.
Bullock, Capt. W. E. born in Northumberland, England, March 30, 1845 - 1916.
Butler, Addie Ingle. 1831-1906.
Butler, Alice. --- Feb. 23, 1922.
Butler, George Griffin. 1822-1908.
Butler, Helen V. Died 1925.
Butts, J-Anna (or Joanna), dau. of Francis and Emma Butts, consort of Rev. J. D. Blackwell. 1834-1868.
Bywater, Mamie. 1833-1923.
Bywater, Mildred. 1908-1927.

Carr, Herbert Henry, 5th son of William Carr, born at Black Heath, England, March 7, 1867, died 1899, Fauquier Co., Va.

Carter, Cassius. 1835-1914.
Carter, Fanny Foote Green, wife of Cassius Carter. 1839-1893.
Carter, Francis Scott, died 1921, aged 53 years.
Carter, Henry L. 1814-1905.
Carter, Isaiah. 182- - 1874.
Carter, Richard. 1826-1882.
Carter, Shirley, M.D. 1835-1928.
Chilton, Joseph. Died 1841, aged 70 years.
Chilton, Lucy Stephen. 1810-1904.  Ann Chilton Johnson -- See Johnson
Cockrill, Hugh S. 1883-1883.
Cockrill, Mary E. 1851-1917.
Cockrill, R.A. 1852-1916.
Connelly, Cornelius, born Cork, Ireland, died 1899, aged 65 years.
Crown, Hannah, wife of Rev. James Crown. 1845-1927.
Crown, Rev. James Henry, born 1834 in Montgomery Co., Md., died 1890.

Dade, Baylor Gurynnetta, dau. of J.W. Tyler. Died 1883. See Tyler.
Day, Alexander. 1843-1862.  (Day -- See Swift)
Day, Baldwin. 1797-1852.
Day, Douglas. 1829-1875.
Day, Virginia Turner, wife of Douglas Day. 1839-1910.
Dent, Mary Ann. 1811-1891.
Dent, William. 1807-1890.
DeShields, Elizabeth. 1811-1884.
De Shields, James. 1804-1862.
Douglas, Martin Guthrie, born in Maryland. 1869-1920.
Drysdale, Christian, died June 1901.
Drysdale, Thomas. 1876-1880.

Edmonds, Adeline, wife of Edward G. 1834-1907.
Edmonds, Edward G. 1836-1897.
Edwards, Ann, died 1902, aged 82 years.
Edwards, W.W. 1812-1900.
English, Elizabeth Roe. 1790-1881.
English, Joseph Marion, son of James and Elizabeth R. English. 1824-1861.
English, Maria C., daughter of James and Elizabeth Roe English. 1826-1903.
Evans, Frances. 1836-1906.
Evans, Mildred Moore Campbell. 1850-1866. (See Campbell)
Evans, Sarah, 1797-1887.

Fallen, Margaret, died 1887---
Fallen, Patrick. Died 188-- aged 84 years.
Finks, Ann Rebecca, adopted daughter of John W. and Lucy Finks. 18-- - 1853.
Finks, John W. 1818-1877.
Finks, Lucy A. 1822-1911.
Fisher. A large stone with name of FISHER upon it and the graves of Annie E. Johnson (1845-1899) and J.D. Ashton (1842-1914).
Fisher, Elizabeth. 1810-1895.
Fisher, Fannie. 1849-1815.
Fisher, John. 1801-1884.
Fisher, Marh H. 1839-1907.
Fisher, Robert. 1888-1923.
Fisher, Robert W. 1835-1908.
Fletcher, A.D. 1814-1890.
Fletcher, Georgie O'Latham, wife of Thaddeus N. 1847-1895. (On Fletcher lot is grave of Sallie W. Withers, wife of Albert. 1850-1878.)
Fletcher, Hugh. 1877-1905.
Fletcher, Mrs. Louisa. Died 1893, aged 75 years.
Fletcher, Manley. 1845-1870.
Fletcher, Manley. Died 1873, aged 7 months.
Fletcher, Thaddeus Norris. 1843-1920.
Fletcher, V.A. "In Memory of Aunt Nish." Died 1849, aged 45 years.
Flynn --- 1838-1910.
Flynn, Mable. 1884-1916.
Flynn, Rachel Hunter. 1845-1919.

Fontaine, Elizabeth. 1845-1864.
Fowler, Col. W. F. 1810-1896.
Francis, Fannie. 1830-1901
Furlong, Edward P. 1834-1854.
Furlong, Isabella. 1857-1915.

Gallaway, C. F. 1842---
Gallaway, Susannah. 1841-1901.
Gaskin, Sophrona. 1850-1931. (See Triplett)
Ghlette, Mrs. Phebe. Died 1889, aged 62 years.
Glasscock, wife of John Samuel Glasscock, and dau. of Ludwell and Agnes Lake. 1830-1892
Glasscock, Helen Smith. 1872-1917.
Glasscock, John Samuel, 1828-1886, son of Henry and Jane Glasscock.
Goodwin, Dr. Le Baron. April 21, 1800 - Nov. 7, 1859. On Goodwin lot stones broken and only word "Ann" legible.
Gowhig, Bridget. 1815-1831.
Gowhig, Dennis. 1813-1890.
Gowhig, Ellen, dau. of Dennis and Bridget, born at Melrose Station, 1855-1879.
Gowhig, Hannah. Jan. 1840 - July 1916.
Gowhig, Mary H. Dau. of William and Hannah. Oct. 2, 1863 - 1913.
Gowhig, Patrick John. 1857-1898.
Gowhig, William. April, 1833- July, 1919.
Gowhig, William, son of Dennis and Bridget, July 1864-1884.
Gowhig, William H. 1873-1890.
Graham, J. Barbour, wife of James M. Died 1904, aged 57 years.
Graham, James M. Dec. 1844-1916.
Gray, Emma E. 1886-1915.
Gray, James William. May 16, 1854-1927.
Gray, Mary E. 1848-1912.
Gray, Newton Lee. 1889-1919.
Gray, Mrs. Virginia. Died 1904, aged 44 years.
Green, Bernard. 1842-1902.
Green, Charles T. 1820-1897.
Green, Lucy, wife of Charles T. 1831-1875.
Green, Thomas. 1838-1899.
Guthrie, Eliza D. Died 1855, aged 77 years.

Hamilton, Betty Peace. 1874-1905.
Hamilton, George Stanton. 1830-1912.
Hamilton, Hugh. 1841-1928.
Hamilton, Isabella Voss. 1840-1927.
Hamilton, Marianna Scott. Died 1918, in 90th year of age.
Harris, H. Ashby. 1862-1928.
Harris, James K. Died 1862, aged 18 years. 5th Texas Regiment, mortally wounded at 2nd Battle of Mannassa.
Hays, Edward. 1865-1878.
Heflin, Alfred, son of Lawson and A. E. 1889-1908.
Heflin, Ann Eliza. 1804 (?) - 1895.
Helm, Edward. 1841-1863.
Helm, Eramus. 1819-1864.
Helm, Frances. 1848-1972 [?].
Helm, Fraspins. Born in Kentucky. Died 1872.
Helm, Mary, wife of Fraspins. 1813-1882.
Helm, Robert. 1845-1864.
Helm, Virginia, wife of Eramus. 1812-1852.
Helm, Virginia Asquith. Died 1841, aged 18 years.
Hendricks, Elizabeth (See Pollock). 1843-1914.
Hicks, Nannie Fitzhugh Randolph, wife of Maj. Robert I. Hicks. 1838-1893.
Hicks, Robert. 1831-1920. Major of C. S. A.
Holt, Fred. Died 1910.
Holtzclaw, 1868-1878.
Holtzclaw, Amon (Almon) Seabury. 1867-1889.
Holtzclaw, Elizabeth. 1820-
Holtzclaw, Frank. 1854-1885.
Holtzclaw, George. 1815-1885.

Holtzclaw, Grace. 1857----
Holtzclaw, Howard. 1868-1878.
Holtzclaw, Willie Baldwin. 1851-1912.
Horner, Alfred Byrnes, son of Gustavus and Mary A. Byrnes Horner. 1861-1934.
Horner, Anne Brown. 1836-1921.
Horner, Ann Maria Lovell, wife of Dr. Frederick Horner. 1816-1898.
Horner, Charles Gustavus, son of Gustavus and Mary A. Byrnes Horner. 1869-1914.
Horner, Elizabeth. 1811-1850.
Horner, Ellen Ashton. Died 1876.
Horner, Frances Scott, wife of Robert Downman. 1837-1900.
Horner, Frederick. 1816-188-
Horner, Dr. Frederick. Assistant surgeon, U.S.N. 1828-1902.
Horner, Gustavus Richard, son of William and Mary Edmonds Horner. 1804-1892.
Horner, Joseph. 1807-1886.
Horner, Maria Sherman, wife of Dr. Fred. Horner. Oct. 5, 1849 - 1920.
Horner, Mary Agnes, wife of Gustavus R. and dau. of Charles and Emeline Byrnes. 1815-1884.
Horner, Mary McClenachan Robb, wife of William. 1828-1916.
Horner, Richard Henry. 1839-1899. (C.S.A.)
Horner, Robert Braxton. 1867-1910.
Horner, Robert Littleton. 1825-1910.
Horner, Seignora Peyton, died 1876.
Horner, Virginia Cary, wife of Richard Henry Horner. 1844-1904.
Horner, William. -----
Howey, John A. Died 1900, aged 87 years.
Hurst, Rosalie, wife of George. Died 1897.
Hutton, Margaret. 1827-1908.
Hyde, Ellen, wife of Philip. Died 1902, aged 65 years.
Hyde, Mannie (sister), died in 22nd year of age.
Hyde, Philip. Born in County Cork, Ireland. 1829-1893.

Isabell, Jonas, born in the North of England. Died 1850, aged 88 years.

James, John. 1819-1892. (On Smith lot)
Jameson, Frederick G. 1915-1919.
Jeffries, James Payne. Died 1908, aged 55 year.
Jeffries, James Payne, son of James P. and M.H. Jeffries. 188-1890.
Jeffries, James Penfield, son of James P. and M.H. Jeffries. 1892-1925.
Jeffries, Mary H. Wyer, wife of James P., dau. of Henry and Anne Powell Wyer. 1856-1920. (See Wyer)
Jennings, Dr. Louis. Died 1860, aged 32 years.
Jennings, Louisa A., wife of W.A. Jennings, dau. of Dr. Turner and Harriett Adams of Zanesville, Ohio. 1840-1904.
Jennings, Mrs. Lucy, relict of Thomas O. Jones, Esq. Died Jan. 25, 1862, aged 70 years
Johns, Edward Lovell, son of Edward L. and Sarah, 1864-1906.
Johnson, Mrs. James. Died 1838, aged 30 years.
Johnson, Cora, wife of T.S. Johnson. 1845-1904.
Johnson, Eppa H., son of D.M. and L.F. 1871-1903 (?).
Johnson, Harry Mauzy. 1845-1908.
Johnson, Ida M., wife of T.F. 1869-1920.
Johnson, Iram (?). 1875-1876.
Johnson, James F. B. & D. 1887.
Johnson, Katherine, dau. of P.L. 1878-1899.
Jolly, Annie Owen, wife of J.D. Jolly. 1867-1917.
Jones, Infant of John and Elizabeth. 1885.
Jones, Elizabeth. Born July 20, 1856; Died Oct. 27, 1914.
Jones, Honora, wife of Richard B. 1853-1931.
Jones, John B. 1856-1906.
Jones, Richard B. 1852-1915.

Keith, Isham, son of Thomas and grandson of Rev. James Keith, of Scotland. 1801-1862.
Keith, James S., son of Isham Keith and wife Sarah A. Keith. 1869-1918. (See Chilton)
Keith, Juliet Chilton, wife of Isham Keith, and dau. of Joseph Chilton. 1800-1887.
Keith, Sarah, wife of Isham Keith. 1837-1912.
Kemper - "Memory of Father and Mother."

Kemper, Col. John. 1768-1856.
Kemper, Martha. 1769-1847.
King, Edwin B., Jr., only son of Edwin B. and Mary S.F. King. 1911-1915.
King, Josie E., wife of F.A. Merriman. (See Merriman)
King, William. 1825-1907.
Kirby, Caroline Sims, wife of John G. 1870-1934.
Kirby, Capt. James. 1838-1906.
Kirby, John G. 1876-1933.
Kirby, Julia C. (Claggett). 1844-1921.
Kirby, Virginia Sims. 1898-1924. (See Sims)
Kirkpatrick, Delia Catherine, wife of Enoch. 1841-1911.
Kirkpatrick, Enoch J. 1846 ----.

Lake, Isaac. 1837-1905.
Lake, John. 1840-1913. Capt. C.S.A.
Lee, Charles. Died 1815, aged 57 years. U.S. Atty. Gen. 1797-1801. (See Pollock)
Lee, Julian. 1840-1901.
Lee, Meta Wallace. 1850-1886.
Legg, Daisy. Died 1908, aged 24 years.
Limerick, Mary, wife of James -- 1837 -- illegible.
Lomax, Elizabeth Winter Payne, wife of Lindsay Lundsford Lomax. 1850-1932.
Lomax, Lindsay Lundsford. 1835-1913. Major Gen. of Army of Northern Virginia.
Luke, Elizabeth. Died 22 February, 1908.
Lunceford, Amanda. 1841-1898.
Lunceford, B.F. 1856-1891.
Lunceford, Benjamin. 1837-1900.

Maddux, James Henry. March 14, 1818 - 1899.
Maddux, James Kerfoot. 1853-1930. Cora Virginia Johnson on Maddux lot.
Maddux, Theodore, son of James and Jane. 1859-1887.
Maddux, Thomas L., son of James H. and Jane Maddux. 1856-1885.
Mann, Jesse L., son of Joel. Died 1888, aged 22 years.
Mann, Joel. 1822-1912.
Mann, Sally A. 1832-1903.
Marr, Catherine Inman, wife of John Marr. 1797-1878.
Marr, Frances Harrison. 1835-1918.
Marr, James Ripon. 1832-1879.
Marr, Jane Blackburn. Feb. 4, 1840 - 1929. "The last of her generation and a noble representative of Old Virginia."
Marr, John. June 6, 1788 - 1848.
Marr, John. 1825-1861.
Marr, John Blackburn. 1840-1927.
Marr, John Quincy. 1825-1861. C.S.A.
Marr, Margaret, 1830-1903.
Marr, Margaret Moore. 1830-1903.
Marr, Sally, eldest dau. of John and C. Marr. 1817-1895.
Marr, Wallace Marion. Died Nov. 26, 1844, aged 24 years.
Marshall, Alexander J. 1803-1862.
Marshall, Maria Rose, wife of Alexander Marshall. 1803-1904.
Marshall, R.I. Taylor. 1835-1862.
Maxheimer, Elizabeth B., wife of Joseph. Born in Scotland. 1851-1912.
Maxheimer, Joseph. 1849-1916.
Mayhugh, John Thomas. 1864-1928.
McLearen, Thomas Coleman. 1812-1886.
Merriam, Fred K. 1833-1833.
Merriam, Josephine. 1855-1888. (See King)
Merriam, Josie E. King, wife of F.A.
Mountjoy, J.W. 1838-1922.
Mountjoy, M.S. 1886-1911.
Mountjoy, R.R. Born March 15, 1842. Died 1864. Capt. of Company D, Battalion Virginia Cavalry, Mosby men. Monument erected by his comrades. C.S.A.
Mountjoy, S.F. 1847-1922.
Muller, Ernest, aged 5 years.
Muller, Frank. 1862-1917.
Muller, Susan, born in London, England. 1836-1895.

Muller, William, born in England. 1810-1884.
Muller, William. Born in Devonshire, England, Jan. 2, 1866; died in New York, 1892.

Nagle, Mrs. Mary. April 20, 1821 - 1896.
Neal, Ann Amelia, wife of George Neal. 1835-1886.
Neal, George H. 1829-1891.
Nelson, Rev. G.W. 1840-1903.
Nelson, George W., Jr. 1875-1928.
Nelson, Joseph. 1873-1883.
Nelson, Margurite. 188-1895.
Nelson, Marvin, 1886-1908.
Nelson, Mary Scollay, wife of Rev. George W. 1850-1923.
Nelson, Nadine. 1879-1883.
Newby, Georginana, wife of Robert. 1824-1868. (Graves of several children on this lot)
Newby, Robert C. 1822-1884.

O'Hara, Isabelle Byrne. 1844-1895.
O'Hara, Mary Emeline. 1863-1902.
O'Reilley. 1879-1900. (Robert)
O'Reilley, Brian. 1868-1886.
O'Reilley, Margaret. 1844-
O'Reilley, Miles. 1886 - 1 year.
O'Reilley, Nicholas. 1876-1894.
O'Reilley, Philip. 1866-1887.
O'Reilley, Robert. 1832-1905.
O'Reilley, Thomas. 1873-1904.

Page, Helen Stuart. 1839-1858.
Page, John --- illegible.
Page, Sarah E., wife of John. Died 1871, aged 58 years.
Palmer, Maj. F.Gendron. Mortally wounded at the 2nd Battle of Manassa. Died Nov. 4, 1862.
Parkinson, J.W. 1817-1904.
Parkinson, L.A. 1829-1892.
Pattie, C.C. 1854-1878.
Pattie, Jenny, wife of William Pattie. 1822-1859.
Pattie, Otho H.W. 1844-1877.
Pattie, V.A. 1831-1857.
Pattie, William. Born 1849; died 1859.
Payne, Alexander Dixon, son of Richard and Alice Fitzhugh Dixon Payne. 1837-1893.
Payne, Charles Edward Fitzhugh. 1841-
Payne, Charles Fitzhugh. 1877-1928. 1st Lt. Aero Squadron, A.E.F.
Payne, Harry Fitzhugh, son of Brig. Gen. W.H.F. Payne and Mary Winston Payne. 1857-1933.
Payne, Inman H. 1822-1905.
Payne, Jeane Morrison Brook, wife of G.E.F. 1850-1921.
Payne, John D., M.D. Born in Tuscumbia, Ala., died in Fauquier Co., Va., 1881.
Payne, John Daniel. 1862-1901.
Payne, John Massie, son of Inman. 1852-1921.
Payne, John Winston, son of William H. and Mary, b. 1858 - 1937.
Payne, Markham Brooke, son of Inman Payne. 1865-1902.
Payne, Mary Ann, wife of Inman Payne. 1924-1900.
Payne, Mary E., wife of Gen. W.H.F. Payne, dau. of Col. William Winter and Minerva Winston Payne. 1831-1920.
Payne, Minerva Winston, wife of William Winter Payne, dau. of Col. John Winston, of Alabama. 1811-1882.
Payne, Sarah Robb Tyler, dau. of A.H. (?) and Mary E. 1865-1875.
Payne, Rev. T. Alexander, son of Inman and Mary Payne. 1863-1898.
Payne, William Fitzhugh. "Not for empire or renown, but for right and commonwealth." Son of Arthur Morson and Mary Mason Fitzhugh, born Jan. 27, 1830; died March, 1904. He entered the Confederate Army as Capt. of Black Horse Troop, and rose to be Brig. Gen. of the 2nd Brigade of Fitzhugh Lee's division.
Payne, William Winter. 1807-1874.
Pierson, Lizzie, wife of Rev. William Pierson, of New York. Died 1880, aged 24 yrs.
Pollock, Rev. A.D. 1807-1890.

Pollock, Charles Lee. Died 1888, aged 39 years.
Pollock, Elizabeth Gordon, 1812-1894 (?), wife of Rev. A. D. Pollock, daughter of
  Charles Lee. (See Lee)
Pollock, Elizabeth Hendrick, daughter of Rev. A. D. Pollock. 1843-1914.
Pollock, Thomas Gordon. Died 1863, aged 24 years - killed at Gettysburg.
Portman, Frederick Arthur Berkeley. 1867-1907.

Reed, Margaret. 1810-1885.
Richardson, Alexander. 1788-1862.
Riley, Annie. Died 1888, aged 75 years.
Robinson, Sarah E. Died 1903, aged 63 years.
Robinson, William E. 1842-1915. C.S.A.
Rush, Charles C. 1858-1931.
Rush, Lucy E. (mother). 1834-1911.
Rush, Mary E. 1858-1931.
Rush, Peyton L. (father). 1835-1898.
Russell, Samuel and Eliza --- inscriptions illegible.

St. Clair, Cornelia. 1838-1915.
St. Clair, Robert. 1856-1915.
Saunders, John A. Company "D", Mosby Virginia Cavalry, C.S.A.
Saunders, Mary E., wife of Thomas. 1820-1887.
Saunders, T.E. 1822-1906
Saunders, Thomas. Company "D", Mosby Virginia Cavalry, C.S.A.
Schwab, Anton. 1834-1906.
Schwab, Joseph, son of Anton Schwab. 1863-1886.
Schwab, Susan E. 1837-1930.
Scott, John, son of Judge John Scott and wife Elizabeth Pickett. 1820-1907.
Scott, John Gordon, son of Col. John Scott and wife Augusta Caskie. 1859-1932.
Scott, Lucinda. Died 1850.
Sedwick, Benjamin. Died 1875, aged 64 years.
Sedwick, Cora Elizabeth. Jan. 17, 1857 - 1869.
Shellman, John. Died 1862, aged 20 years.
Shepherd, John. Died 1849.
Sims, Alice Mosby. 1865-1928.
Sims, Marian Louise. 1848-1907.
Sinclair, Ann Maria. Died 1892 - aged 69 years.
Sinclair, Maria Louisa. Sept. 13, 1829 - 1889.
Smith, Amanda, wife of P.A.L. 1821-1903.
Smith, Annie E. Jan. 11, 1801 - 1881.
Smith, Frank P. 1854-1907.
Smith, George Summer. 1849-1819.
Smith, Jenny. 1849-19---.
Smith, John. 1797-1863.
Smith, John. March 3, 1817 (or 1812) - Feb. 11, 1892.
Smith, John Thomas. Died 1872, aged 56 years.
Smith, William. 1866-1908.
Sower, Mary. 1844-1922.
Sower, Richard. Dec. 1837 - 1910. C.S.A.
Sower, William Summer. 1869-1931.
Spellman, Annie Heyward, wife of H. Conway Spellman. Died June 22, 1905.
Spellman, H. Conway. Died Feb. 1917.
Spellman, Hayward North. June 1889 - 1935. (World War soldier)
Spicer, Maude. 1875-1913.
Spicer, Wade. 1871-1909.
Sudduth, Mary. Died 1851, aged 33 years.
Sullivan, Maggie, daughter of Dennis and Ellen Sullivan. 1876-1892.

Tongue. "In memory of Johnzie Tongue, Priscilla Tongue, Thomas L. Tongue,
  Martha Tongue, Ann L. Tongue. 1798-1872."
Tongue, Frances. 1818-1891.
Tongue, James R. 1809-1881.
Tongue, Johnzie. 1845-1925.
Tongue, Rosa Neal. Died 1928.
Tongue, T. William. 1846-1918.

Triplett, Arthur W. 1846-1927.
Triplett, Ella, wife of Arthur W. Triplett. 1843-1908.
Triplett, Landies (?). 1853-1881.
Triplett, P. H. 1849-1919.
Triplett, Spillman L. 1901-1928.
Turner, Harriett, wife of late Dr. John A. Turner, Dec. 27, 1884, aged 77 years.
Tyler, Constance Horton. 1848-1922.
Tyler, Guennetta Baylor Dade, daughter of John Webb Tyler. Died 1883.

Utterback, Addison D. Died 1896.
Utterback, Annie. Died in Lynchburg, 1905.
Utterback, Virginia. Died 1920.
Utterback, William Warren, son of John and Mary. 1890-1920.

Vose, Laura G., wife of F. G. Vose and sister of F. G. Anderson. Sept. 1865-1918.

Waller, John Tyler. 1845-1865.
Ward, Berkeley. April 1783 - 1860.
Ward, Harriet ----- illegible.
Ward, Henry C. 1829-1861. 1st Lt. of Fauquier County Guards. Killed at first
    Battle of Mannassa.
Ward, Dr. John. June, 1826 - 1885.
Ward, Mary Grace, widow of Dr. John Ward, born in Baltimore, Md; died 1898, in
    Washington D. C.
Washington, Estelle ---- inscription illegible.
Washington, Georgianna Langhorne Baylor, widow of Temple Washington, dau. of
    Jane Alexander Dade (?) and G -- Walker Baylor. March 13, 1808 - Jan. 14, 1908.
Washington, Mildred Jane, wife of Robert Washington. 1824-1926.
Washington, Robert. 1812-1852.
Weaver, Richard. Died 1862, aged 39 years. C. S. A.
Wells, H. 1833-1905.
White, Charles Mason. 1855-1911.
White, D. B. D. 1893.
White, Gamilla, wife of John White, 1821-1892.
White, Hamden. 1812-1888.
White, Jane H., wife of D. B. White ---
White, John L. 1817-1899.
White, Mary, dau. of Charles G. and Helen White, 1888-1890.
White, Rev. Robert. 1850-1905.
White, Sallie Warren, wife of Rev. Robert White. 1855-1925.
Williamson, Catherine. Died 1905. This stone was erected in "Loving memory of
    mother, Susan, and brother, Robert Bruce."
Williamson, Louisa F. 1852-1933.
Williamson, Louisa R. F. 1852-1933.
Williamson, Thomas Vowell and Sarah Brook Williamson --------
Williamson, W. W. Died 1903.
Williamson, Rev. William. Died 1848, aged 83 years.
Wine, James. 1834-1909.
Wine, Sarah G. 1833-1909.
Wingfield, Thomas Smith. 1813-1897.
Winmill, Albert. 1852-1904.
Winmill, Josephine. 1855-1910.
Wise, George C. 1848-1922. U. S. Navy.
Withers, Sallie W., wife of Albert Withers. 1850-1878.
Withers, Dr. Thomas. 1790 (or 1796) - 1865.
Wood, Daniel. 1852-1924.
Woodzell, Emma D. Died 1908, aged 38 years.
Woodzell, George. 1842-1933.
Woodzell, Martha Clark. 1847-1924.
Woodzell, Mary. 1878-1918.
Wyer, Ann E. Powell, wife of Rev. H. Wyer. 1833-1905.
Wyer, Rev. Henry. 1829-1901.
Wyer, Henry Halstead, son of Rev. Henry Wyer. 1870-1906.
Wyer, John Powell, son of Rev. Henry Wyer. 1863-1905.
Wyer, Walter Penfield. 1860-1922.

# FAUQUIER COUNTY RENT ROLL - 1770

-- D'Butts 30
Adams, Isaac 150
Allen, Archibald 188
Allen, John 187
Allen, John, dec'd. 1043
Allen, Thomas 187
Allen, Ursley 230
Allen, William 148
Anderson, John 584
Aris, John 160
Arnold, John 150
Asberry, William 201
Ashby (Frederick Co.) 340
Ashby New deed 424
Ashby, Capt. John 1055
Ashby, John, Jr. 375
Ashby, Nimrod 100
Ashby, Robert 916
Ashby, Stephen 135
Ayers, Thomas 350

Bailey, James 100
Bailey, John 100
Bains, John 183
Baisey, John 200
Ball, Benjamin 160
Ball, William 600
Barber, John 200
Barby, Andrew 145
Barker, William 197
Bartell, Thomas 200
Basey, Edmond 125
Beach, Margaret 135
Beach, Peter 200
Bell, James 600
Bell, John (from Culpeper Co.) 800
Benson, Pane 250
Berry, George 170
Berryman, Maxmillian 1163
Bethell, Thomas 250
Blackmore, Joseph --
Blackwell, Joseph 1180
Blackwell, Col. William 538
Boswell, George 648
Bradford, Daniel 810
Bramlett, Henry 250
Bramlett, Reuben 150
Bramlett, William 123
Bronaugh, Thomas 150
Bronaugh, William 410
Brooke, Humphrey 150
Brooke, William 200
Brown, John (Heirs) 300
Buckner, Ruth 1000
Bullitt, Benjamin 300
Bullitt, Cuthbert 300
Burdette, Frederick 100
Bushaw, James 570

Butler, John 423
Buttell, Joseph 287
Button, Harmon 164
Carom (Carson), Champe 227
Carr, John 150
Catlett, John 358
Chapman, Constance 3068
Chichester, Richard (?) 1600
Chichester, William, Charles, John, Stephen & Thos. 765
Chilton, John 463
Chinn, Thomas 829
Churchill, Armistead 1690
Churchill, Henry 200
Churchill, John (chil. of) 1582
Conway, Thomas 1648
Conway, William 200
Conyers, John 489
Conyers, Samuel 200
Cooledge, Judyson 1748
Coppage, Moses 275
Coppage, William 830
Cortney, John 300
Cortney, William 182
Coventon, Richard 150
Crockett, James 134
Crosby, George 226
Crump, Benjamin 375
Crump, George 470
Crump, John 188-93 609
Cummins, Simon 150

Darnall, Mathew 223
Darnold, David 150
Darnold (Darnall), Jermi. 600
Delaney, Joseph 680
Dodd, Nathaniel 196
Dodson, George 100
Dodson, William, Sr. 192
Doggett, Bushrod 800
Downman, Raleigh 630
Duff, James 100
Duncan, Charles 242
Duncan, John 100
Duncan, John 125
Duncan, John 188
Duncan, John, Sr. 325
Duncan, Joseph 328
Edmonds, Elias 885
Edmonds, William 500
Edwards, Garrett 219
Edwards, John 100
Ellis, John ---
Embry, Robert 482
Etherington, John 200

Eustace, William 1960
Eves, Thomas 200
Eves, William 100
Fegan, Daniel 130
Ferry, Ann 443
Fishback, Frederick 60
Fishback, Harmon 100
Fishback, John 257
Fishback, Josiah 257
Fishback, Phil 257
Flory, Daniel 150
Foley, James, Sr. 117 & 300
Fox, Samuel 394

Garner, Charles 100
Garner, James 400
Garner, Vinson 400
Genn, James Heirs 774
Gent, Widow 639
Gent, George 100
George, Parnie (?) 150
Gibson, Jonathan 1050
Gibson, William 50
Glasscock, -- 900
Grant, George (Of Pr. George Co.) 100
Grant, William 300
Green, Duff 570
Grigsby, Samuel 177
Grinnan, ---- 186
Grubbs, Richard 207
Gunning, Thomas 150

Hackley, Francis --
Hackley, Lott 246
Hackley, Richard 100
Hall, Widow 200
Hampton, Ruth 500
Hardin, Martin 965
Harley, Richard 100
Harmon, Fishback 179
Harper, John 230
Harrell, Daniel 100
Harrison, Col. Thomas --
Helm, Thomas 388
Hening, George 100
Henson, Robert 117
Hewit, Susannah 200
Hewit, Susannah 150
Hitt, Harmon 500
Hitt, John 216
Hitt, John, Jr. 53
Hitt, Joseph 214
Hitt, Peter, Jr. 275
Hitt, Peter, Sr. 200
Hogan, James 175
Hogan, William 124
Hogan, William 413
Holtzclaw 185
Hottzclaw, Benjamin 130

71

Holtzclaw, Henry 987
Hopper, Blagrove 325
Hord, Thomas 235
Hudnal, John 125
Hudnal, John (Heirs of) 375
Hudnal, Joseph 200
Hudnal, Thomas 500
Hudnal, William 375
Humston, Edward 175
Hunter, James 200
Hunter, William 400

Jacob, Morris 211
James, John 50
James, John Capt. 376
James, Thomas 980
Jeffries, John 227
Jennings, Augus 308
Jennings, William 31
Jett, Francis 150
Johnson, Jeffries 1038
Johnson, Moses 150
Johnson, William 100
Jones, Brenentom (?) --
Jones, John 153

Kemper, Harmon 184
Kemper, Henry ---
Kemper, Jacob 163
Kemper, John 363
Kemper, Peter 298
Kenner, George 180
Kenner, Howson 775
Kernes, William 418
Kirk, William --

Lampkins, George 925
Lawerence, Edward 317
Leach, Joseph 100
Lewis, Zachariah 268
Luttrell, Austin 80
Luttrell, James 124
Luttrell, John 70
Luttrell, Mary 80
Luttrell, Michael 70
Luttrell, Richard 58
Luttrell, Robert 74
Luttrell, Samuel 70
Luttrell, Susannah 80

Markham, John 100
Marrs, Ann (widow) 1135
Martin, Charles 171
Martin, Eve 100
Martin, Henry 163
Martin, John 100
Martin, Joseph 150
Mathis, Robert (?) 127
Mathis, Thomas 350
Mauzy, Betty 14
Mauzy, Henry 220, 434
Mauzy, John (Heirs) 590
McCarty, Jerrett 50
McClanahan, William 194

McCormack, John 100
McCormack, Stephen 100
McKee, John 66
Miller, Simon (dec'd.) 575
Miller, William 100
Minter, Joseph 213
Morehead, Charles 306
Morehead, John (dec'd.) 450
Morgan, James (Heirs) 174
Morgan, John 166
Morgan, Charles, Jr. 500
Morgan, Charles, Sr. 127
Morgan, Simon 463
Morgan, William 622, 865
Morgan, William, Jr. 147
Morris, William --
Murray, James 630

Neavil, Capt. George --
Nelms (Helms ?), Samuel 112
Nelson, John 298
Nelson, John, Sr. -
Nevill, John (Heirs) 227
Nevill, Joseph 116
Newgent, Edward --
Newgent (Nugent), Thomas --
Newland, Daniel 140
Newport, Peter 100

Obannon, John, Jr. ---
Obannon, William ---
Obannon, William Mrs. --
Obannon, William, Sr. --
Otterback (Utterback), Henry --
Otterback, John 80

Page, Thomas 100
Parker, Dr. 452
Pierce, Peter (Heirs) 70
Peters, John 800
Pickett, William (Exrs.) (Of Culpepper Co.) 500
Porter, Samuel 235

Randolph, William 680
Ransdell, Wharton 896
Ransow (Rousan), John 260
Rector, Harmon 100
Rector, Henry 100
Rector, Jacob 100
Rector, John 337
Rector, Nathaniel 100
Redding, Timothy 50
Reiley, Thomas 200
Right (Wright), Capt. John 236
Robertson, Joseph 100
Rousan, William 250
Routt, John --
Routt, Peter (of Stafford Co.) --
Russell, William 100
Rust, John 200

Savage, Dr. (of Markham) 1834
Scott, Capt. James 2000
Scrows (?) Heirs ----
Sears, John 576
Seirs (Sears), James 122
Settle, George 100, 153
Settle, Isaac 22
Settle, Joseph 147
Settle, William 507
Shumate, Daniel 100
Sinckler, John (dec'd.) 213
Singleton, Stanley 200
Smith, Alexander (Heirs) 461
Smith, Augustine 255
Smith, Caleb 75
Smith, James --
Smith, John 156
Smith, Joseph 88, 600
Smith, Thomas 100, 100
Smith, William ---
Snelling, Aquilla 232
Snelling, Benjamin 38
Spielman, Jacob (Heirs) 264
Stamps, William 630
Stephenson, James 268
Stewart, James 476
Stone, Thomas 159, 159
Strothers, Daniel 100

Terrall (?), Francis 100
Thomas, Jacob 264
Thornberry, Thomas 586
Thornton, William 55
Triplett, William 434

Waller, Charles (Heirs) 400
Waugh, Joseph 600
Waugh, William 150
Weaver, Elizabeth Ann 160
Weaver, John 150
Weaver, Tillman 311
Welthy (?), Widow 134
Whily (?), Allen 300
Wilburn, Edward 138
William, Jonathan (Heirs) 174
Williams (One of D. Chambers' heirs) 200
Williams, George 134
Williams, Paul 241
Withers, James --
Withers, John 500
Withers, Thomas 718
Withers, William 600
Wood, Joseph 100
Wood, Joshua 130
Wood, Nehemiah 80
Wright, Capt. John 236
Wright, William 185

Young, James 250
Young, Original 159

RENT ROLL - 1738

Prince William County, Va.

Fauquier Co. was formed in 1759, being taken from Prince William Co., and named after Francis Fauquier, Governor of Virginia. Many of the following names given on the Rent Roll of Prince William Co. (1738) are to be found later in Fauquier Co.

Abbott, Roger
Arrington, Wansford
Ash, Francis
Ashmore, Widow

Baker, Charles
Ball, Alexander
Barton, Thomas
Barton, Thomas
Baylis, William
Berry, Thomas
Billings, Jasper
Bland, John
Brinbett (?), Henry
Bronaugh, Jeremiah
Bronaugh, Capt. Jeremiah
Brooks, Thomas
Buchanan, Joseph, dec'd.
Buckner, Richard
Bush, John

Calk, James (or Joseph)
Calvert (Colvert), George
Calvert, George, Jr.
Calvert, Sarah
Canterbury, John
Carr, John
Champ, John
Champ, Major John
Chambers, Joseph
Chapman, Joseph (Heirs)
Chilton, Capt. Thomas
Clemont (Clement), Alexander
Combs, Emmanuel
Combs, Joseph
Compton, William
Comyers, Davis
Coram, William
Corbin, John
Cornwell, Charles
Cottonwell, Thomas
Crouch, William
Crump, John
Cruppner, Richard
Cummings, Malachi

Darmott, Michael

Earle, Samuel
Edy, Samuel

Farrow, John (orphan)
Farrow, William
Ficklin, William
Floyd, Henry
Foster, William
French, James

Garner, John (orphan)
Garner, Thomas
Garner, Vincent
Gibson, John, Gent. of N. Carolina
Glascock, John
Goslin, John, dec'd.
Graham, Howard
Grant, John (inspector)
Grayson, Benjamin
Grayson, Capt. Benjamin
Grigg, John
Grubbs, Richard

Hall, Widow
Halley, Henry
Hancock, Scarlett
Harper, George
Harrison, Burr
Harrison, Thomas
Harrison, Thomas, Jr.
Hedges, John
Holtzclaw, Jacob & John
Hopper, Blagrove
Hopper, John
Hudnall, Joseph, William & Thos.

Johnson, Jesse
Johnson, John
Johnson, Tolito (?)

Kamper, Howson
Kamper, James
Kamper, John
Kent, ------
Kinchloe, John

Lambert, Hugh

Linton, Widow
Linton, John
Linton, Moses
Ludwell, Philip

Marr, Chris.
Marr, Daniel
Marr, John
Martin, Joseph
McComkry, Rev. William
McDonald, Donald
Minton, Joseph
Morgan, Charles
Moss, Mathew

Neale, Roswell
Nevill, George
Nounan, Widow

Page, John

Routt, William
Russell, William

Sarlson (?), Nicholas
Smith, William
Spiller, William
Stamps, Thomas
Stone, Thomas
Stribbling, Capt. Thomas
Strothers, William

Tackett, Lewis
Taylor, Charles
Thorn, William
Toward, Orphans

Veale, Morris
Vicars, Orphans

Wallace, Burr (widow of)
Welch, Thomas
Whitledge, John
Whitledge, Thomas
Whitledge, William
Williams, Jonas
Williams, William
Winwright, John
Wright, Joseph

# FEES - 1827

A list of fees due Isaac A. Williams, Clerk of Fredericksburg Chancery Court, in the County of Fauquier, Virginia.

Allen, Henry
Armistead, Ann B.
Armistead, John
Armistead, Robert

Ball, George
Baylis, John T.
Bayliss, William
Baylor, Ann D.
Beale, John G.
Bishop, Joshua
Blackwell, Frances
Bogess, Henry
Brooke, F.W.
Bruce, Alexander
Byrne, William

Chapman, George, Jr.
Chilton, Mark A.
Comly, J.A. & Allen, W.S.
Corbin, James
Cross, James
Crowne, Thomas

Dearing, George
Digges, Edward
Digges, Whiting
Dodd, Ann

Edmonds, William F.
English, James

Farrow, Benjamin
Farrow, Nimrod
Fishback, ---
Fitzhugh, Battaile
Floerie, James (Joseph)
Foote, George W.
Foster, Thomas
Frazier, James

Gibson, William
Gillison, -----
Glascock, Benjamin
Glassell, John
Gordon, Samuel

Graham, Benjamin
Grigsby, Aaron
Grigsby, Baylis
Grigsby, Nathaniel

Handy, William
Handy, William
Haraway, Richard
Hart, Robert
Hayes, John
Hayes, John
Hickerson, Elizabeth
Hickerson, Hosea
Hitch, Aquilla
Holtzclaw, Charles
Hudnal, Mary
Hume, Robert
Hunton, Thomas

James, David
Jennings, Thomas
Johnson, Turner M.

Kelly, Alexander D.
Kelly, James W.
Kemper, John
Kemper, William
King, Vincent

Latham, George
Latham, Jere D.
Lee, Hancock
Lewis, Henry M.

Maddux, Grover
Mallory, Edward
Mallory, William
Marshall, James M.
Martin, George
McCormick, Stephen
McNean & Cowles
Moore, Thomas
Murphy, William S.
Murphy, William S.
Murray, William & John

Obannon, Benjamin

Obannon, James
Obannon, Joseph

Payne, William
Phillips, William F.
Pickett, -------
Poe, William
Porter, John

Richards, Edward D.
Rogers, Notley W.
Rose, Robert H.
Russell, Marcus

Scott, Alexander B.
Scott, John
Shacklett (?), John
Shaw, Neale
Smith, Joseph
Smith, Thomas
Smith, Walter A.
Smith, William
Sinkler, William (?)
Strother, Enoch
Strother, John (by next friend)
Strother, Susannah

Thompson, Elizabeth
Thornhill, Elijah
Triplett, Frances
Triplett, William
Turner, Thomas
Turney, Lewis
Tutt, Thomas

Warde, Berkeley
Weaver, John
Welch, Sylvester
Wharton, Samuel
Wheatley, James
Winn, Jemina
Withers, Daniel
Withers, Jesse
Withers, Spencer

Yorby, William G.

(The above list was given merely as an index of the names of some of the families living in Fauquier County in 1827.)

## TENANTS OF THE MANOR OF LEEDS

### Fauquier County - 1777

Allen, Archibald 100
Allen, John 104
Allen, Reuben 200
Allen, William 120

Barbey, Andrew 126
Barbey, Joseph 200
Barton, David 150
Barton, John 100
Bennett, Daniel 100
Bolt, Robert 200
Briggs, William 163
Brown, Dixon 213
Browning, Jacob 100
Burgess, Garner 200

Cook, William 200
Corder, William 200
Crawley, Richard 200
Crim, John, Jr. 100
Crim, John, Sr. 200

Day, William 200
Dearing, John 100
Devlin, William 200
Douglas, Benjamin 130

Ellis, John 100
Ellis, Sarah 105

Flelkins, William 150
Fletcher, William 200
Flinn, Valentine 200

Garrett, A. 200
Grant, John 120
Grimsley, Joseph 130
Grimsley, William 100
Gudrage, Allen 100

Hamrick, John 134
Harris, Samuel 250
Hefflin, James 140
Hefflin, Simon 200
Heminger, William 105
Hitt, Joseph 158
Hume, Andrew 200
Humston, John
Husht (?), Rosannah 100

Jeffrey, George 100
Jett, Francis 250
Jett, James 150
Jett, John, Sr. 238
Jett, William 100
Johnston, John ---
Jones, Charles 200
Jones, Henry 100
Jones, John 170

Laurence, Edward 200
Laurence, Peter 105
Linegar, William 118
Littlejohn, Charles 150
Lovell, Sarah 100
Luttrell, Samuel 150

Marshall, Widow 150
Marshall, John 146
McCormack, John 200
McQuin, John 100
Morgan, Charles 197
Morgan, William ---
Murphy, Miles 200

Neale, Benjamin 200
Nichols, Samuel 200
Norman, Clement 140
Norman, Clement 200
Norman, Jesse 140

Oldham, Mary 200

Payne, Francis 200
Payne, John 100
Payne, Reuben 140
Payne, Reuben 200
Payne, Thomas 200
Pickett, William 275
Pinkard 140
Priest, John 200
Pyior, Benjamin 200

Rand olph, Richard 150
Riley, John 200

Settle, George 134
Shumate, John 200
Sinclair, John 200
Smith, John 200
Smith, William 200
Smoot, John 200
Snelling, Hugh 100
Stone, Thomas 250
Sudduth, James 128
Sullivan, David --
Swain, Charles --

Taylor, Charles 120
Thompson, Jesse 100

Walker, William 100
Waller, Charles 250
Weaver, Jacob 100
Welch, David ---
Williams, Joseph 200
Wood, Dickerson 100
Woodyard (Woodard?), Lewis 200

## PENSION RECORDS

Name, rank, service, when placed on pension roll, commencement of pension, and age

| | | | | | |
|---|---|---|---|---|---|
| Beale, Richard E. | Pri. | Va. Mil. | 12.17.1832 | 3.4.1831 | 74 |
| Blackwell, David | Pri. | Va. Mil. | 4.24.1833 | 3.4.1831 | 84 |
| Canady, John | Seaman | Va. St. Navy | 2.15.1833 | 3.4.1831 | 70 |
| Combs, Robert | Pri. | Va. Conti. | 6.17.1833 | 7.4.1833 | 81 |
| Edmonds, David | Pri. | Va. St. Troop | 11.21.1833 | 3.4.1831 | 77 |
| Ethell, Anthony | Pri. | Va. Conti. | 6.8.1833 | 3.4.1833 | 77 |
| Groves, Philip | Pri. | Va. Mil. | 10.11.1833 | 3.4.1831 | 78 |
| Jeffries, Alexander | Pri. | Va. St. Troops | 2.5.1833 | 3.4.1831 | 72 |
| Kemper, Charles | Pri. | Va. Mil. | 2.26.1833 | 3.4.1831 | 78 |
| McClanahan, William | Pri. | Va. Conti. | 4.1.1833 | 3.4.1831 | 72 |
| Merry, Philip | Pri. | Va. Mil. | 4.4.1834 | 3.4.1831 | 85 |
| Moffitt, Jesse | Pri. | Va. St. Troop | 4.18.1833 | 3.4.1831 | 75 |
| Monroe, George | Pri. | Va. St. Troops | 5.23.1833 | 3.4.1831 | 71 |
| Morrison, Edward | Pri. | Va. Cav. | 7.19.1833 | 3.4.1831 | 76 |
| Murphy, John | Pri. | Va. St. Troops | 4.18.1833 | 3.4.1831 | 102 |
| Obannon, Thomas | Pri. | Va. Mil. | 8.18.1833 | 3.4.1831 | 76 |
| Payne, Augustine | Pri. | Va. Mil. | 2.25.1833 | 3.4.1831 | 72 |
| Payne, William | Sergt. | Va. Mil. | 2.28.1831 | 3.4.1831 | 75 |
| Payne, William | Capt. | Va. St. Troop | 2.23.1833 | 3.4.1831 | 80 |
| Rawles, Kenag | Pri. | Va. Mil. | 10.4.1833 | 3.4.1831 | 70 |
| Riddle, William | Pri. | Va. Mil. | 10.12.1833 | 3.4.1831 | 84 |
| Rowles, William | Pri. | Va. St. Troops | 3.20.1833 | 3.4.1831 | 75 |
| Thompson, John | Pri. | S. Car. Mil. | 1.24.1833 | 3.4.1831 | 77 |
| Tomlin, William, Sr. | Capt. | Va. Conti. | 8.21.1832 | 3.4.1831 | 76 |
| Welch, Sylvester | Pri. | Va. Conti. | 4.2.1833 | 3.4.1831 | 79 |
| Wickliffe, David | Pri. | Va. Conti. | 3.11.1833 | 3.4.1831 | 80 |
| Withers, Jesse | Pri. & Sergt. | Va. Mil. | 9.26.1833 | 3.4.1831 | 74 |
| Withers, Spencer | Sergt. | Va. Conti. | 4.10.1833 | 3.4.1831 | 88 |

# INDEX

---, Ann 65
  Ben 36
  Caty 55
  Daniel 35
  D'Butts 71
  Elizabeth 37, 53
  Jack 37
  Lucy 31
  Polly 58
  Sam 37
  Samuel 35
  Solomon 18
  Will 37

--- A ---

Abbott, Roger 73
Abell, Ephiram 40, 45
Adams, Ann 45
  Carly 39
  Charles 39, 45
  Elizabeth 17, 60
  Franky 55
  Gavin 45
  George 17, 31, 45
  Harriett 66
  Isaac 71
  John 8, 9, 11, 14, 17, 45
  John, Dr. 63
  John T. 63
  Josias 17
  Mary 63
  Nancy 39
  Polly 53
  Sarah 63
  Susannah 17, 55
  Thomas 42
  Turner, Dr. 66
  Virginia 63
  Walter 38
  William 38
Aden, Lydia 37
Adie, Mary 28
Alexander, Ellis 45
  Sarah 51
  William 7
  William, Esquire 24
Alford, William 45
Allanson, William 39
Allen, --- 45
  Ann 47
  Archibald 71, 75
  Azariah 45
  Betty 12
  Edmund 63 (2)
  Henry 45 (2), 74
  James 3, 11
  John 3, 30, 44, 45, 71 (2), 75
  Joseph 3, 30
  Margaret 44, 59
  Margaret E. 63
  Martha 22
  Mary 38
  Reuben 75
  Susan 24
  Ursley 71
  Ursulla 30
  Thomas 3, 30, 71
  W.S. 74
  William 3, 10, 30, 44, 45 (2), 71, 75
Allison, David 16, 43
  Mary Semour Hall 43

William 16, 43
Allsup, Dorothy 9
Ambler, David 45
  William 45
Ambrose, Elizabeth 3
Amiss, Dolly 50
Anderson, Agga 45
  Andrew 8
  Cornelius 45
  F.G. 70
  John 71
  Joseph 45
  Mary 54
  Nancy 49
  Sally 45
  Samuel 20
  Theophiles 45
  Thomas 45
Andrew, Alice 63
Anner, Eleanor 47
Aramsmith, William 45
Ardeb, Aaron 45
Argle, Jenny 52
Aris, John 71
Armistead, Ann B. 74
  John 74
  Robert 74
Armitage, Mary Ann 63
Arnold, Benjamin 16, 18, 32
  Elijah 41
  Isaac 27, 45
  James 4, 21
  Jemina 54
  John 16, 71
  Nancy 59
  Samuel 45 (2)
Arrington, Wansford 73
Asberry, William 71
Asbury, George 45
Ash, Ann 47
  Dorothy 59
  Eleanor 57
  Elizabeth 9, 42
  Eon 9
  Francis 9, 42, 45, 73
  George 9
  Harriett 42
  Jane 45
  John Richard 42
  Juliet 42
  Kitty 42
  Littleton 9
  Lucy 42
  Maria 42
  Molly 9
  Nancy 42
  Peggy 48
  Sarah 42
  Susannah 42
  Thornton 42
  Uriel 9, 45
  William 9, 42
Ashby, --- 71 (2)
  Alexander 28
  Ann 61
  Benjamin 28, 45
  Dolly 54
  Enoch 28
  H. 65
  John 14, 17, 21, 28, 45 (2)
  John, Capt. 71
  John, Jr. 12, 71
  Leannah 32
  Lucy 32
  Martin 28

Milly 50
Nathaniel 45
Nimrod 28, 43, 71
Patty 62
Robert 28 (2), 45 (2), 71
Sally 28
Stephen 71
Thomas 28
William 28, 45
Winnifred 57
Ashford, Bayliss 28
Ashley, Enoch 9
  John 3
  Robert 9
Ashly, Ann 60
  Nimrod 45
Ashmore, ---, Widow 73
  Sarah 25
Ashton, Ellen 66
  J.D. 64
  Lawerence 45
Askins, John 25
Asquith, Virginia 65
Athel, Molly 28
Athey, Joshua 45
Atkinson, Elenn 59
Atterburn, Polly 61
Atwell, Francis 45
Atwood, John 45
Auberry, Thomas 45
Austin, John 45 (2)
  Nancy 57
Ayers, Elizabeth 60
  Thomas 71

--- B ---

Babson, Polly 60
Bailee, Andrew 23
Bailes, Will 17
Bailey, Am... 42
  Ann 61
  Betty 7
  Carr 7
  Catherine 2
  Elizabeth 58
  George 45
  Green 45
  Hannah 54
  James 7, 45, 71
  Jenny 61
  John 7, 15, 45, 71
  Joseph 7, 24, 45
  Mary 7
  Moses 19
  Nancy 40
  Samuel 45
  Sarah 47
  Simon 45
  Stephen 45
  Thomas 7, 45 (2)
  William 7, 45 (3)
  Wright 15
Bains, John 71
Baisey, John 71
Baker, Charles 73
  Elizabeth 58
  John 15
  Lettice 59
  Richard 36, 42
  Samuel 15
Bale, James 45
  Jane 50

Bales, John 45
Baley, Mary 12
Balis, Henry 45
  William 45
Ball, Alese 42
  Alexander 73
  Anne 39
  Benjamin 30, 39, 45, 71
  Clementine 55
  David 30, 39
  Edward 7
  Elizabeth 31
  George 74
  Hannah 30
  James 25, 31
  John 31, 42
  Judith 60
  Judy 31
  Lucy 31
  Nancy 31
  Peggy 60
  Sarah 39, 45, 48
  Shoaltial 31
  Talliaferrio 31
  Thomas 30
  William 46 (2), 71
  William, Capt. 19
Ballard, John 46
  Mary 23
  Mary Nugent 52
  William 14, 23, 27
Ballenger, Edward 46
Banks, Gerrard 11
Banley, Nathan 8
Bannister, Augustine 28
  Frances 5, 48
  Mary 6
Bannon, George 12
Barbee, Andrew 32, 33
  Andrew Russell 33
  Anna 48
  Edward 46
  Elizabeth 33
  Jane 33
  John 4, 33, 46
  Jonathan 43
  Joseph 33, 37, 46 (2)
  Thomas 33
  William 46
Barber, Elizabeth 62
  John 4, 71
  Nancy 53
Barbey, Andrew 75
  Joseph 75
  Thomas 11
Barby, Andrew 71
Barhan, Betsy 16
  Celia 16
  Elijah 16
  Molly 16
  Peter 16
  Rawleigh Chinn 16
  Sukey 16
Barker, Ann 31
  Charles 26, 40, 46
  Chloe 31
  Edward 63
  Elizabeth 31
  Hannah 57
  Jemina 54
  John 10, 17, 19, 22, 31, 46
  Lillie Maddux 63
  Mary 31
  Milly 31
  Nanny 26
  Peter 14
  Sarah 31, 54
  Susannah 26
  William 26, 40, 71
  Willim 33
Barler, Edward 63
Barnes, Betsy 45
  Dinah 51
  John 46
  Mary 39
Barnett, Achilles 46
  Ambrose 9, 29, 46
  Charles 36
  James 46
  Joseph 46
  William 46
Barnough, John 46
Barr, Elizabeth 46
Barracks, Asey 46
Barratt, Mary 6
  Nancy 52
Barrett, Ambrose 9
  James 9
  John 9
  Judith 9
  Milly 9
Barry, Greenberry 46
  Julia 63
  Robert 63
  Willis 46
Bartell, Thomas 71
Barten, Margaret 38
Bartenstein, Edward 63
  Elizabeth 63
  Ferdinane 63
  L. A. 63
  Sarah Fitzhugh 63
Bartlett, Ann 46
  James 11, 46
  John 46, 63
  Martha Ann 63
  Mary Ann 63
  Sarah 25
  Thomas 11, 46
Barton, David 75
  John 75
  Thomas 2, 73 (2)
  William 46
Basey, Edmond 71
Bashaw, Betsy 46
  Celia 47
  Frances 46
  Mary 62
Bates, Robert 46
Batson, Elizabeth 41
  James 41
Battaile, Sarah 35
Battaley, Ann 21
  Fielding 21
  Hannah 21
Battaly, Hannah 61
Batterson, Robert 46
Baxter, John 46
Bayley, William 46
Baylie, Catherine 24
Baylis, Jean 58
  John T. 74
  William 45, 73
Bayliss, William 74
Baylor, Anne Bridges 63
  Ann D. 74
  Fanny Courtneay 63
  G... Walker 70
  John Walker 63
Bayse, Hannah 54
  Isaac 46
  Josiah 46
  Josias 19
  Nancy 43
  Richard 46
Beach, Ann 15
  John 15
  Lettice 15
  Margaret 71
  Mary 15
  Peter 15, 71
  Sarah 15
Beadle, John 46
Beale, Charlotte 51
  John G. 74
  Margaret 31
  Richard E. 76
  Richard Eustace 31
Beard, Andrew 3
Beatty, John 46
Beckham, Alexander 63
  John G. 63
  Mary 63 (2)
Beckman, James H. 36
Becksler, William 63
Beckwith, Marmaduke, Sir 23
Bedle, John 46
Beech, Alexander 4
  Margaret 4
  Mary 4
  Peter 4
  Sarah 4
  Thomas 4
  William 4
Bell, Frances 33
  James 16, 71
  John 5 (2), 6, 22, 71
  William 33
Benam, Diana 61
Benard, Henry 42
Bencer, Clacy 59
Bendall, R. T. 63 (2)
  Virginia 63
  Virginia Stone 63
  Virginius Oldner 63
Benjey, Sarah 27
Benn, Rachel 55
Bennett, Daniel 75
  George 6
  John 6
  Sanford 46
Benson, Ann 57
  Charles 46
  Elizabeth 58 (2)
  Franky 46
  Pane 71
  Robert 46
  Zachariah 46
Bentles, Annie E. 63
Benum, Diana 61
Berditt, Peggy 56
Berry, Elijah 46
  George 46, 71
  Reuben 20
  Thomas 46, 73
  William 21, 46
Berryman, Benjamin 46
  Elizabeth 47
  Francis 46
  Mary 59
  Maxmillian 3, 21, 71
Bethel, Ann 54
Bethell, Thomas 71
Bigbie, --- 54
Billings, Jasper 73
Billingsby, Ellander 57
Billingsley, Clement 34
  James 46
Birciram, Conty 7
Bird, Lena 58
  Mary 53
  Mitchell 41
Bishop, Daniel 46
  Elizabeth 62

James 46
Joshua 74
Bitts, Benjamin 35
Black, Nancy 49
Blackaby, George 46
Blackburn, John 63
    Thomas 24
Blackerby, --- 55
    Elizabeth 55
    Jeduthon 46
    Joseph 21
Blackman, William 46
Blackmore, Ann 9
    Joseph 71
Blackwell, Alice 51
    Ann 25, 46, 57, 58
    Ann Grayson 28
    Ann Lee 51
    Bettie 48
    Betty 25
    Celia 49
    David 38, 76
    Eleanor Foote 63
    Elizabeth 44
    Frances 63, 74
    Frances Grayson Smith 63
    George Steptoe 25
    Hannah 10
    J.D., Rev. 63
    James 46
    John 10, 12, 21, 22, 25, 35, 40
    John, Col. 35
    John, Gen. 43
    John D. 63
    John Davenport 63 (2)
    Joseph 10 (2), 15, 25, 38, 46, 71
    Joseph, Jr. 12, 15
    Judah 25
    Judith 10, 54
    Lucy 10 (2), 25, 51, 60
    Mary 51
    Nancy 38
    Samuel 10, 25, 29, 39, 46 (2)
    Samuel, Jr. 15
    Sarah 10
    Thomas 39, 40, 46
    William 10, 35, 38
    William, Col. 71
Bland, Betty 19
    Catherine 26
    Charles 19
    Esther 19
    Jacky 19
    James 19, 26, 46
    Jane 26
    John 73
    Mary 19, 26
    Thomas 26
Blauset, John 12
    William 12
Blithe, Mary 56
Bogers, Rodham 46
Bogess, Henry 74
Boggs, Hannah 8
    Jeremiah 8
    Richard 8
    Thomas 8
Boley, Elijah 46
    Elizabeth 52
Bolling, Elizabeth 30
    John A. 42
Bolt, Robert 75
Bolton, Malinda 57
Boon, Squire 22
Boorman, Elizabeth Duvall 63
    Robert 63
Borain, Peter 46

Borden, Sarah 62
Borein, Peter 46
Boscarver, Susanna 54
Boswell, George 71
    Molly 47
    Susannah 49
Bowen, James 46
    Sally 56
Bower, Rachel 46
Bowers, Ann 52
    Betsy 38
    Margaret 60
    Michael 38
    Molly 38
    Peggy 38
    Peter 38
    Rachel 38
    Rosannah 38
    Susan 38
    Violet 50
    William 38
    Williams 38
Bowling, Thomas 46
Bowman, George 46
    Rebecca 61
Bowmer, Jemina 57
    Polly 48
Boyce, Richard 46
Boyd, John 46
    Molly 47
    Samuel 12, 16, 46
Bradford, Alexander 1, 3, 10, 20 (2)
    Ann 1, 30
    Austin 46
    Baldwin 30
    Benjamin 20, 47
    Caty 29
    Charles 38
    Daniel 1, 2, 10, 20, 38, 71
    Elizabeth 13, 21, 56
    Enoch 38
    Fielding 38
    H. (A.) 2
    Henry 1, 21
    Jane 56
    John 38
    Katy 38
    Lucinda 53
    Mary 1, 20 (2), 45, 50, 54, 56
    Sarah 33, 38
    Simon 38
    Violetta 38
    William 1, 38, 47
Bradley, Hugh 26, 29, 47
Brady, Amelia 19
    Sukey 35 (2)
Bragg, David 47
    Dozier 47
    Dozzer 38
    Elizabeth 57
    Joseph 22
    Mary 45, 46
    Peggy 38
    Phoebe 45
Brahan, James 11
    John 10
    Lettice 11
    Thomas 11
    William 11
Bramlett, Henry 12, 14, 47, 71
    Reuben 31, 71
    William 47, 71
Branan, Hannah 26
Brangham, Thomas 47
Brannin, Mary 60
    Polly 62
Branthan, Richard 47
Bray, John 47

Bredwell, Teba 47
Brent, Alexander 38
    Ann 38
    Christopher Neale 38
    Elizabeth Mary 38
    George 38
    Mary Waddy 38
    Thomas 38
    William 22, 38
Brian, James 47
Briant, Amelia 46
Bridges, Anne 63
Briggs, William 75
Brimm, John 47
    Thomas 47
Brinbett, Henry 73
Brink, Alexander 47
Bristraw, Elizabeth 6
Broadbent, James 47
Broadhurst, Joseph 47
    William 47
Bronaugh, Benjamin 34
    Jeremiah 73
    Jeremiah, Capt. 73
    John 13, 40
    Margaret 13, 34
    Mary Ann 13
    Mary Mason 13
    Sympha Rosenfield 13
    Thomas 21, 47, 71
    William 13, 31, 47, 71
Bronaunt, Martha 12
    Sarah 12
Bronbaugh, Francis 8
    Nancy 53
Brook, Jeane Morrison 68
    Sarah 70
Brooke, Ann S.H. 63
    Annie Amelia 63
    F.W. 74
    Francis 43
    Francis Calvin 63
    George 33, 47
    H.L. 63
    Humphrey 71
    James V. 63 (2)
    Lucy 33
    Mary E. 63
    Molly 46
    Nancy 43
    Reuben 63
    Richard Harris 63
    Sarah 54
    Virginia 63 (2)
    Virginia Dandridge 63
    William 47, 71
Brooks, Ann 1, 40
    Anne 33
    Danckus 1
    Dorcas 32
    Elizabeth 1, 32
    Frances 27
    Francis 33, 40
    George 33
    H. 5, 27
    Hannah 1
    Humphrey 7
    Humphreys 40
    John 32
    Lucy 53
    Mary 1, 32
    Mathew 33
    Mathew Whiting 40
    Milly 40
    Molly 54
    Sarah 1
    Thomas 1, 32, 73
    William 1, 32

Winny 57
Brough, Catherine 57
Brown, Alexander 27
  Anabelle 63
  Ann 55
  Ann Ireland 39
  Anne 66
  Charles 17
  Daniel 23
  Dixon 3, 75
  Elizabeth 32, 57, 61
  F. Turner 63
  Florence H. 63
  Frances 55
  Francis 47
  G.R. 23, 39
  George 23
  Gustavus, Jr. 39
  Hannah 58, 63
  John 3 (2), 27, 47 (2), 71
  Jonathan 23, 29, 37
  Lillie Maddux 63
  Margaret 57
  Marmaduke 13, 23
  Martha 23
  Martin 23
  Mary 23, 33, 37, 46, 54
  Molly 33
  Peggy 23, 46
  Rebecca 23
  Robert 33, 47
  Sally 32
  Sibby 23
  Susannah 27
  Thomas 47 (4)
  W. Judson 63
  Will 3
  William 23, 37, 47, 63 (2)
  Winnifred 48
Browning, Alice 51
  Caleb 27
  Elizabeth 45
  Henry H. 63
  Henry R. 63
  Jacob 75
  Maria 63
Bruce, Alexander 74
  Charles 11
  Margaret 58
  Robert 70
Bruin, Elizabeth 22
Brumm, John 47
Bryan, Battaley 21, 47
  Michael 44
  Rachel 57
Bryant, Anna 46
Buchanan, Hannah 37
  James 32
  John 6, 37
  Joseph 73
  Mary 37
  Michael 37
  Thomas 37
Buckley, William Lawerence 47
Buckman, Sarah 62
Buckner, Catherine Talliaferro 60
  George, Jr. 29
  Judith 22
  Richard 73
  Ruth 71
Bullitt, Barsheba 29
  Benjamin 1, 5, 61
  Benoni 5
  Burwell 5
  Cuthbert 5, 12, 16, 24, 71
  Elizabeth 5, 51, 58
  George 5
  John 5
  Joseph 5, 12, 29
  Parmenas 5
  Sarah 5
  Thomas 5, 12
  William 5
Bullock, Lilly 63
  W.E., Capt. 63 (2)
Bulton, Jacob 47
Burdell, John 1
Burdette, Frederick 22, 71
  John 22
  Joseph 47
  Mary 30
  Nancy 51
  William 47
Burditt, William 5
Burger, Eleanor 49
Burgess, Ann 7
  Anne 27
  Dawson 7
  Edward 27, 33, 47
  Elizabeth 45
  Francis 7
  Garner 11, 27, 75
  James 27
  Jane 7, 53
  John 27
  Nancy 27
  Peggy 27
  Ruth 7
  Susannah 27
Burke, Ann 42
  Elizabeth 42
  George 42
  Jane 42
  John 42
  Polly 42
  Sarah 42
  Susan 42
  Susannah 42
  William 42 (2)
Burnett, Frederick 22
Burras, William 47
Burroughs, Judith 60
Burton, James 47
Bush, John 73
Bushaw, James 71
Bussey, Cornelias 38
  Cornelius 39
  Jane 38
  Peggy 47
Butcher, Catherine 60
Butler, Addie Ingle 63
  Alice 63
  Ann 21
  Benjamin 25
  Elizabeth 2, 4, 25
  George Griffin 63
  Helen V. 63
  John 3, 20, 25, 71
  Joshua 18
  Nancy 27
  William 15, 47 (2)
Buttell, Joseph 71
Button, Catherine 27
  Harmon 2, 27, 71
  Jacob 27, 47
  Rebecca 27
  Sarah 60
  Susan 27
Butts, Emma 63
  Francis 63
  J-Anna (Joanna) 63
Byrn, Thomas 47
Byrne, Isabelle 68
  William 74
Byrnes, Charles 66
  Emeline 66

Bywater, Mamie 63
  Mildred 63

--- C ---

Cahoon, Prudence 60
Cain, Mary 32
Calk, James (Joseph) 73
Callahan, James 47
Calmes, Lucy 9 (2)
  Marquis, Jr. 47
Calvert, Charity 50
  George 37, 73
  George, Jr. 73
  Sarah 37, 73
Calvin, Henry 47
  Mary 52
  William 47
Camack, Henry 47
Campbell, Catherine 23
  Mildred Moore 64
  Nancy 54
  Owen 47
  Sarah 45
Camragg, David 47
Camron, Angus 47
Canady, John 76
Cannon, John 47
Canor, Mathew 47
Canterbury, John 73
Caram, Champ 12
Carle, Elizabeth 11
Carlin, Milly (Molly) 48
Carom, Champe 71
Carpenter, Benjamin 23, 28, 38, 47
  Sarah 8
Carr, Herbert Henry 63
  John 71, 73
  William 16, 63
Carroll, Sanford 47
  Sarah 46
Carson, Champe 71
Carter, Ann 49
  Cassius 64 (2)
  Dale 47
  Daniel 32
  Elinor 62
  Fanny Foote Green 64
  Francis Scott 64
  George 29
  Henry L. 64
  Isaac 47
  Isaiah 64
  James 47 (2)
  John 47
  Richard 64
  Shirley 64
  William 24, 29, 47
Carthron, John 47
Carvell, Anna 11
  Dempsey 11
  Elizabeth 11
  James 47
  John 16
  Judith 16
  Porter 11
  Sally 11
Cary, Virginia 66
Caskie, Augusta 69
Catlett, Alexander 13
  Elizabeth 13
  John 4, 13, 26, 47, 71
  Susannah 24
  William 13
Cavanaugh, Michael 26
Cave, John 35

Rhody 35
Samuel 35, 37
Sarah 35
Thomas 35
Chaddick, Charles 47
Chadduck, Charles 16
Chadwell, Cinthia 60
　Elizabeth 41
　John 41, 48
　Lucy 51
Chamberlain, Eliz. 57
　Margaret 53
Chamberlayne, Mary 46
Chambers, D. 72
　Joseph 73
Chamlayne, James 21
Champ, John 73
　Major John 73
Chandler, William 48
Channel, James 36
Chapman, Constance 71
　George, Jr. 74
　Joseph 73
　Thomas 16
Chappelle, Margaret 52
Chester, Mary 47
Chewnor, John 48
Chichester, Charles 71
　John 71
　Richard 7, 9, 71
　Sarah 9
　Stephen 71
　Thos. 71
　William 71
Childs, James 48
Chilton, --- 66
　Betty 10
　Charles 12 (2), 16, 21, 24, 26, 27, 48
　Charles, Dr. 38
　George 12
　John 10 (2), 12, 71
　Joseph 10, 12, 40, 48, 64, 66
　Lucy 12
　Lucy Stephen 64
　Mark A. 74
　Nancy 12, 59
　Samuel 37
　Thomas 12, 38
　Thomas, Capt. 73
　Will 10
　William 10, 33
Chinn, Ann 61
　Betty 25
　Catherine 56
　Charles 25
　Chichester 48
　Christopher 25
　Elijah 25
　Elizabeth 48
　Hugh 39, 48
　Jenny 62
　Joseph 25
　Margaret 25
　Mary 58
　Nancy 25
　Penelope 25
　Raleigh 25
　Rawleigh 25
　Rawleigh, Sr. 25
　Seth 25
　Sukey 25
　Susan 32
　Thomas 48, 71
　William Ball 25
Chirley, Mary 47
Chrisman, George 48
Christian, Martin 48

Christy, Charles 48
Chunn, Andrew 43
　Charles 43
　John 17
　John T. P. 11
　John Thomas 43
　Thomas 14
　Zach 43
Churchill, Ann 48
　Armistead 15, 71
　Henry 71
　John 4, 71
　Milly 45
Claggett, Julia 67
　Sam 39
　Samuel 39
Clark, Benjamin 34
　Dolly 54
　Elizabeth 34
　Harriet 57
　James Thomson 16
　John 28
　Martha 70
　Mary 34 (2)
　Nancy 51
　Sukey 29
　Thomas 34
Clarke, George 48
　John 48
Clarkson, Milly 43
Claypool, Anne 45
Clayton, John 48
　Philip 48
　William 48
Clemans, Mary 58
Clemence, --- Glascock 39
Clement, Alexander 10, 73
Clemont, Alexander 73
Clendenning, Geo. 51
　Nancy 49
　Nelly 58
　Peggy 58
Cleveland, Fanny 59
Clifton, Rebecca 14
Climan, Ann 56
Coale, William 44
Cochran, Richard 37
Cockran, Nathan 20, 48
Cockrell, Anderson 20, 28
　Anne 11
　Mary 20
　Roannah 53
　Rosanna 28
　Sally 28
　William 28
Cockrill, Hugh S. 64
　Mary E. 64
　R. A. 64
Cockrin, Rosey 29
　William 29
Collier, John 4
Collins, Ann 25
　Betsy 51
　George 25
　James 25
　Joseph 48
　Lilly 50, 52
Colvert, Charity 50
　George 73
Colvin, Sarah 45
Comb, Ennis 35, 36
　Margaret 36
Combs, Betty 17
　Catherine 45
　Cuthbert 12, 17
　Emmanuel 73
　Ennice 36
　Evis 17

Heland 17
Hetheland 17
John 5, 14, 17
John, Jr. 17
Joseph 17, 73
Margaret 36
Nannie 17
Nimrod 17
Robert 76
Sarah 17
Sith 5, 12
Comly, J. A. 74
Compton, Richard 48
　William 73
Comyers, Davis 73
Congrove, Lydia 61
　Moses 7
Connay, Peter 38
　William 5
Connelly, Cornelius 64
Conner, James 48
　William 48
Constable, Jemima 52
　Nancy 47
Conway, Ann 19
　Elizabeth 44
　Henry 22
　James 22
　Joseph 22, 48
　Mary 13
　Peggy 52
　Peter 1, 15, 22, 25, 29, 40 (2), 44
　Sarah 46, 50
　Thomas 1, 6, 20, 22, 24, 29, 44, 71
　William 19, 22, 23, 71
Conyers, John 71
　Samuel 71
Coodnick, Alice 53
Cook, Betty 53
　Giles 19
　John 2
　Littleton 19
　Nancy 45
　Sarah 2
　Thomas 19
　William 75
Cooke, Ann 58
　John 28, 29, 40, 48
Cooksey, Philip 35
Cooledge, Judyson 71
Cooper, Elizabeth 53
　Mary 48
　Vincent 48
Cope, William 44
Coppadge, Charles 29
　John 26
Coppage, Jane 13
　John 9, 48
　Moses 13, 71
　William 48, 71
Coppedge, Elizabeth 4
　John 4, 8, 16
　Sally 4
　William 4, 8, 32, 48
Coram, Champ 18
　Richard 14, 18
　William 73
Corbin, Elisha Hall 10
　Hannah 10
　James 74
　John 48, 73
　Martha 10
Corder, Bulis 48
　Eve 62
　John 3 (2), 48
　Minna 49

81

Nelly 49
William 75
Cornelia, Absalom 6
Cornelias, Peggy 48
Cornet, Richard 48
Cornwell, Charles 73
   David 11
   Franky 51
   Jacob 11, 48
   Jarvice 11
   Mary 11
   Peter 11, 14
   Peyton 48
   Sarah 11
   Simon 11, 42
Cortney, John 71
   William 71
Corum, Catherine 4
   Mary 4
Cottonwell, Thomas 73
Courtneay, Fanny 63
Courtney, James 48
   William 48
Coventon, Richard 71
Covert, Asa 48
   Martin 48
Cowles, --- 74
Cox, Abraham 41
   Allinda 51
   Ann 41
   Elenor 37
   Elizabeth 41
   James 37, 41 (2)
   Thomas 41
   William 41
   Zachariah 41
   Zachary 41
Crafford, George 48
   Lucy 55
Craig, Ann 54
   James 6, 21, 39
   Joseph 39
Cramp, Benjamin 11
Cranch, John 48
Crawford, Eliz. 52
   William 48
Crawley, Margaret 47
   Richard 75
Creek, Peggy 46
Creel, Rachel 33
Crees, Judith 55
Cremon, Anne 46
Crim, Dosha 36
   John, Jr. 75
   John, Sr. 75
Crisman, George 48
Crockell, Sally 53
Crockett, James 22, 71
   Mary Ann 51
Crosby, Ann 59, 61
   Enoch 29
   Frances 56
   Franky 50
   George 22, 48 (2), 71
   Mary 61
   Susannah 22
   Uriel 12
   William 24
Crosley, Hannah 28
Cross, James 74
   Joseph 39
Crosson, John 48
Crouch, Jane 50
   William 73
Crown, Hannah 64
   James, Rev. 64
   James Henry, Rev. 64
Crowne, Thomas 74

Crum, Delia 31
   Joseph 31
Crump, Ann 54
   Benjamin 3, 11, 26, 44, 71
   Catherine 26
   Daniel 26
   Frances 47
   George 3, 26, 44, 71
   Hannah 44
   John 26, 44 (2), 71, 73
   Joseph 44
   Mary 61
   Sarah 26, 51
   Susannah 59
Crupper, Ann 34
   John 48
   Molly 61
Cruppner, Richard 73
Cummings, Alexander 7
   Daniel 48
   Elizabeth 7
   John 7, 18
   Levi 48
   Malachi 73
   Peter 7
   Simon 7
   Thomas 18, 19 (2)
Cummins, George 48
   Mary 49
   Sally 52
   Simon 71
   William 48
Cundiff, Isaac 38
   James 38
   Lettes 38
Cundiffe, Elizabeth 23
   William 17
Cunningham, Elizabeth 30
   Timothy 48
Curtice, Elijah 43
   John 42, 43
   Lewis 43
Curtis, Chester 48
   Elizabeth 46
   Mary 59
Cushenberry, Ann 52

--- D ---

Dade, ---, Mrs. 17
   Baylor Gurynnetta 64
   Jane Alexander 70
Dairs, Mary 61
Dale, --- 43
   James 43
   Daniel, John 48
Dareing, John 25
Dargan, Ann 7
Darmott, Michael 73
Darnale, Delia 57
Darnall, Catherine 31, 32
   Caty 32
   David 3, 25, 48
   Diana 61
   Elijah 15
   Elizabeth 5
   Isaac 5
   James 17
   Jeremiah 2 (3), 11, 12, 15, 32
   Jermi. 71
   John 5, 25
   Joseph 2, 32, 48
   Joshua 48
   Mary 25, 59
   Mathew 71
   Morgan 5

   Morgan, Jr. 5
   Raleigh 48 '
   Rosamond 32
   Susannah 59
   Waugh 5
   William 7, 48
   William D. 39
Darnold, David 71
   Jermi. 71
Davidson, Ann 54
Davis, A. 35
   Charles 36
   Eli 48
   Elizabeth 36, 39
   Ezekiel 32
   Frances L. 46
   George 48
   Griffith 36
   James 48
   John 36
   Levi 36, 48
   Lydia 36
   Richard 36
   Ruth 59
   Thomas 6, 48
   William 13, 36
Dawson, John 30
   Margaret 60
   William 48
Day, Alexander 64
   Baldwin 64
   Cossom 31
   Cossun 39
   Douglas 64 (2)
   George 49
   John 49
   Virginia Turner 64
   William 29, 49, 75
Deal, Lucy 51
Dealls, Ann 40
Dean, John 49
Deane, Charles 7
Dearen, Bettie 49
Dearing, Conrad 49
   Fanny 61
   George 74
   John 30, 75
Debell, Ann 61
   Elizabeth 61
De Bell, Lewis 49
   William 49
Delaney, Joseph 71
   William 11
   William W. 3
Delgram, John 13
Dells, John 49
Dennally, Thomas 49
Dennis, Isaac 49
   James 32
   Samuel 34
   Susannah 49
Dennison, Henry 49
   John 49
   Mary 51
Dent, Mary Ann 64
   William 64
Dermont, William 49
Deros, Eliz. 47
De Shields, Elizabeth 64
   James 64
Devers, William 49
Devlin, William 75
Dews, Eliz. 47
Dialls, Ann 40
Dickman, Joseph 35
Digges, Edward 35, 74
   Edward, Jr. 35
   Elizabeth 40

Thomas 33
Whiting 74
Diggs, Elizabeth 33
  Thomas 37
Dillard, Molly 61
Divis, Aquilla 33
Dixon, Alice Fitzhugh 68
  Jenny 49
Dobie, James 18
Dobin, James 49
Doby, Ann 39
  James 39
  John 39
  Margaret 38
Dodd, Allen 22
  Ann 74
  Benjamin 22
  Daniel 49
  Elizabeth 22, 59
  James 22
  John 22
  Mary 55
  Nathaniel 22 (2), 71
  Sarah 22
Dodds, Sarah 15
Dodson, Abraham 6
  Barbarby 12
  Barbarey 6
  Elijah 6
  Enoch 6, 12
  George 71
  Grantham (Granthane) 6
  Greenham 6
  Greenhane 12
  Jodeph 6
  Tabitha 6
  William, Sr. 71
Doggett, Bushrod 71
Doleas, Polly 60
Donaldson, Daniel 49
  Stephen 13
  Stephens 49
  William 13
Donnelly, Thomas 49
Donphan, Alexander 44
  Mary 44
Doty, Elizabeth 52
Doubtman, Nancy 58
Douglas, Benjamin 75
  Martin Guthrie 64
  Sarah 61
Dowdall, Browner 49
  James 13
  Thomas 49
Dowell, Elizabeth 55
  Nehemiah 49
Downing, Winnifred 50
Downman, Raleigh 71
  Robert 66
Downs, Henry 34
Drake, Dennis 49
  Jean 46
Drummon, Sukey 12
Drummond, Aaron 49
  Frances 54
  Joshua 32, 49
  Susannah 60
  William 49
Drysdale, Christian 64
  Thomas 64
Duff, Ann 50
  James 15, 71
  John 49
Duffy, B. 37
  Bernard 36
Dugan, Ann 7
  John 7
Dugard, John 13

Dugarde, John 11
Dulaney, Charles 30
Dulin, Charles 39
  Clemence 39
  Edward 39, 49
  Elizabeth Haddox 39
  George 39
  John 39, 49
  Lewis 49
  Lydia 57
  Mary 53
  Philip 39
  William 3, 30, 39
  William Elzey 39
Duncan, Archibald 49
  Benjamin 49
  Betty 57
  Catherine 12
  Charles 31, 49, 71
  Christopher 49
  Elizabeth 51, 60
  Enoch 31
  Franklin 49
  Gollop 28
  Housen 35
  Houser 30
  Jesse 49
  John 2, 31, 33, 71 (3)
  John, Sr. 71
  Joseph 30 (2), 35, 49 (3), 71
  Leanna 61
  Leroy 49
  Lucinda 31
  Lydia 30, 35, 49
  Mary 62
  Milly 31, 33, 51, 52
  Moses 31, 33, 35
  Nancy 22, 52
  Nimrod 49
  Peggy 58
  Priscilla 46
  Rose 49, 56
  Wilky 31, 33
  William 49
  Willis 31 (2)
Duvall, Elizabeth 63
Dye, Martin 49
  Sarah 51
Dyson, Elizabeth 43
  Mary 46
  Winnifred 43


--- E ---

Eady, Benjamin 49
Earle, Samuel 3, 73
Eastham, John 38
Easthane, Catherine 54
Eaton, Abigail 45
  Samuel 49
Edge, Forrester 49
  John 7, 20
  John, Jr. 49
  Sinty 7
Edmond, Mary 53
Edmonds, Adeline 64
  Ann 6, 53
  Betty 6
  David 76
  Edward G. 64 (2)
  Eli 8
  Elias 3, 6, 22 (2), 24,
    33, 38, 49, 71
  Elias, Sr. 12
  Elizabeth 22, 46
  Frances 49, 51

George 38
James 33
John 33, 38
John, Jr. 38
Judith 6
Mary 66
Peggy 38
Sophia 45
William 6, 15, 38, 49, 71
William, Jr. 33
William F. 74
Edmonson, Ann McCarthy 53
Edrington, John 7
Edwards, Ann 64
  Benjamin 38
  Betty 27
  Charity 43
  Elizabeth 24
  Garret 5
  Garrett 71
  George W. 49
  Gerrard 3
  James 5
  John 5, 8, 16, 71
  Martin 49
  Thomas 27
  W.W. 64
  William 49
Edy, Samuel 73
Einsor, George 49
Elgin, Casandra 52
Elias, James 41
Ellett, Mary 56
Elley, Esther 52
Elliott, Ann 7, 61
  Anne Roberson 17
  Benjamin 7, 9
  Eleanor 7
  Elizabeth 17
  Jemina 17, 58
  Mildred 17
  Molly 17, 48
  Reuben 16, 17, 23
  Ruth 16
  Sally 55
  Samuel 41
  Sarah 7, 18
  Sary 60
  Thomas 9, 17
  William 7, 17, 49
Ellis, Ann 15
  James 42
  John 15, 71, 75
  Jonathan 15
  Joseph 42
  Molly 47
  Owen 15
  Reuben 49
  Sarah 75
  William 15, 49
Ellitt, Elizabeth 23
Embrey, Ann 27
  Charles 27
  John 27
  Leanna 61
  Robert 27 (2)
  Sarah 48
Embry, Jesse 49
  Nancy 55
  Robert 27, 71
  Sarah 60
  Thomas 27
  William 49
Emmons, Agattha 33
  James 49
  Joseph 33
  William 33
Emory, Ann 55

English, Elizabeth R. 64
  Elizabeth Roe 64 (2)
  James 64, 74
  Joseph Marion 64
  Maria C. 64
Eskridge, Samuel 15
Estham, John 38
Etcheson, Letty 59
Ethell, Anthony 76
Etherington, Elizabeth 12
  John 71
Eustace, Ann 39, 50, 54
  Hancock 39
  Isaac 34, 49
  Mary 39
  William 39, 49, 71
  William, Jr. 26, 31
Evan, David 32
  Margaret 46
  Thomas 10
Evans, Elizabeth 62
  Frances 64
  John 49
  Mildred Moore Campbell 64
  Samuel 49
  Sarah 64
Eves, Thomas 71
  William 71
Evins, Martha 23
Evinston, Francis 49

--- F ---

Fallen, Margaret 64
  Patrick 64
Fanbeon, Jacob 8
Fanbin, Sally 47
Fannin, John 49
Fant, Armistead 50
Faraguson, Molly 28
Ferguson, William 50
Farrow, Ann 28
  Benjamin 28, 74
  Dolly 51
  John 73
  Nimrod 74
  William 73
Feagan, John 38
Feagin, Cleary 16
  Edward 16
  Elizabeth 16
  Frances 16
  John 16
  Mary 16
  Sarah 16
  Susannah 16
  William 16
Feagins, Sally 38
Fegan, Clara 46
  Daniel 50, 71
  Edward 28, 50
  Mary 54
  Susannah 46
Fenner, Lettice 31
Ferguson, John 31
  Lewis 50
  William 50
Ferry, Ann 71
Feunce, William 50
Fever, Moses 19
  Thomas 19
Fewell, Benjamin 50
  James 50
Ficklin, William 73
Fidler, Rebecca 52
Fielding, Edwin 21

Nancy 21, 48
Fields, Ann 19
  Daniel 19
  Elizabeth 19, 58
  Fieldon 19
  George 19
  Hannah 19
  Henry 50
  John 12, 19, 23
  Lewis 19
  Margaret 23
  Mary 19
  Milly 19
  Reuben 50
  Sarah 19
  Thomas 50
Finch, Elizabeth 61
  Polly 59
  William 37
Finks, Ann Rebecca 64
  John W. 64 (2)
  Lucy 64
  Lucy A. 64
Finnie, Ann 3, 61
  Hannah 3, 13
  John 3
Fishback, --- 74
  Franky 55
  Frederick 2, 71
  Harmon 71
  Jacob 2, 50
  James 26
  James W. 39
  John 17, 22, 28, 71
  Josiah 25, 71
  Josias 22, 26, 35
  Lilly Tibbs 57
  Lucy 30
  Lydia 58
  Milly 58
  Nanny 22
  Patty 35
  Phil 71
  Philip 22, 25, 43
  Polly 56
  Sarah 26, 48, 56, 57
Fisher, --- 64
  Elizabeth 64
  Fannie 64
  John 64
  Marh H. 64
  Martha 54
  Richard 30
  Robert 64
  Robert W. 64
  Samuel 50
  Susannah 54
Fitzgerald, Milly 6
Fitzhugh, Alice 68
  Battaile 74
  Dudley 35
  George 35, 63
  Mary 35
  Nannie 65
  Sarah 63
  Sarah Battaile 35
  Thomas 24, 28, 50
  W. 43
  William 35
Flelkins, William 75
Fleming, Archibald 50
  James 14
Fletcher, A.D. 64
  Aaron 21, 33
  Ann 45
  Benjamin 50
  Elizabeth 29
  Georgie O'Latham 64

Hugh 64
  John 29, 30 (2), 50
  Louisa 64
  Lydia 61
  Manley 64 (2)
  Nish 64
  Richard 30, 50
  Sarah 49
  Thaddeus N. 64
  Thaddeus Norris 64
  Thomas 30
  V.A. 64
  William 1, 75
Flinn, Valentine 75
  William 50
Floerie, James (Joseph) 74
Florence, Hannah 54
Flory, Daniel 71
Flourence, Sarah 57
Floweree, Daniel 2
  William 50
Flowerell, John 50
Flowers, John 50
  William 50
Floyd, Henry 50, 73
Flynn, --- 64
  Mable 64
  Rachel 33
  Rachel Hunter 64
  William 33
Foard, Thomas 50
Fogan, Edward 36
  Mary 36
Fogg, Nathaniel 50
Foley, Bryant 34
  Elizabeth 34
  Enoch 34
  James 12, 34, 50 (2)
  James, Sr. 71
  John 50 (2)
  John James 34
  Lettice 49
  Mary 33
  Molly 34
  Oglevie Lettice 34
  Oglevie P. 34
  Oglivie Leah 34
  Sarah 9, 54, 61
  Susannah 34
  Thomas William 34
Fontaine, Elizabeth 65
Foote, Bethelon 1
  Celia 10
  Elizabeth 1
  Fanny 64
  Frances 1, 56
  George 1, 10, 14
  George W. 74
  Gilson 1, 4, 7
  Henry 1
  Hester 10, 49
  Mary 1, 61
  Richard 1, 16
  Richard, Jr. 7
  William 1, 16, 50
Ford, Ann 61
  George 6, 50
  Henry 18, 50
Forrester, John 32
Foster, Andrew 50
  Ann 58
  Elizabeth 50
  George 50
  Robert 50
  Thomas 74
  William 50, 73
Fowkes, Ann Harrison 9
  Chandler 9, 18, 50

Elizabeth 18, 55, 57
Enfiets 18
George 18
Gerrard 17
Mary 8, 9, 18, 59
Nancy 55
Sarah 59
Thomas 9
Thomas Harrison 9
William 18
Fowler, Ann 20
W.F., Col. 65
Fox, Charles 50
  James 34
  John 31
  Nancy 32
  Samuel 71
Frances, Joseph 50
Francis, Fannie 65
Frazier, Charles Haynes 20
  Daniel 20
  James 74
Freeman, Charlotte 45
  Elizabeth 50, 60
  Garrett 28, 29, 34
  Gollop 28
  Hannah 49
  Harris 50
  James 28, 29, 50 (2)
  John 6
  Margaret 25, 28
  Mary 51
  Nathaniel 28, 29
  Sally 28
  William 18, 29, 50
French, Daniel 20, 25
  James 73
  John 25
  Margaret 61
Frie, Susan 61
Froggett, Andrew 50
Frye, Abraham 50
  Elizabeth 55
Fullers, Sally 48
Fulton, James 50
Furlong, Edward P. 65
  Isabella 65
Furr, Elizabeth 19
  John 50
  Mimey 38
  Nancy 45, 50
  Thomas 19
  William 38
Furrow, Molly 54

--- G ---

Gabriel, George 50
Gallaway, C.F. 65
  Susannah 65
Gant, Ambrose 50
Garner, Ann 41
  Benjamin 21, 27
  Celia 49
  Charles 71
  Daniel 21
  Diannah 27
  Elizabeth 33
  James 27, 71
  Jemina 33
  Jesse 33
  John 4, 33, 73
  Jonas 33
  Joseph 50
  Nancy 58
  Sarah 22
  Smith 50
  Thomas 73
  Vincent 27, 33, 50, 73
  Vinson 71
  William 33
Garrett, A. 75
  James 50 (2)
  Nimrod 50
Gaskin, Sophrona 65
Gavner, Sally 59
Gear, Elizabeth 31
Gellerson, Daniel 41
Genn, Celie 25
  James 25, 71
Gent, ---, Widow 71
  George 71
George, Aaron 50
  Abner 50
  Ann 47
  Elizabeth 15
  Joseph 15, 35, 50
  Lydia 15
  Margaret 15
  Nicholas 15
  Painick 13
  Parnach 34
  Parnie 71
  Reuben 50
  William 15
  Wilmouth 15
German, Michael 50
Ghlette, Phebe 65
Gibson, Abraham 38
  Alexander 50
  Alse 55
  Ann 39
  Ann Grayson 9, 46
  Catlett 9
  Elizabeth 10
  Isa 52
  Jacob 39
  John 9, 28, 39, 73
  John, Jr. 50
  Jonathan 1, 5, 8 (2), 9 (2), 14, 28, 37, 71
  Jonathan, Capt. 23
  Jonathan Catlett 28
  Joanathan Catlett 28
  Margaret 49
  Margaret Catlett 28
  Mary 28
  Moses 50
  Robert 23, 29, 50
  Susanna 28
  Susannah 9
  Thomas 8, 9, 28, 35, 51
  Thomas, Capt. 31
  William 51, 71, 74
Gilbert, Felix 51
Giles, Elizabeth 50
  Pensela 48
Gillison, --- 74
  Ann 9
  James 22
  James, Sr. 36
  John 37, 51 (2)
  Margaret Gibson 49
  Mary 49
  Peggy 46
Gilson, John 39
Gladstone, Arthur 51
Glascock, Agatha 30
  Alice 60
  Am. 61
  Anna 51
  Benjamin 74
  Catherine 60
  Downing 51
  Fanny 49
  Gregory 39
  Hezekiah 37 (2)
  James 30
  Jenny 56
  John 51, 73
  Lydia 56
  Margaret 56
  Mary 20
  Molly 51
  Peter 51
  Phebe 56
  Sarah 46
  Susannah 51
  Teally 58
Glass, Mikel 21
Glasscock, --- 65, 71
  Archibald 51
  Frances 20
  George 22
  Gregory 39
  Helen Smith 65
  Henry 65
  Hezekiah 22
  Jane 65
  John 20, 22, 31, 51
  John Samuel 65 (2)
  Michael 51
  Sally 48
  Thomas 20, 22
  William 51
Glassell, John 74
Glendenning, Betsy 38
  Geo. 51
Godley, John 51
Goe, Robert 51
Goff, William 51
Golden, Joseph 51
Goldsmith, Benjamin 33
Goodin, Mary 53
Goodwin, Le Baron, Dr. 65
Gordon, Samuel 74
Gore, Caty 60
  Jonah 51
Gorman, Michael 50
Goslin, John 73
Gough, Bailey 51
  Gladah 47
Goulding, Vincent 51
Gowhig, Bridget 65 (3)
  Dennis 65 (3)
  Ellen 65
  Hannah 65 (2)
  Mary H. 65
  Patrick John 65
  William 65 (3)
  William H. 65
Goyston, M.B. 63
Graham, Benjamin 74
  George 51
  Howard 73
  J. Barbour 65
  James M. 65 (2)
Grant, Aggy 53
  Ann 51
  Chapman 41
  Elizabeth 55, 56
  George 51, 71
  John 73, 75
  Joseph 51
  Judith 46
  Mary 54
  Peter 21, 22, 23, 25, 33, 38
  Robin 51
  Sarah Ann 51
  Susan 14
  Susannah 23
  William 13, 51, 71

Graves, Duncan 51
   Nathaniel 40
   Thomas 51
Gray, Emma E. 65
   Garrett, Jr. 28
   James William 65
   Mary E. 65
   Nathaniel 51 (2)
   Newton Lee 65
   Thomas 51
   Virginia 65
Grayer, George 51
Grayson, Benjamin 73
   Benjamin, Capt. 73
   Frances 63
   Susanna 28
Green, Ann 51
   Bernard 65
   Charles T. 65 (2)
   Duff 5, 71
   Elizabeth 28, 58 (2)
   Fanny Foote 64
   Frances 58
   Gabriel 42, 51
   George 51
   James 51 (2)
   John 28, 51
   Lucy 65
   Mary 56
   Moses 51
   Robert 51
   Thomas 37, 65
   William 51 (2)
Greening, Franky 48
Greenwood, Daniel 32
   Henry 51
Gregory, Winny 59
Grey, Charles 12
Griffin, George 51
   Margaret 62
   Mary 58
   William 36
Griffith, Dennis 33
   Elijah 33
   Evan 16, 21, 33
   John 33
   Peggy 33
   Sarah 33
   Sarianne 33
   Susannah 33
   Willoughby 33
Grigg, John 73
Grigsby, Aaron 51, 74
   Ann 17
   Baylis 74
   Bayliss 26
   Benjamin 31, 51 (2)
   Eady 26
   Edith 50
   Elizabeth 57
   James 17
   Lewis 26
   Mary 61
   Nathaniel 26, 74
   Rachel 56
   Samuel 17, 51, 71
   Susannah 52, 60
   Taliaferrio 51
   William 17, 26, 51
   Winnifred 26
   Winny 61
Grimsley, Joseph 75
   Nimrod 51
   William 75
Grinnan, --- 71
   Elizabeth 48
   Sarah 60
   Vashti 53

Grogan, Elizabeth 16
Groves, John 51
   Mary 48
   Philip 76
Grubbs, Richard 17, 71, 73
Gudrage, Allen 75
Gunning, Thomas 71
Guthrie, Eliza D. 65
   James 16
Gutridge, Allen 51
   Elijah 41
   Elizabeth 48
   Peter 51
   Reuben 51
Guttridge, William 41
Guy, Ann 53
   Sarah 54


--- H ---


Hackley, Francis 38, 71
   Jael 38
   James 28, 51
   Joel 38
   Lott 38, 71
   Mary 28
   Richard 71
Haddocks, Charlotte 19
Haddrick, Charlotte 57
Haddux, Abraham 51
Hagan, John 51
Hailey, Anthony 51
   John 51
   William 51 (2)
Hainer, George 52
Hainey, Winnifred 47
Hale, Jane 47
   Joseph 34
   Martha 58
   Sally 57
   Honor 26
Hall, ---, Widow 71, 73
   Catherine 60
   Henry 2
   Jane 47
   John 51
   Joseph 2
   Molly 54
   Richard 10, 11
   William 51
Halley, Henry 73
Hambucks, James 15
Hamilton, Betty Peace 65
   George Stanton 65
   Henry 26
   Hugh 65
   Isabella Voss 65
   Marianna Scott 65
   Robert Mandeville 63
   Sarah 54
   William 26
Hammit, Hannah 22
Hammons, John 51
Hampleton, Presley 40
Hampton, Alfred 41
   Ann 46
   Charlotte 9
   Elizabeth 5, 59, 60
   Frances 27
   Francis 41
   Gale 5
   George 52
   Jeremiah 41
   Joanna 9
   John 41
   Joseph 41, 52

Lawson 41
   Martha 5
   Mary 27
   Minny 41
   Molly 41
   Richard 5, 9, 10
   Ruth 71
   Sally 56
   Sarah 5
   Susannah 9, 27, 41
   Thomas 52
   William 5, 7, 10, 43, 52
Hamrick, Gilson 52
   James 6
   John 75
   Mary 16
Hancock, Lena Ann 54
   Scarlett 73
   William 52
Hand, John 52
Handy, William 74 (2)
Haney, Thomas 52
Hanor, Harmon 30
   Mary 30
Hansborough, Gabriel 40
   James 40
   John 52
   Molly 40
   Morris 11
   Peter 40, 52
   William 52
Hanson, Ann 39
   Samuel 39
   Samuel, Col. 39
Haraway, Richard 74
Hard, Elizabeth 46
Hardewicke, Elizabeth 54
Hardin, Benjamin 52
   John 2
   Martin 1, 2, 4, 5, 71
   Mary 62
   Nancy 48
Hardistrees, Susannah 36
Hardiwien, William 10
Hardwicke, Sukey 55
Harley, Joseph 52
   Phebe 50
   Richard 71
Harmon, Fishback 71
Harper, George 73
   Isaac 52
   John 71
   Rachel 59
   Sally 53
Harrell, Daniel 71
Harrill, --- 52
   John 4, 20
Harrilland, Daniel 7
Harrington, John 52
Harris, Arthur 52
   Catherine 52
   Elisha 52
   Elizabeth 55
   George 52
   H. Ashby 65
   Henry 34 (2), 52
   James K. 65
   Jemina 26, 33
   Martha 52
   Samuel 52, 75
   Susanno W. 39
   Thomas 33
   William 22, 33
Harrison, Ann 9, 52
   Benjamin 8, 9, 12, 14, 26, 28, 35 (2)
   Burr 8, 9, 52, 73
   Cuthbert 9, 16

David 35
Frances 9, 67
Jane 55
Lucy 9, 55
Lydia 50
Mary 35, 50
Mathew, Jr. 28
Sarah 9
Sith 9
Thomas 8 (2), 73
Thomas, Col. 71
Thomas, Jr. 73
William 8, 9, 52
Hart, Robert 74
Hatfield, Stewart 52
Hathaway, --- 51
  Dolly 25
  Dorothy 57
  Eliza 57
  Eliz. 53
  Elizabeth 25
  Francis 25
  James 9 (2), 18, 52
  Joanna 9
  John 15, 17, 24, 25
  Juday 25
  Margaret 52
  Molly 25
  Nancy 25
  Sarah 24, 25
  Sarefta 56
  Sarepta 25
  Susannah 25
Haugh, James 52
Hawkins, Benjamin 52
  Jesse 52
  Sally 48
Haydon, James 24
Hayes, Betsy 48
  Jacob 52
  John 74 (2)
  Molly 48
  Parthenia 51
Hayne, Jonathan 52
Haynes, Charles 20
Haynie, Maxmillian 6
Hays, Edward 65
Hazlerig, Samuel 24
Head, Cornelius 52
  Richard 52
Headley, James 29, 52
  Lucy 29
  Robert 52
Heale, Mildred 56
  Priscilla 47
Healey, John 25
  Mary 25
Heaton, James 52
  Thomas 52
Hedengran, Peter 7
Hedges, John 73
Heffering, Augustin 31
  Nancy 31
Hefferling, Susannah 51
Hefflin, Ann 51
  James 75
  Simon 75
  William 52
Heflin, A. E. 65
  Alfred 65
  Ann Eliza 65
  Anna 41
  Darkey 41
  Lawson 65
  Peggy 46
  Polly 41
  Sally 45
  William 41

William, Jr. 41
Heiner, George 52
Helm, Edward 65
  Eramus 65 (2)
  Frances 65
  Fraspins 65 (2)
  Mary 65
  Richard 10
  Robert 65
  Sarah 46
  Thomas 22, 23, 34, 71
  Virginia 65
  Virginia Asquith 65
  William 52 (2)
Helms, Ann 9
  Letty 9
  Samuel 72
Heminger, William 75
Henderson, Elizabeth 60
  Pierce Bayley 52
Hendley, John 22
Hendricks, Elizabeth 65
Hening, George 71
Hennie, Michael 8
Henry, Joseph 21
  Nancy 57
  Sally 51
  Tabitha 50
Hensley, Dudley 51
Henson, Robert 71
Hermons, James 10
  John 10
  Mary 10
  Susannah 10
Herndon, George 52
Herring, Catherine 55
Hetch, Peggy 60
Hewit, Susannah 71 (2)
Hewlett, Susannah 44
Heyward, Annie 69
Hich, Christopher 24
  Rebecca 24
Hichlhorn, Eve 58
Hickerson, Ann 46
  Elizabeth 74
  Hosea 74
  John 40
  Mary 49
Hickman, John 17, 52 (2)
  Sarah 60
  William 52
Hicks, Nannie Fitzhugh Randolph 65
  Robert, Major 65
  Robert I., Maj. 65
Hickson, Daniel 38
Higgison, Walter 52
Hilburn, Elizabeth 49
Hilkins, Margaret 52
Hill, James 52
  Mary 31
  Sarah 56, 60
Hinson, Dennis 52
  George 52
  Hanley 49
  James 40, 52
  Jesse 52 (2)
  Robert 40
  Tapley 40
Hinton, Fanny 52
  William 16
Hitch, Aquilla 74
  Elizabeth 45
  John 52
  Petty 60
  Rebecca 45
  Susannah 60
  Wise 52

Hite, Elizabeth 3
  Isaac 32
  Jacob 3
Hitt, Alexander 42
  Alice Katherine 2
  Elizabeth 8, 42
  Fanny 42
  Hannah 42
  Harman 2, 15
  Harmon 8, 71
  Harrison 42
  Henry 8
  Isaac 32
  John 8, 52, 71
  John, Jr. 71
  Joseph 8, 71, 75
  Lucy 52
  Mary 2, 42, 46
  Miriam 52
  Nancy 42, 56
  Peter 2, 8 (2), 42, 52
  Peter, Jr. 71
  Peter, Sr. 71
  Presley 42
  Pressley 42
  Sarah 13
  Susannah 42, 51
  Thaddeus 42
Hoard, Thomas 11
Hockman, Ann 27
Hodo, Peter 23
Hogain, Bathasheba 56
  Rawley 24
Hogan, Barbara 60
  James 13, 71
  Margaret 5
  Mary Ann 13
  Rawleigh 52
  William 71 (2)
Holder, David 3
  Dorris 52
  Susannah 48
Holiday, Samuel 18, 39
Holly, Rolly 52
  Sally 58
Holm, Lynaugh 7
Holmes, Edmond 21
  Sebrasta 50
Holt, Fred 65
Holton, Alexander 18
  Elizabeth 18
  William 18
Holtzclaw, --- 65, 71
  Amon (Almon) Seabury 65
  Amos 52
  Archibald 52
  Benjamin 71
  Charles 74
  Eliz. 57
  Elizabeth 65
  Frances 39
  Frank 65
  Franky 52
  George 65
  Grace 66
  Harman 2
  Henry 2, 72
  Howard 66
  Jacob 2, 6, 22, 73
  John 2, 73
  Joseph 2
  Milly 6
  Nathaniel 52
  Susannah 54
  Willie Baldwin 66
Home, E. E. 4
Homes, Edwin 52
  James 52

Hooe, Robert, Col. 23
Hooes, Henry Dade 37
Hoomes, Nathaniel 52
Hopp, Thomas 53
Hopper, Blagrove 72, 73
    John 3, 53, 73
    William 53
Hopwood, Fanny 55
    Sally 52
Hord, James 53
    Peter 53
    Sarah 53
    Thomas 72
Horner, Alfred Byrnes 66
    Anne Brown 66
    Ann Maria Lovell 66
    Catherine 39
    Charles Gustavus 66
    Elizabeth 39, 66
    Ellen Ashton 66
    Frances 39
    Frances Scott 66
    Fred., Dr. 66
    Frederick 66
    Frederick, Dr. 66 (2)
    Gustavus 66 (2)
    Gustavus Brown 39, 53
    Gustavus R. 66
    Gustavus Richard 66
    John 39
    Joseph 66
    Maria Sherman 66
    Mary A. Byrnes 66 (2)
    Mary Agnes 66
    Mary Edmonds 66
    Mary McClenachan Robb 66
    Richard Henry 66 (2)
    Robert 39
    Robert Braxton 66
    Robert Downman 66
    Robert Littleton 66
    Seignora Peyton 66
    Virginia Cary 66
    William 39, 53, 66 (3)
    William Edward 39
Horton, Augustine 41
    Benjamin 41
    Catherine 28
    Charles 53
    Craven 53
    Elijah 53
    Finton 56
    Nancy 54
    Tyler 70
Hotten, William 53
Howell, Benjamin 53
    Franky 47
    Letty 55
Howey, John A. 66
Hubbard, Ann 22
    Epaphroditus 53
    Ephiram 53
Hudnal, John 72 (2)
    Joseph 72
    Mary 74
    Thomas 72
    William 72
Hudnall, Alice 48
    Jemina 14
    Joseph 53, 73
    Molly 62
    Nancy 49
    Thos. 73
    William 53, 73
Hudson, Sarah 48
Huffman, Catherine 45
    William 53
Hughes, Abraham 53

    Agatha 55
    John 6
Hulett, Leroy 19
Hume, Agatha 52
    Andrew 40, 75
    Elizabeth 60
    Frances 53
    George 40
    Hannah 40
    James 17
    John 40
    Margaret 13
    Patience 57
    Robert 40, 74
Humes, Alecy 49
    Charles 53
    Hannah 13
    Mary 48
Hummins, Sally 52
Humphrie, John 53
Humstead, Edward 10
    Susana 8
    Susanah 8
Humston, Edward 3, 53, 72
    Jane 52
    John 75
    Thomas 34
Hunter, James 72
    Rachel 64
    William 72
Hunton, Hannah 36
    James 23, 27, 36
    Melinda 59
    Polly 47
    Thomas 36, 74
    William 7, 11, 12, 23, 25, 27, 43
    William, Jr. 27
Hurill, Elizabeth 48
Hurley, Daniel 53
Hurst, George 66
    Henry 30
    Jane 31
    Rosalie 66
    Rosanna 30
Husht, Rosannah 75
Hutcherson, --- 5
Hutton, Margaret 66
Hyde, Ellen 66
    Mannie 66
    Philip 66 (2)

--- I ---

Igram, Lucy 40
Iles, Absalom 11
Ingle, Addie 63
Ingram, Thomas 53
Inman, Catherine 67
Innes, Elizabeth 24
Ireland, Ann 39
    James 53
Isabell, Jonas 66
Isarel, Sabbatiah 22

--- J ---

Jackman, Adam 18
    Hannah 37
    Hester 2
    Joseph 18
    Richard 18, 53
    Thomas 2, 18
    William 18

Jackson, Daniel 53
    Dempsey 53
    Ephiram 53
    Francis 22
    Lydia 60
    Magdalen 8
    Molly 35
    Peggy 53
    Robert 20
    Samuel 53 (2)
Jacob, Morris 72
    William 53
Jacobs, Moring 62
James, Agatha 11
    Aldridge 40
    Ann 46
    Benjamin 13, 42, 53
    David 40, 74
    Dinah 13, 44
    Elizabeth 11, 28, 40, 42
    Franky 61
    George 11
    Hannah 28, 53
    Isaac 53
    James 11, 13
    John 3, 11, 13, 14, 21, 26, 34, 40, 42, 44, 53 (2), 66, 72
    John, Capt. 72
    Joseph 42, 53
    Margaret 11, 40, 47
    Margaret Bruce 58
    Mary 11, 40, 53
    Molly 11
    Peggy 58
    Phebe 49
    Susannah 13, 49
    Thomas 11, 13 (2), 18, 28, 42, 53, 72
Jameson, Enoch 41
    Frederick G. 66
Janaway, Margaret 44
Janny, Aquilla 37
Jeffers, Sarah 7
Jefferson, Joseph, Jr. 38
Jeffrey, George 75
Jeffries, Agnes 59
    Alexander 76
    Anderson 53
    Briant 53
    Ephiram 53
    Henry 53
    James P. 66 (3)
    James Payne 66 (2)
    James Penfield 66
    John 53, 72
    Joseph 28, 53
    Lettice 47
    Lucy 50, 52
    M.H. 66 (2)
    Mary 28, 59
    Mary H. Wyer 66
    Molly 54
    Thomas 53
Jenkins, John 53
    Peggy 59
    Susannah 48
    Thomas 53
    William 22
Jennings, Alexander 53
    Augus 72
    Augustin 14
    Augustine 14, 25
    Baylor 14, 34
    Banjamin 14
    Berryman 12, 14
    Betty 14, 22
    Cloe 62
    George 14

Hannah 14, 49
Lewis 14, 53
Louis, Dr. 66
Louisa A. 66
Lucy 66
Milly 60
Sally 14
Thomas 74
W.A. 66
William 14, 53, 72
Jermert, Joshua 53
Jett, Catherine 59
Francis 72, 75
James 53, 75
John 6
John, Sr. 75
Nancy 51
Peggy 51
Sally 58
Susan 51
William 2, 75
John, Benjamin 53
Johns, Edward L. 66
Edward Lovell 66
Sarah 66
Johnson, --- 66
Alexander 20
Ann Chilton 64
Annie E. 64
Archibald 53
Bailey 20
Baldwin 36
Betsy 46
Betty 8
Bushby 53
Charles 53
Cora 66
Cora Virginia 67
D.M. 66
David 53
Elizabeth 20, 49
Eppa H. 66
Frances 57
Hannah 6, 53
Harry Mauzy 66
Ida M. 66
Iram 66
Isaac 36
James 20, 66
James F. 66
Jeffrey 20
Jeffries 72
Jesse 73
John 18, 53, 73
Katherine 66
L.F. 66
Letty 43
Lucy 38
Lydia 36
Margaret 14, 56
Minor 53
Moses 8, 72
Nimrod 53
P.L. 66
Presley 20
Sally 47
Sarah 20
Smith 30
T.S. 66
Tennis 53
Thomas 1, 19, 53
Tolito 53
Turner M. 74
Wilfred 53
William 72
Y. 29
Johnston, Aaron 3
Charlotte 42

Daniel 42
David 42
Duanna 42
Elizabeth 54
Francis 3
Jemina 34
John 42, 75
Margaret 3
Mary 26
Molly 42
Moses 42
Moses, Sr. 42
Nelly 57
Nimrod 42
Jolly, Annie Owen 66
Jones, --- 43, 66
Ann 60
Benjamin 8
Betty 9, 52
Brenentom 72
Cary 40
Charles 75
Darkes 20
Edward 53
Elizabeth 36, 51, 60, 66 (2)
Frances 50
George 9
Hannah 40, 60
Henry 75
Honora 66
Isaiah 54
James 40, 54
John 21, 54(3), 66, 72, 75
John B. 66
John Warner 54
Joseph 54
Levi 54
Lewis 42
Lucretia 40
Mary 40, 57
Moses 54
Polly 52
Richard 54
Richard B. 66 (2)
Robert 54 (2)
Sarah 40
Sol 9
Solomon 9
Thomas O. 66
William 9, 24, 33, 39, 40, 54
Jordan, Nancy 32
Judson, W. 63

--- K ---

Kampe, Peter 54
Kamper, Frederick 54
Hannah 54
Harman 2
Henry 2, 5
Howson 73
James 73
John 73
Judy 25
Philip 5
Sarah 47
Kearne, Elizabeth 56
Kearns, Henry 32
Lydia 48
Kearton, Anthony 42
Elizabeth 42
Fanny 42
John 42
Thomas 42
Keas, Ann 46
Keating, Gerrard 36

Jemina 36
Kebbie, William 54
Kebble, Mary 54
Keen, Mathew 32
Keith, Alexander 34 (2)
Betty 25
Catty 34
Caty Gallashue 25
Charlotte 25
Charlotte Ashmore 25
Elizabeth 51
Isham 12, 25, 26, 66 (4)
James, Rev. 66
James S. 66
John 14, 21, 25
Judith 25
Juliet Chilton 66
Mary Isham 25
Obannon 34
Sarah 66
Sarah A. 66
Thomas 12, 25, 26, 33, 38, 54, 66
William 34
Kelley, Joseph 21
Kelly, Alexander D. 74
James W. 74
John 21
Joseph 21
Thomas 21
Kemper, --- 66
Agnes 55
Ann 2, 36
Anna 54
Anney 36
Catey 36
Charles 27, 36, 76
David 54
Elias 36
Elizabeth 36
Fanny 55
Harmon 72
Henry 72
Jacob 72
Jacob, Jr. 36
Jacob, Sr. 27, 36
John 2, 22, 36, 54, 72, 74
John, Col. 67
John, Sr. 27
Joseph 36
Lewis 54
Martha 67
Martin 54
Mary 36
Moses 36
Nancy 54
Peter 30, 36, 72
Rosanna 54
Susannah 36, 43
Thomas 54
Tilman 36
William 74
Kendall, Jesse 54
Lucretia 47
Kennaday, Rachel 54
Kennedy, Sarah 58
Kennard, Frances 51
George 14
Joshua 36
Kenner, Betty 37
Catherine 55 (2)
Elizabeth 56
Francis 14, 15
George 72
George Turville 14
Howson 14, 15, 72
Judith 29
Lawerence 29

Lucy 29
Mary 59
Robert 19, 54
Rodham 14, 15, 19, 23, 29, 54
Samuel 15
Sarah 58
Susannah 6, 15, 56
Kenny, Andrew 54
Kent, --- 73
Kenton, John 21
  Simon 25
Kernes, Ann 41
  Benjamin Horton 41
  Daniel 41
  John 41
  John M. 41
  William 41, 72
Kerns, Jacob 54
  John 7
  Thomas 54
Kerr, Asenth 34
  Betsy 36
  Betty 34
  Dorcas 34, 57
  John 13, 23, 30, 34, 35
  John, Jr. 34
  Lucy 34
  Peggy Smith 34
  Sarah 34
  Sarah Crosby 34
  William 34 (2)
Kerrs, John 7
Key, James 19
  Price 54
  Thomas 54
Keys, Ann 46
  James 14
  Margaret 48
  Naomi 48
Kibble, William 54
Kidwell, Fanny 60
  Mary 32, 49
  Thomas 54
  William 32
Kinchloe, Cornelius 6
  Hannah 19, 51
  James 54
  John 10 (2), 73
  William 10, 15
Kines, John 33
King, --- 67
  Cornelius 42
  Edwin B. 67
  Edwin B., Jr. 67
  Elizabeth 38
  George 54
  Henry 38
  John 54
  Joseph 38
  Joshua 54
  Josie E. 67 (2)
  Mary Ann 55
  Mary S. F. 67
  Orphy 42
  Thomas 7
  Vincent 74
  William 67
Kirby, Caroline Sims 67
  James 54
  James, Capt. 67
  John G. 67 (2)
  Julia C. (Claggett) 67
  Virginia Sims 67
Kirk, Elizabeth 16
  William 16, 72
Kirke, Elizabeth 58
  Sarah 16
Kirkpatrick, Delia Catherine 67

Enoch 67
Enoch J. 67
William 54
Kish, Peggy 49
Kittson, John 54
Knight, John 54
Knowland, John 54
Knowlong, John 54
Knox, Janet 23
  John 23
  Robert 23
  Robert Dade 23

--- L ---

Lacy, M. 41
  Moses 54
  Nathaniel 54
Lake, Agnes 65
  Cloe 46
  Isaac 67
  John, Capt. 67
  Ludwell 65
  Vincent 54
Lambert, Hugh 73
  Sarah 39
Lamkin, Betty 57
  James 54
Lampkin, Peggy 59
Lampkins, George 72
Lane, James 6
Lanketer, Alexander 54
Lansdown, John 26
Larrance, Edward 32
  John 54
  Richard 32
Latham, George 74
  Jere D. 74
Lathane, Elizabeth 50
  Francis 28
Laurance, Ann 47
  Elizabeth 46
  Peter 15
Laurence, Edward 24, 75
  John 24
  Peter 24, 75
  Richard 24
  Rodham Tullos 24
Lawerence, Edward 54, 72
  Edward, Jr. 1, 4
  Edward, Sr. 4
  Eliz. 54
  Janney 59
  Lydia 50
  Mary 6
  Mason 54
  Peter 1
  Richard 4
  Rodham 54
  Sally 58
  Teanny (Feanny) 1
  William 16
Lawler, James 23
  Polly 60
Laws, Betty 38
  John 38
Lawson, Ann Stepham (Steptoe) 10
  Elizabeth 10
  Epaphroditus 10
  Gavin 16, 24, 39
  Harry 10
  James 31
  John 10, 35
  Mary 10
  Petty 25
  Thomas 31

William 39
Leach, Elizabeth 47
  George 54 (2)
  George, Jr. 26
  George, Sr. 26
  J... 54
  Joseph 72
  Marshall 54
  Nancy 59
  Sarah 45, 52
  Susannah 61
  Valentine 54
Leachman, Mary 62
  Susannah 62
Leake, Ann 46
  Bazie 54
  Milly 50
Lear, Molly 45
  William 54
Lears, Hannah 7
Lee, Arthur 27
  Charles 67, 69
  George 27
  Hancock 27, 54, 74
  Hancock, Capt. 35
  James 54
  Julian 67
  Kendall 27
  Mary 54
  Meta Wallace 67
  Priscilla 27
  Richard 27
  Susannah 58
  William 27
Leer, Molly 25
Lees, Mary 21
  Molly 25
Legg, Daisy 67
  Davenport 3
Lewis, Acke♦ 48
  Ann 26
  Britain 40, 54
  Henry M. 74
  Jacob 54
  James 40
  Jane 40
  Lovey 54
  Sarah 13
  Thomas 13
  William 40
  Zach 11
  Zachariah 72
Limerick, James 67
  Mary 67
Linegar, William 75
Lingham, Richard 5
Linn, Alexander 54
  Joseph 54
  Mary 47
Linton, ---, Widow 73
  John 73
  Moses 73
  Nancy 57
Lion, John 54
Little, Jordan 55
  Susannah 52
Littlejohn, Charles 75
Lloyd, George Emory 55
  James 35
  Joseph 37, 55
Logan, Henry 55
  John 55
Loman, John 2
Lomax, Elizabeth Winter Payne 67
  Lindsay Lundsford 67 (2)
Lombard, Elizabeth 41
Love, William 55
Lovell, Ann Maria 66

Sarah 75
Lowe, Jesse 55
  John 55
  Mary 50
Lowry, Daniel 55
  Mary 56
  William 55
Luckett, Douglas 37
  Ignatus 37
  John 37
  Lyons 31
  Mary 37
  Nancy 37
  Richard 37
  Thomas 37
  William 37
Ludwell, Philip 73
Luke, Elizabeth 67
Lunce, Hester 45
Lunceford, --- 45
  Amanda 67
  B.F. 67
  Benjamin 67
  George 19
Lunsford, John 55
  Rodham 55
  Roldy 55
  Margaret 44
  William 44
Luttrell, Abner 14
  Austin 72
  Betty 14
  Dinah 14
  Dolly 14
  Elizabeth 56
  Hannah 14
  Heland 17
  Hetheland 17
  James 4, 12, 72
  John 4, 14, 20, 55, 72
  Lot 14
  Lydia 14
  Mary 4, 14, 72
  Michael 4, 14, 72
  Nannie 17
  Nathan 14
  Nelson 55
  Nimrod 17
  Richard 4 (2), 6, 14, 72
  Robert 4, 14, 72
  Samuel 4, 11, 72, 75
  Sarah 4, 14
  Susannah 4, 72
  Unstips 4
  Winnifred 24
Lynn, Fielding 31
  Francis 31, 55
  John 31
  Lewis 31
  Thompson 31

--- M ---

Mackarel, James 55
Mackie, Thomas 6, 25
Macklan, Joseph 6
  William 6
Maddox, Elizabeth 8
  George 28
Maddux, Easter Sally 20
  Fanny 20
  Frances 23
  George 55
  Grover 74
  James 67
  James H. 67
  James Henry 67
  James Kerfoot 67
  Jane 67 (2)
  Jesse 55
  Jethrofield 20
  Lazarus 20
  Lillie 63
  Margaret 20, 62
  Mary 49
  Mathew (Martin) 20
  Nathaniel 20, 55
  Theodore 67
  Thomas 14, 20
  Thomas L. 67
  William 20
Mahoney, Benjamin 55
  Eliza 45
  Frances 56
  Misten (Martin 55
Majors, Alexander 55
Mallory, Clement 43
  Clement P. 36
  Edward 74
  James 55
  L. 34
  Philip 55
  William 55, 74
Maorgan, Elizabeth 21
Manly, Sarah 13
Mann, Jesse L. 67
  Joel 67 (2)
  Sally A. 67
Manrony, Mary 1
Manuel, Abbe 30
  Francis 30
  Zachariah 30
Markham, Catey 15
  J.W. 6
  James 55
  John 1, 44, 72
  Jonathan 13
  Mary Ann 15
  William 55
Markwell, Mildred 31
  William 31
Marr, Ann 3
  C. 67
  Catherine Inman 67
  Chris 10
  Chris. 73
  Daniel 22, 73
  Frances Harrison 67
  James Ripon 67
  Jane Blackburn 67
  John 67 (4), 73
  John Blackburn 67
  John Quincy 67
  Margaret 67
  Margaret Moore 67
  Mary 13
  Sally 67
  Wallace Marion 67
Marrs, Ann 72
Marshall, ---, Widow 75
  Alexander 67
  Alexander J. 67
  Alice 57
  Charles 37, 40, 41, 42, 43 (2), 55
  George 19
  James 16
  James M. 74
  John 55, 75
  Judy 47
  Lucy 43
  Maria Rose 67
  Mary Ann 5
  Nancy 56
  R.I. Taylor 67
  Sarah 53
  Simon 55
  Thomas 2 (2), 7, 10, 21
  Thomas, Jr. 55
  William 1, 2
Martin, Alexander B. 23
  Benjamin 30
  Caty 48
  Charles 24, 25, 30, 55 (2), 72
  Elinor 15
  Elizabeth 15, 59
  Elizabeth Mountjoy 24
  Enoch 30
  Eve 72
  George 55, 74
  Hannah 49
  Henry 72
  Hosea 30
  James 55
  John 26, 30, 32, 72
  Joseph 72, 73
  Joseph, Sr. 30
  Katherine 30
  Nancy 62
  Nimrod 55
  Tillman 2
  Tilman 15
  Verlinda 23
Marvel, Eliz. 60
Marvet, Eliz. 60
Mason, Ann 62
  Colbert 55
  Jesse 55
  Margaret 24
  Mary 32, 62, 68
  Thomas 55
Massey, Thomas 55
Massie, Asa 40
  Ase 40
  Benjamin Morehead 40
  Dollie 40
  Dolly 40
  John 40
  Josias 40
  Nimrod 40
  Robert 40
  Samuel 40
  Thomas 40
Masters, Ann 23, 50
Mather, Benjamin 55
Mathers, Robert 55
Mathew, Elpha 49
  John 22
  Sally 29
Mathews, John 35
  Mary 35
  Simon 55
Mathis, Alice 6
  Ann 6
  Chichester 6
  Elizabeth 6
  Griffin 6
  John Dudley 6
  Nancy 6
  Newman 6
  Robert 6, 72
  Sarah 6
  Thomas 72
Matthew, Polly 47
  Rachel 59
Mauzy, Betsy 62
  Betty 20, 43, 72
  Elizabeth 43, 44
  George 43
  Henry 20, 43, 55, 72
  Jemina 35, 48
  John 6, 20, 28, 30, 35, 43,

44, 72
John, Jr. 44 (2)
Joseph 43
Margaret 20
Mary 6, 44
Michael 43, 44
Molly 20, 51
Myrna 30
Peggy 20, 45
Peter 6, 20, 43, 44, 55
Polly 58
Richard 43
Sally 6, 22
Thomas 43
William 43
Maxheimer, Elizabeth B. 67
Joseph 67 (2)
May, James 26
Maybin, David 55
Mayes, Henry 55
Mayhugh, John Thomas 67
Mays, Nancy 45
Mcall, Samuel 56
McBee, Benjamin 55
Fanny 49
John 55
Susan 45 (2)
McCabe, Hanson 60
McCanahan, Jane 60
McCaron, Daniel 55
McCarthy, Ann 53
McCarty, --- 24
Cornelius 55
Jerrett 72
McChosney, Ann 19
McClanahan, David 55
Gerrard 55
Jane 48
John 55
Lettice 55
Molly 59
Patty 58
William 55, 72, 76
McClenachan, Mary 66
McCloud, Martin 55
McComkry, William, Rev. 73
McConchi, Robert 55
McConchie, Dorothy 53
McCormack, Ann 49
Betsy 45
Eliz. 55
John 72, 75
Margaret 52
Stephen 6, 72
McCormick, James M. 2
John 24
Margaret 24
Stephen 24, 74
McCoy, Daniel 55
Elizabeth 50
Joseph 55
McDaniel, John 56 (2)
William 3
McDonald, Archibald 56
Donald 73
Eleanor 62
Jared 56
Lydia 56, 62
Mary 45
McEndress, William 37
McEntree, William 56
McFarland, Jane 41
John 41
Robert 41
McFeavor, Elizabeth 56
McGraw, Isaiah 56
McIoar, Elizabeth 16
James 16

John 16
Mary 16
McKay, Ann 50
Betty 22
Isaac 22
Priscilla 57
McKee, John 72
McKenney, Alice 32
Elizabeth 32
Francis 32
John 32
Mary 32
Susannah 32
McKenny, Mathew 56
McKenzey, Franklin 14
McKinney, Mary 50
McKinsey, Elizabeth 47
McKonkey, Catherine 45
Milly 48
McLearen, Thomas Coleman 67
McMecklin, Margaret 42
McMeeker, Archibald 56
McMeekin, --- 53
Mary 59
McNeal, William 56
McNean, --- 74
McNeel, John 39
Mcoboy, Peggy 19
McPherson, Richard 2
McQueen, Elizabeth 60
McQuin, John 75
McVeigh, Jesse 41
Meoll, Samuel 56
Merr, Ann 3
Merriam, F.A. 67
Fred K. 67
Josephine 67
Josie E. King 67
Merriman, F.A. 67
Merry, Philip 76
Metalfe, Asa 55
Metcalf, Charles 31
Margaret 8
Metcalfe, Betsy 18
Charles 19, 55
Christopher 12
Elias 55
Eliz. 56
John 21, 55
Sally 35
William 18, 34, 35, 36
Michael, Caty 60
Jenny 60
Middleton, Studley 56
Millar, Will 23
Millard, William 18
Miller, Ann 3
Elizabeth 2
Harman 2
Henry 56
John 6, 56
Molly 53
Simon 6, 72
Susannah 45
William 72
Milton, Mary 56
Minor, Armistead 30
George 56
Minter, Anthony 12
Betty 45
Elizabeth 12
Hannah 8, 62
Jacob 8, 12
John 12
Joseph 12, 72
Mary 12
William 12
Minters, Joseph, Jr. 7

Minton, Joseph 73
Mintor, Jacob 10
John 10
Joseph 10
Mary 10
William 10
Miskel, William 14
Mitchell, John 22, 56
Joshua 56
Moffett, Henry, Jr. 18
J. 11
Jesse 20, 28
John 9
Lucretia 62
William 56
Moffitt, Charlotte 50
Jesse 76
Milly 51
Monday, Charles 56
Millah 48
Monroe, Alexander 41
Elizabeth 48
George 76
James 56
John 18, 20, 31
Molly 45
Sarah 51
Montgomerie, Thomas 29
Moon, McLanahan 56
Moore, Ann H. 48
Frances 6
Francis 56
Henry 34
Margaret 61, 67
Mildred 64
Samuel 56 (3)
Thomas 74
Morcy, John 26
Morehead, Alexander 6, 22
Ann 24
Anne 24
Armistead 21
Benjamin 40
Cary 49
Charles 1, 5, 6, 7, 15, 16, 19, 21, 34, 56, 72
Dressley 6
Eliz. 58 (2), 61
Elizabeth 21, 34
George 56
James 21
John 6, 15, 25, 34, 40, 72
John, Sr. 30
Karenhappach 21
Lida 22
Lucy 52
Lydia 34
Mary 15, 21, 34, 57, 58
Molly 55
Peggy 34
Polly 58
Presley 16
Pressley 21
Samuel 6, 34
Susan 61
Thomas 15
Turner 19, 21
William 6
Wilmarth 34
Moreland, Nancy 46
Morgan, Abel 8
Abraham 8
Alice 5
Anne 5
Benjamin 5, 56
C. 56
Charles 5, 29, 56, 73, 75
Charles, Jr. 72

Charles, Sr. 5, 72
Daniel 39
Elizabeth 55
Enoch 8
Francis 56
Grace 8
James 5, 72
Jeremiah 21, 26, 29
John 5, 8, 56, 72
Joseph 18, 20, 21, 29, 56
Martha 8
Mary 5, 8
Phebe 50
Polly 50
Randle 8
Randle, Jr. 8
Rosanna 59
Sally 55
Simon 5, 29, 31, 72
Spencer 56
William 4, 5, 72, 75
William, Jr. 72
Moring, John 56
Morman, Frances 59
Morris, --- 43
  Anne 56
  Benjamin 6
  David 56
  David W. 39
  Elizabeth 20
  Sanders 43
  William 72
Morrison, Daniel 17
  Edward 76
  Jeane 68
  John 56
Mosby, Alice 69
Moseless, Henry 4
Moss, Daniel 56
  Mary 60
  Mathew 73
  Meredith 13
  Moses 37
  Tealy 56
  William 56
Mott, William 56
Mouffett, Henry 1
Mountjoy, J.W. 67
  M.S. 67
  R.R. 67
  S.F. 67
  William 44 (2)
Mourse, George 56
Moxley, Hannah 43
  James 43
  Jeremiah 43
  Sebella 43
  Solomon 43
Muller, Ernest 67
  Frank 67
  Susan 67
  William 68 (2)
Munney, John 19
Murphew, John 56
Murphy, Darly 44
  David 56
  Jane 54
  John 76
  Leander 56
  Miles 75
  Teny 26
  William 56
  William S. 74 (2)
Murray, Enoch 56
  Esther 57
  Francis 29
  James 4, 12, 72
  John 74

Lydia 59
Mary 23
Reuben 42
William 74
Murry, Alice 59
  Benjamin 56
  Dorcas 19
  James 1, 20
  John 20
  Lydia 20
  Ralph 20, 23, 25
  Reuben 20, 56
  Sary 17
Myers, Michael 56
  Peggy 37
Myoratt, Sarah 7

--- N ---

Nagle, Mary 68
Nalle, William 23
Nalls, William 56
Nash, William 56
Nay, Joseph 56
Neal, Ann Amelia 68
  George H. 68
  Mary 27
  Mathew 32
  Matthew 11, 27 (2)
  Richard 43
  Rosa 69
Neale, --- 43
  Ann 22
  Ben 24
  Benjamin 22, 24, 75
  Berry 15
  James 43 (2), 56
  Jesse 24
  Joanna 22
  Joseph 22
  Judah 22
  Judith 55
  Lettice 56
  Mary 22, 50, 59
  Mathew 22, 34
  Moses 24
  Nancy 57
  Roswell 73
  Sarah 22
  Thomas 56
  William 43
Neaoble, Peggy 9
Neavil, George, Capt. 72
  Joseph 56
  Thomas 56
Neavill, Gabriel 6
  George 6, 9
  Henry 6
  John 6
  Judith 46
  Mary 6, 9, 53
  Peggy 9
  Robert 6
  Sarah 18
  Thomas 6
Neaville, Lettice 52
Neigh, Isaac 36
Nelms, Samuel 72
Nelson, Betty 45
  Catherine 12, 53
  Caty 9
  G.W., Rev. 68
  George W., Jr. 68
  George W., Rev. 68
  James 28, 56
  Jemina 22, 61

Jesse 22
John 11, 15, 22, 23, 28 (2), 56 (2), 72
John, Jr. 28
John, Sr. 22, 72
Joseph 28, 56 (2), 68
Lettice 22
Margaret 22
Margurite 68
Marvin 68
Mary 28
Mary Scollay 68
Nadine 68
Sarah 22
Thomas 14, 28, 56
William 22, 26
Nevill, George 73
  Joanna 52
  John 72
  Joseph 72
Newby, Betty 29
  Georginana 68
  Hannah 45
  Nancy 46
  Robert 68
  Robert C. 68
  Sinah 50
Newell, Benjamin 18
  John 18
  Nancy 18
  Richard 18
Newgent, Edward 72
  Thomas 72
Newhouse, Polly 53
Newlan, Daniel 3
  Jane 3
Newland, Daniel 72
  William 56
Newman, Ethel 43
Newport, Peter 72
  Sarah 52
Nichols, Samuel 75
Nickols, James 39
  Mary 39
  Nathan 39
  Thomas 39
Noble, John 41
Norman, Barsheba 29
  Clement 24, 75 (2)
  George 56
  Jesse 75
  Judy 59
  Sally 49
  Tabitha 53 (2)
  William 2
Norris, Cathering 40
  Elizabeth 40
  Ellin 40
  Hannah 40
  John 16, 40 (2), 57
  Joseph 40
  Mary 40
  Samuel 40
  Sarah 40
  Septimus 40, 57
  Susannah 58
  Thaddeus 42
  William 13, 40
Northcutt, Benjamin 57
  John 57
  Winny 32
Nouman, Molly 61
Nounan, ---, Widow 73
Nugent, Ann 23
  Edward 23, 27
  Mary 52
  Thomas 23, 27, 72
Nutt, Richard 41, 57

Winny 41

--- O ---

Oar, Sally 50
Obannon, Andrew 9, 57
  Benjamin 9, 57, 74
  Betty 56
  Bryan 3
  Bryant 9
  Catherine 56
  Elias 34
  Fanny 14
  George 11
  Isham 34, 42
  James 9, 34, 74
  John 3, 6, 9, 17, 30, 34, 35, 41
  John, Capt. 11
  John, Jr. 72
  John, Sr. 9
  Joseph 9, 34, 57, 74
  Joyce 54
  Lydia 30, 34, 35
  Nancy 54
  Sally 57
  Samuel 3, 9, 12
  Sarah 3, 9
  Stelle 12
  Susannah 48
  Thomas 3, 9, 12, 57, 76
  William 3, 9, 34, 41, 72
  William, Mrs. 72
  William, Sr. 72
Obanon, Jemina 53
Odor, Sarah 53
Ogleby, Elizabeth 50
O'Hara, Isabella Byrne 68
  Mary Emeline 68
O'Latham, Georgie 64
Oldacres, Hannah 46
  Nancy 49
Oldaker, Abraham 32
  Hester 32
Oldham, Mary 75
Oliman, Ann 56
Oliver, Josias 57
  Mary 62
  Samuel 57
  Walter 41
Oneal, Thomas 57
Orear, Daniel 37
  Jesse 57
O'Reilley, --- (Robert) 68
  Brian 68
  Margaret 68
  Miles 68
  Nicholas 68
  Philip 68
  Robert 68
  Thomas 68
Orr, Sally 50
Orsley, Hannah 28
Otterback, Henry 72
  John 72
Owen, Annie 66
  Bethelon 57
  John 21
  Rebecca 57
Owens, Aaron 57
  Amelia 33
  Bethel 57
  Elizabeth 57
  Jane 21
  Jeremiah 21
  Johnson 12
  Mason 57

Nancy 57
Thomas 57
William 57
Owing, Jean 30

--- P ---

Page, Elizabeth 2
  Helen Stuart 68
  John 68 (2), 73
  Sarah E. 68
  Thomas 72
Paine, William 57
Palmer, Elizabeth 46
  F. Gendron, Maj. 68
  Mary 55
Parker, ---, Dr. 72
  Abraham 57
  Alexander 3, 5, 6, 10, 24
  Amy 24
  Ann 10
  James 26
  John 15
  Joseph 57
  Judith 10
  Judy 24
  Lucy 24
  Martin 57
  Mary 26, 47
  Richard 10, 24, 26, 34
  Sarah 53
  Thomas 15, 57
  William 10, 24
Parkinson, J.W. 68
  L.A. 68
Parklow, Sarah 46
Parlow, Elizabeth 28
Parmer, Isaac 57
Parr, James 30
Parson, Matilda 48
Parsons, William 57
Patterson, James 57
Pattie, C.C. 68
  Jenny 68
  Otho H.W. 68
  V.A. 68
  William 68 (2)
Paulie, Issachar 57
Payne, --- 63
  A.H. 68
  Alexander Dixon 68
  Alice Fitzhugh Dixon 68
  Ann 60
  Arthur Morson 68
  Augustine 57, 76
  Benjamin 36, 57
  Charles Edward Fitzhugh 68
  Charles Fitzhugh 68
  Coldton 57
  Elizabeth Winter 67
  Francis 75
  G.E.F. 68
  George 36
  Harry Fitzhugh 68
  Inman 68 (3)
  Inman H. 68
  Jeanne Morrison Brook 68
  John 75
  John D., M.D. 68
  John Daniel 68
  John Massie 68
  John Winston 68
  Lucy 56
  Markham Brooke 68
  Mary 60, 68 (2)
  Mary Ann 68

Mary E. 68 (2)
Mary Mason Fitzhugh 68
Mary Winston 68
Merryman 57
Minerva Winston 68 (2)
Molly 50, 57
Nancy 50
Patty 51
Reuben 75 (2)
Richard 68
Sarah Robb Tyler 68
Susannah 36, 51
T. Alexander, Rev. 68
Thomas 19, 75
W.H.F., Brig. Gen. 68
W.H.F., Gen. 68
William 74, 76
William, Capt. 76
William, Jr. 57
William Fitzhugh 68
William H. 68
William Winter 68 (2)
William Winter, Col. 68
Peach, John 57
Peake, Elizabeth 16
  John 13
  John, Jr. 16
  Mary 13, 16 (2)
  Sally 16
  Thomas 16
  William 17
Peakes, John 16
Pearce, Jacob 21
  John 21
  Lelia 21
  Peter 21
  Rosannah 21
  Susannah 21
Pearl, Elijah 23
  Elizabeth 23
  Martha 23
  Richard 23
  Samuel 23
  William 23
Pearle, Samuel 23, 29, 34, 57 (3)
  William 23, 57
Pearse, William 7
Pearson, Elizabeth 54
Peirce, Peter 72
Pendleton, Edward 39
  Robert 57
Penny, James 57
Peny, James 5
  Sarah 5
Peper, Winnifred 28
Pepper, Ann 50
  Elijah 57
  Hannah 45
  Jeremiah 57
  Jesse 57
  Lucy 30
  Molly 50
Perkins, Jonathan 20
Perry, Sally 57
Petcher, John 44
Peters, Betty 17, 43
  Elizabeth 48
  James 17 (2), 43, 57 (2)
  John 9, 17, 33, 36, 37, 40, 57, 72
  Lewis 17
  Mary 34
  Nancy 17, 36
  Nimrod 17
  Sally 62
  Sarah 17
  William 17
Pettet, Nathaniel 57

Samuel 57
Thomas 57
Petty, Marshall 57
Peyton, Chandler 41
  Cuthbert 57
  Henry 17, 26
  Henry, Jr. 32
  Henry, Sr. 32
  Margaret C. 41
  Mary 53
  Richard Henry 41
  Seignora 66
  Thomas 38
  Valentine 57
  Yelverton 41
Pharis, Samuel 9
Phillips, Caty 59
  Drusilla 45
  Elizabeth 18, 47
  Fielding 57
  Ruth 58
  Sarah 46
  William 28, 57
  William F. 74
Pickard, Mary 50
Pickett, --- 74
  Agatha 52
  Ann 15, 35
  Betsy 43
  Charles 41
  Daniel 35
  Elizabeth 5, 69
  George 5, 40, 43
  George Blackwell 43
  Hannah 22
  James 35
  John 5, 35, 43, 57
  Lucy 52, 55
  Martha 35
  Martin 5, 15, 25, 43, 57
  Martin, Major 12
  Molly 53
  Reuben 5
  Sally 55
  Sanford 35
  Sarah 5, 62
  Sebba 59
  Steptoe 43
  William 5, 16, 25, 31, 35, 43, 72, 75
  William Sanford 19, 36, 57
Pierce, John 57
  Judith 27
  Peter 21
Pierson, Lizzie 68
  William, Rev. 68
Pilcher, Steven 57
  William 57
Pinchard, William 30
Pinckard, Sarah 56
Pinkard, --- 75
  Mildred 22, 39
  William 39
Pinkstone, Anna 58
Piper, B. 19
Pitcher, Chloe 19
Poe, William 74
Pollard, Abner 57
Pollock, --- 65, 67
  A.D., Rev. 68, 69 (2)
  Charles Lee 69
  Elizabeth Gordon 69
  Elizabeth Hendrick 69
  Thomas Gordon 69
Pope, Benjamin 57
  William 13, 15
Popkins, Jehu 57
Pore, Mary 24

Porter, Agatha 42
  Betty 37
  Catherine 62
  Charles 37, 57
  Christopher 58
  Ebenezer 35
  Edwin 37, 38, 58
  Eli 37, 58
  Elizabeth 58
  Eppa 58
  Eve 2
  Frances 47
  Hannah 30, 35
  Joan 30
  John 28, 30, 37, 58, 74
  Martin 42, 58
  Mary 45
  Samuel 2, 58, 72
  Susannah 58
  Thomas 37, 38, 58
  William 37, 38
Portman, Frederick Arthur Berkeley 69
Powan, William 58
Powell, Ann E. 70
  Anne 66
  Burr 40, 41
  Catherine 40
  Henry 58
  Kitty 33
Powers, Patrick 58
  Thomas 58
Prage, John 58
Pragh, Elizabeth 49
Prainer, Philip 58
Pratt, Henrietta 54
  Zephania 58
Preston, Sarah 59
  William 3, 7
Price, Ann 15
  Bennett 15
  Elizabeth 15
  Judith 15
  Rebecca 59
  Richard 58
  Samuel 58
Prichard, Peggy 15
  Stephen 15
Priest, Elizabeth 23, 49
  Eveles 17
  Frances 13
  George 17
  John 17, 75
  Mary 32
  Mason 58
  Nancy 54
  Peter 32
  Richard 17, 24
  Samuel 17
  Sarah 24, 32
  Sarry 17
  Thomas 6, 17, 32
  William 17
Pritchett, Jane 2
Putman, Elizabeth 58
Pyior, Benjamin 75

--- Q ---

Quarles, Betty 8
  Elizabeth Minor 8
  John 8
  Susannah 53
Queens, Sally 54
Quisenberry, Ann 52
  Gracey 31

Zaccheus 40

--- R ---

R..., Richard 58
Race, William 58
Railey, Thomas 12
Rakestraw, Nancy 52
Raley, Peggy 48
Ralls, Charles 58
  Edward 11
  Joel 58
Ramsdell, Charles Morehead 24
  Edward 24
  John 24
  Major Thomas 34
  Margaret 24
  Sarah 24
  Thomas 24
  Thomas, Sr. 24 (2)
  Wharton 24
  Wharton, Jr. 24
  William 24
  William, Jr. 24
Randall, Hannah 46, 55
  Margaret 55
Randolph, Elizabeth 61
  Nannie Fitzhugh 65
  Richard 75
  William 72
Ransdell, Betsy 51
  Chilton 11
  Edward 11
  Jenny 21
  Mary 48, 58
  Sally 51
  Thomas 11, 58
  Wharton 5, 10, 11, 58, 72
  William 11
  William, Sr. 11
Ranson, Betty 6
  William 1, 6
Ransow, John 72
Ratcliffe, Elizabeth 50
Rawles, Kenag 76
Rawlins, John 31
Read, Mary 56
  Theophielus 58
  Thomas 58
Reading, Timothy 4
  William 3
Really, Sarah 48
Reaves, Elizabeth 21
Recter, Nathaniel 41
Rector, Benjamin 8, 14, 18
  Betty 52
  Catherine 8, 51
  Caty 37
  Charles 8
  Daniel 8
  Darius 61
  Edward 37
  Elijah 37
  Elizabeth 8
  Enoch 18
  Frederick 8, 18
  Hannah 58
  Harman, Jr. 18
  Harman, Sr. 18
  Harmon 8 (2), 72
  Henry 1, 8, 18, 37, 72
  Jacob 8, 72
  John 8, 18, 37, 72
  Lewis 58
  Mary 8, 22 (2)
  Mary Ann 37

Moses 58
Nathaniel 72
Pencey (Percy) 37
Polly 37
Sally 48 (2)
Spencer 37, 58
William 18
Rectors, Harmon 26
Redd, Allen 58
  Barbary 45
  Joseph Bullitt 29
  Permercis 29
  Priscilla 29
  Susan 29
Reddin, Timothy 2
Redding, Reuben 58
  Timothy 72
  William 30
Redman, Richard 1
  Sarah 6
Redmon, John 33
Reed, Margaret 69
  Samuel 38
  Winny 60
Reiley, Thomas 72
Renas, Zeky 58
Rennolds, James 11
  John 21
  Margaret 11
Reno, Lila 25
Renoe, George 58
  Zeky 58
Resen, Thomas 58
Rhodes, Elizabeth 59
  Hezekiah 58
  Jacob 58
  John 58
Rice, Bailey 58
Richards, Edward D. 74
Richardson, Alexander 69
Rickard, William 58
Rickett, James 58
Riddle, Kitty 45
  William 76
Ridley, John 26 (2), 58
Right, John, Capt. 72
Rile, Sallie 7
Riley, Annie 69
  Betsy 61
  Catherine 31
  Charles 31
  Eave 25
  Edward 25, 31
  Elizabeth 51
  George 31
  Hugh 31
  John 31, 75
  Lettice 49
  Nancy 53
  Susan 31
  Thomas 31
Ringo, Burtis 58
Rings, Burtis 58
Rixby, Richard, Jr. 58
Roach, George 25, 58
  John 58
  William 13
Roady, James 29
Robb, Mary McClenachan 66
Roberson, Anne 17
  Lucy 38
Robert, Elizabeth 58
  John 58
Roberts, Amelia 51
Robertson, Alec 7
  Benjamin 58
  James 15
  John 15, 58

Joseph 72
Robey, Betsy 54
Robinson, Benjamin 13, 23
  Berryman 19
  Catherine 19
  David 58
  Dixon 23, 58
  Elesha 23
  Elijah 23, 58
  George 23, 58
  Hannah 19
  James 23, 58
  Jenny Argle 52
  Jesse 19
  John 19, 23
  Joseph 14, 19
  Katy 53
  Lucy 19, 45
  Lydda 23
  Lydia 50
  Martha 19
  Mary 23, 56
  Maxmillian 19, 58
  Molly 19, 58
  Nancy 62
  Nathaniel 23
  Peggy 19
  Sarah E. 69
  Stephen 23
  Susannah 40
  William 19, 58 (2)
  William E. 69
Roe, Elizabeth 64
  Lydia 56
  Original 58
  Steven 58
  William 58
Roger, Betty 29
  Edward 29
  George 29
  Henry 58
Rogers, --- 12
  George 7, 12, 34, 41
  Henry 32
  James 3
  John 32
  Kissy 61
  Margaret 55
  Mary 32
  Molly 59
  Notley W. 74
  Rodham 46
  Sally 55
  Sarah 32
  Stephen 32
Roley, Betsy 54
  Thomas 41
Rollins, Peggy 61
Rookhard, Elizabeth 37
  Hiram 37
  Nancy 37
  Robert Carter 37
  Thomas 37
Roose, Aaron 58
  Nicholas 58
Roper, Elizabeth 20
  John 9, 20
  Letty 20
  Nancy 20
  Priscilla 43
  Richard 20
  Sally 20
  Sarah 20
  Sukey 20
  Violet 20
  William 20
  Winny 20
Rose, Robert 43 (2)

Robert H. 74
  Sarah 20
  Susannah 62
Rosenfield, Sympha 13
Roser, John 9
  Mary 9
Ross, Hector 13
Rosseau, Susannah 57
Rossen, John 58
Rosser, Hannah 62
  Mary 56
Rossey, Thomas 58
Roswell, Mary 53
Rouins, James 59
Rousan, Henry 20, 36
  John 20, 36, 72
  Lydia 36
  Priscilla 36
  Sarah 36
  William 20, 36, 72
Rousann, Ann 57
Rout, Fanny 26
  Jane 26
  Richard 26
Routt, Hannah 46
  James 25, 29
  John 72
  Nancy 52
  Peter 59, 72
  Rachel 47
  William 73
Routte, Daniel 59
Rowan, William 58
Rowles, William 76
Roy, Willy 18, 31, 35, 37, 59
Rozier, Elizabeth 56
Runnelis, Ann 46
  John 59
Rush, Charles C. 69
  Lucy E. 69
  Mary E. 69
  Peyton L. 69
Rusley, George 59
Russell, Benjamin 12
  Daniel 59
  Eliza 69
  George 1
  Lucretia 14
  Marcus 74
  Mary 2, 32, 54
  Samuel 69
  Sarah 60
  William 2, 59 (2), 72, 73
Rust, John 13, 59 (2), 72
  Mary 49
  Peter 59
  Sally 55
Ryan, Winifred 44


--- S ---


St. Clair, Cornelia 69
  Robert 69
Sanders, Brittain 27
  Elizabeth 27
  Gabriel 27
  James 27
  Larking 27
  Lewis 27
  Mary 29
  Molly 47
  Robert 7, 23, 27
  Thomas 27, 59
  William 27, 59
Sanford, Bennett 36
  Betty 36

John 36  
Richard 36  
Robert 36  
William 36  
Sarlson, Nicholas 73  
Saunders, John A. 69  
   Mary E. 69  
   T. E. 69  
   Thomas 69 (2)  
Savage, ---, Dr. 72  
Scantland, Fielding 59  
Schwab, Anton 69 (2)  
   Joseph 69  
   Susan E. 69  
Scollay, Mary 68  
Scott, Alexander 16  
   Alexander B. 74  
   Charles 59  
   Cuthbert 16  
   Elizabeth 16, 24 (2), 25, 26  
   Frances 16, 53, 66  
   James 10, 16, 25  
   James, Capt. 72  
   James, Rev. Mr. 26  
   John 17, 24, 41, 69, 74  
   John, Col. 69  
   John, Judge 69  
   John Gordon 69  
   Lucinda 69  
   Margaret C. 41  
   Marianna 65  
   Nancy 16  
   Robert 6, 24  
   Sarah 16, 26, 37  
   Thomas 16  
   William 59  
Scrows, --- 72  
Seabury, Amon (Almon) 65  
Seaman, Thomas 4, 5  
Sear, Molly 45  
   William 54  
Sears, Hannah 7  
   James 72  
   John 72  
Seaton, Alice 42  
   Betty 14  
   Francis 42  
   George 15, 42, 59  
   James 4, 19, 29, 33, 37, 42  
   Jenny 58  
   John 20, 42, 59  
   Lydia 42  
   Margaret 62  
   Mary 14  
   Sarah 59  
   William 14, 19, 21, 33, 42, 59  
Sedwick, Benjamin 69  
   Cora Elizabeth 69  
Seirs, James 72  
Selden, ---, Dr. 37  
Selman, Joseph 25  
   Zack 59  
Settle, Betty 47  
   Edward 8, 11, 16, 18, 32, 59  
   Elizabeth 18, 62 (2)  
   George 72, 75  
   Hannah 49, 51  
   Henry 18  
   Isaac 72  
   Joseph 72  
   Nancy 18  
   Pope Williams 18  
   Rosanna 11  
   Rose 53  
   Sally 50  
   Sarah 18, 27  
   Strother 59  
   William 8, 16, 18, 59 (2), 72  

William Freeman 18  
Settles, Edward 25  
   Gayson 25  
   Mary 25  
   William 25  
Shackleford, B. 27, 33  
   James 10  
   Mary 4, 51  
   Milly 55  
Shacklett, Edward 40  
   John 74  
Shadrack, Elizabeth 1  
   John 1  
Shadwell, Eliza 47  
Shank, Susannah 52  
Shanks, Katy 52  
Shark, Isaac 2  
Sharp, Ann 62  
Sharpe, Ann Nugent 27  
   Elizabeth 50  
   Lincefield 23, 27  
   Spencer 59  
Shaver, John 25, 59  
   Rebecca 53  
Shaw, Charles 59  
   John 59  
   Neale 74  
Sheetzs, Benjamin 32  
   Joseph 32  
Shehogan, Sarah 52  
Shellman, John 69  
Shepherd, John 69  
Sherman, Maria 66  
Shesterson, George 59  
Shipp, Colby 12  
   Elijah 59  
   John 12  
   Joseph 59  
   Laban 12, 13, 59  
   Nancy 12 (2), 46  
   Polly 12  
   Richard 13  
   Richard Wiatt 12  
Shipps, Mary 47  
Shirley, Ajah 12  
   James 59  
Short, John 59  
Shud, Ann 49  
Shultz, Joseph 59  
Shumate, Ann 24  
   Anna 52  
   Bailey 23  
   Benjamin 59  
   Betty 37  
   Daniel 12, 23, 72  
   Elizabeth 37  
   Hohn 59  
   James 23  
   Jane 37  
   Jemina 23  
   John 21, 23, 26, 59, 75  
   John, Sr. 9, 40  
   Joshua 23  
   Judah 23  
   Judith 46  
   Lettice 23  
   Lewis 37  
   Lydia 50  
   Margaret 62  
   Mark 33  
   Mary 12, 57  
   Mason 26  
   Sarah 55  
   Tabitha 12  
   Thomas 23  
   William 23, 59  
Shurley, John 9  
Shurlock, James 59  

Sias, John 16  
Silman, Elinor 29  
   Joseph 29  
   Zack 59  
Simmons, Catherine 47  
   Katy 47  
Simpson, John 44  
   Lydia 59  
   Mary 44  
Sims, Alice Mosby 69  
   Caroline 67  
   Marian Louise 69  
   Virginia 67  
Sinckler, John 72  
Sinclair, Ann Maria 69  
   Elizabeth 32  
   John 75  
   Margaret 32  
   Maria Louisa 69  
   Sarah 46  
Sincleare, Charity 7  
   Daniel 7  
   Elizabeth 7  
   James 7  
   Jimime 7  
   John 7  
   Mary 7  
   Robert 7  
   Sarah 7  
   William 7  
Singer, Nancy 47  
Singleton, Caty 55  
   Elizabeth 62  
   John 31  
   Stanley 72  
Sinklar, Archibald 36  
   Horatio 36  
   Isaac 36  
   James 36  
   John 36  
   Lydia 36  
   Middleton 36  
   Nancy 36  
   William 36  
Sinklear, John 11  
Sinkler, Polly 50  
   Sarah 5, 44  
   William 74  
Sinklers, Dinah 44  
   George 44  
   John 44  
   Samuel 44  
   Thomas 44  
   William 44  
Sinsee, Sarah 27  
Skinker, Samuel 40  
   Thomas 40  
   William 40  
Skinler, Samuel 40  
   William 40  
Skinner, Thomas 26  
Slaughter, Cadwalder 59  
   Cadwaller 24  
   Henry 59  
   Jess 59  
   Joseph 59  
   Judah 43  
   Margaret 56  
   Matthew 59  
   Samuel 59 (2)  
   Stanton 43  
Smallwood, John 41  
Smares, Sarah 23  
Smarr, Andrew 59  
Smedley, William 59  
Smith, Abner 30  
   Alexander 3, 39, 72  
   Amanda 69

Andrew 35
Ann 22, 48, 50, 60
Anna 48
Annie E. 69
Augustine 1, 59 (2), 72
Berryman 59
Caleb 59, 72
Catherine 46
Cleater 13
Delaney 59
Elias 41
Elijah 41
Elizabeth 14, 34, 41, 47
Enoch 30, 41
Frances Grayson 63
Frank P. 69
George 4
George Summer 69
Hannah 1, 18, 35, 55
Hedgman 41
Helen 65
Henry 4
Isham 41
J. H. 11
James 1, 19, 59 (2), 72
Jane 1, 39
Jean 58
Jemime 55
Jenny 69
John 1, 22, 30, 36, 41 (2), 59 (5), 69 (2), 72, 75
John Thomas 69
Joseph 1, 19, 24, 30 (2), 34, 35, 40, 72, 74
Lewis 1, 59
Lucinda 41
Martha 14, 19, 57
Mary 14, 55, 57, 61
Mary Waugh 59
Mathew 19
Matthew 59
Milly 47
Moein 50
Nancy 48, 58
P. A. L. 69
Rand 27
Rebecca 18
Rowley 13, 30
Ruth 30
Sarah 45, 51
Scarlett 60
Subrey 35
Susannah 28, 32, 61
Thomas 3, 19, 36, 60, 72, 74
Walter A. 74
Willamina 30
William 1, 19 (2), 30, 35, 60 (2), 69, 72, 73, 74, 75
William, Capt. 18
Smoot, Charity 57
    Claiborne 60
    Edward 60
    Enoch 42
    Franky 54
    John 60, 75
    Lewis 60
Smoots, Barton 35
    Charity 35
    Clabour 35
    Enoch 35
    Frances 35
    James 35
    John 35
    Leonard 35
    Lewis 35
    Mary Betsy 35
    Tomsen 35
    William 35

Snape, Nathaniel 60
Snelling, Aquilla 72
    Benjamin 10, 72
    Elizabeth 10, 61
    Hannah 45
    Hugh 75
    William 27
Snope, Nathaniel 32
Snyder, Caty 58
    Mary 55
    Nimrod 60
Soddust, Mary 35
Southard, Benjamin 60
    Elizabeth 15
    Francis 15
    George 15
    Jemina 15
    John 7, 15
    Levi 15
    William 15
Sower, --- 63
    Mary 69
    Richard 69
    William Summer 69
Sparks, Elizabeth 51
    James 60
Spellman, Annie Heyward 69
    H. Conway 69 (2)
    Hayward North 69
    John 60
Spenny, Benjamin 41
    William 40
Sperry, Benjamin 41
Spettler, Phillip, Jr. 60
Spicer, Rebecca 59
    Maude 69
    Wade 69
Spielman, Jacob 72
Spille, Philip 35
Spiller, Chloe 60
    Sophia 59
    William 73
Spillman, Jacob 2
    John 18
Spinney, Mary 46
Spring, Nicholas 60
Squire, Susannah 61
Squires, Ann 16
Stacy, Sarah 17
Stadler, Elizabeth 41
Stamps, Elizabeth 4
    George 4
    John 4
    Mary 4
    Molly 4, 55
    Thomas 4, 73
    Timothy 4
    William 4, 7, 72
Stanford, James 60
Stanton, Lucinda 59
    William 60
Stark, Elizabeth 17
    James 17, 60
    John 23
    William 60
Starke, Sally 57
    Sarah Ann 52
Steatard, Joseph 29
    Mary 29
Steele, Henry 29
    Molly 47
    Samuel 29, 34
Steeles, Samuel 41
Steggers, Susannah 43
Stegler, Martha 59
Steigler, Elijah 43
Stenson, James 60
Stephen, Adam 44

Elizabeth 52
Lucy 64
Stephens, Docia 49
    Robert 8
Stephenson, James 72
    Samuel 60
Stephinson, Benjamin 31
Stevens, Allen 60
    James 60
Stevenson, Benjamin 60
    Patty 53
    Peggy 60
    William 60 (2)
Stevinson, Peggy 31
Stevson, James 60
Stewart, Allen 17, 60
    Betty 18, 39
    Charles 18
    Helen 18
    James 16, 17, 18, 37, 39, 72
    James, Jr. 37
    Jane 18, 39
    John 17
    Mary 18, 56
    William 1, 16, 18, 26, 60
    William, Rev. 6
Stiggens, Elizabeth 56
Stigler, Caty 49
    James 38
    John 43
    Lewis 43
    Martha 55, 59
    Mildred 38
    Price 60
    Susannah 43
Stiglers, Elizabeth 43
    Lucy 43
Stinson, Ann 50
Stone, Ann 56
    Benjamin 7 (2)
    Betty 18
    Menoah 28
    Nimrod 60
    Parsiall 48
    Thomas 2, 72, 73, 75
    Virginia 63
Stout, Isaac 60
Stribbling, Thomas, Capt. 73
Stribling, Thomas 60
Striker, Henry 60
Stringfellow, Ann 46
    Betsy 45
    Dolly 47
    George 60
    Harry 60
Strother, Benjamin 23
    Enoch 74
    Jane 39
    John 74
    Nancy 57
    Reuben 23, 36
    Sukey 51
    Susannah 74
Strothers, Daniel 72
    James, Sr. 15
    Sally 58
    William 73
Stukle, George 60
Suddeth, John 7
Suddith, John 60
    Levi 60
Sudduth, Alse 32
    Ann 18
    Francis 18, 32
    George 32
    James 75
    John 18
    Mary 32, 69

William 32
Sullivan, David 75
Dennis 69
Elizabeth 47
Ellen 69
George 21
Maggie 69
Mary 52
Mary Ann 59
Sarah 48
Sylvester 60
William 60
Summers, Isabbell 13
Suthard, Benjamin 60
Suttle, Fanny 45
Sarah 33
William 22, 33
Sutton, John 60
Swain, Charles 75
Swift, --- 64

--- T ---

Tackett, Elizabeth 4
Lewis 4, 73
Tait, Peter 17
Talbert, Ann 49
Talbut, Ann 34
Benjamin 34
John 34
Tallaferrio, Francis, Col. 21
Talliaferrio, Catherine 60
Tapps, Molly 48
Tarlton, Sarah 60, 61
Taylor, Benjamin 32, 60
Charles 2, 73, 75
Daniel 44
Eliza 59
Elizabeth 6, 27, 51
Henry 29
James 60
Jesse 60
John 60 (2)
Joseph 8, 13, 16, 21, 26
Lazarus 1, 2, 3, 44
Mary 45, 53
Nancy 46
R.I. 67
Raleigh 60
Remey 59
Susannah 52
Thomas 60
William 60
Teagle, Susan 61
Tebbs, John 16
Tennill, Francis 2
Tennison, Ann 55
Terrall, Francis 72
Tharp, Jesse 42
Tharpe, Fanny 55
Thatcher, Catherine 20
Thayer, William 60
Thomas, Allenner 36
Ann 48, 59
Anne 56
Benjamin 60
Daniel 36, 60
Elisha 60
Eramus 36
Jacob 72
James 60
John 36
Owen 36
Precious 36
Rebecca 36
Sally 52

Sukey 31
Susannah 54
William 36, 60
Thompson, Aaron 60
Ann 52 (2), 57, 62
Dinah 13
Elizabeth 30, 74
George 32
James 18, 22, 25
Jesse 31, 75
John 76
Sally 31, 59
Thorn, William 73
Thornberry, Margaret 56
Mary 62
Thomas 72
Thornbury, Daniel 37
Elizabeth 37
Francis 37
Henry 37
John 37
Mary 37
Peggy 37
Samuel 37
Thomas 37
William 37
Zachariah 37
Thorndyke, Elizabeth 50
Thornhill, Bryant 23
Charles 23
Elijah 23, 74
Elizabeth 23
James 23
Leannah 23
Parthenia 23
William 23
Thornton, Lettice 34 (2)
Thomas 60
William 72
Threkeld, George 1
Threlkeld, Jesse 2
William 2
Threlkyeld, William 60
Thrift, Hamilton 26
Rebecca 26
Throckmorton, Ann 27
Frances 27
Mary 27
William 27
Tibbetts, Elizabeth 54
Tibbs, John 44
Mary 45
Tidler, Thomas 15
Tiffin, Mary 58
Timberlake, Eppa 29, 33, 41
Sarah 33
Tinsal, John 60
Tippett, William 60
Toff, Elizabeth 52
Tolle, Anne 29
George 16, 29
James 16
Jonathan 16
Roger 16
Sarry 16
Stephen 14, 16, 29
Susannah 16
Tolles, Jonathan 60
Micajah 60
Reuben 60, 61
Stephen 61
William 61
Tolling, Elizabeth 55
Tolls, Anne 53
John 61
Tolton, James 61
Tomkils, Morgan 27
Tomlin, William 12, 61

William, Sr., Capt. 76
Tompkin, Fontanatus 41
Tompkins, Christopher 41
Henry 41
John 41
Tomson, Milly 57
Tongue, --- 69
Ann L. 69
Cloe 37
Frances 69
James R. 69
Johnzie 69 (2)
Joshua 37
Martha 69
Priscilla 69
Rosa Neal 69
T. William 69
Thomas L. 69
Toward, --- 73
Townsend, Rose 23
Tracy, Philip 61
William 61
Traverse, Raleigh 44
Triplett, --- 65
Amelia 31
Ann 31
Anne 31
Arthur W. 70 (2)
Benedicte 31, 61 (2)
Betty 31
Celia 51
Ella 70
Frances 31, 74
Francis 31 (2)
Hedgman 31
Helen 60
John 61
Landies 70
Lawerence 61
Mary 40, 48
P.H. 70
Reuben 61
Robert 31
Spillman L. 70
William 31, 60, 61 (2), 72, 74
Trueman, John 61
Tullis, Ann 13
Tullos, Mary 54
Richard 1
Rodham 61
Tupman, Francis 7
Turberville, George 19
Turley, John 61
Margaret 22
Nancy 62
Turnbull, Robert 27
Turner, ---, Capt. 17
Alexander 61
Anna 45
Charles 15
Edward 16
Elizabeth 45
F. 63
Harriett 70
Hez. 11
Henrietta 43
Hezekiah 17, 26
James 61
John 61 (2)
John A., Dr. 70
Mary 16
Nancy 56
Rebecca 59
Richard 36
Sarah 48
T. 44
Thomas 61, 74
Virginia 64

Zephanie 43
Turney, Lewis 74
Turty, Nancy 61
Tutt, Thomas 74
Twentymen, Alender 2
  Benjamin 2
  Edward 2
Tyler, Benjamin 61
  Constance Horton 70
  Guennetta Baylor Dade 70
  J.W. 64
  John Webb 70
  Mary 6

--- U ---

Underwood, Anthony 61
  John 61
  Maragret 18
  Mary 38
  William 1
Utterback, Addison D. 70
  Annie 70
  Benjamin 61
  Caty 48
  Charles 26, 61
  Elizabeth 26, 56
  Henry 18, 26, 72
  John 70
  Mary 70
  Nimrod 32
  Virginia 70
  William Warren 70

--- V ---

Vanderbilt, Chloe 54
Vaughn, Sarah 50
Veale, Morris 73
Vicars, --- 73
Vorris, Thaddeus 61
Vose, F.G. 70
  Laura G. 70
Voss, Isabella 65
Vowel, Zach 43
Vowells, Zach 43
Vowels, Henry 43
Vowls, John 61

--- W ---

Waddell, Elizabeth 60, 61
  Jane 56
  Mathew 61
  Matt. 26
  William 61
Waddle, Mathew 26
  Susannah 42
  William 26
Waddles, Elizabeth 26
  George 26
  James 26
  John 26 (2)
  Margaret 26
  Polly 26
  William 26
Wade, Frances 24
Wagner, Benjamin Harrison 35
  Margaret Short 35
  Peter, Col. 35
Waite, Jane 31
Wake, John 61

Mary 42
Robert 42
William 42
Walker, Ann 46
  George 37
  James 40
  Sally 49
  William 75
Wallace, Burr 73
  Meta 67
Waller, Charles 35, 61, 72, 75
  John Tyler 70
  W. 19
Walpole, Edward 61
Walter, Elizabeth 44
  George 44
  William 44
Walters, Ann 45
Walton, Ann 44
  Sarah 44
  William 44
Ward, Berkeley 70
  Harriett 70
  Henry C. 70
  John, Dr. 70 (2)
  Mary Grace 70
Warde, Berkeley 74
Warden, Elisha 61
  Henry 40, 61
  John 61
Warren, Sallie 70
Washington, Estelle 70
  Georgianna Langhorne 70
  Lawerence 16
  Mildred Jane 70
  Robert 70 (2)
  Temple 70
  Warner 11
Waters, Thomas 61
Watkins, Elizabeth 50
Watts, Ann 7
  Francis 7 (2), 44, 61
  Hannah Russ 8
  John 7
  Sarah 34, 52
  Thomas 14
Waugh, Joseph 72
  Mary 26, 43
  Peter 44
  Tyler 61
  William 21, 72
  William Mountjoy 44
Weadon, Anne 23
  Elizabeth 23
  John 23
  William 23
Weather, Cloe 14
Weathers, Nancy 14
Weaver, Ann 32
  Catherine 2, 60
  Elizabeth 2
  Elizabeth Ann 72
  Frances 51
  Jacob 2, 61, 75
  John 2, 72, 74
  Richard 70
  Susannah 2
  Tillman 2, 72
  Tillman, Capt. 26
  William 32
Webb, Isaac 61
  John 14 (2)
  Judith 14 (2)
  Priscilla 14
  William 14
Weeden, John 33
  Polly 60
Weedon, Nathaniel 61

Weeks, Elizabeth 55
  Peggy 54, 62
  Thomas 41
Welch, David 75
  Elizabeth 39
  John 61
  Margaret 53
  Mary 56
  Silvester 11 (2)
  Sylvester 61, 74, 76
  Thomas 61, 73
  William 61 (2)
Well, Richard 38, 39
Wells, H. 70
  John 61
Welthy, ---, Widow 72
West, Benjamin 30, 61
  Charles 61
  Ignatus 30
  Jane 31, 61
  Sally 32
  Silby 13
Westall, Mary 26
Wey, Amos 61
  Henry 61
  John 61
Whalon, Patrick 61
Wharton, Long 61
  Samuel 61, 74
  Samuel, Jr. 29
Wheakley, James 5
Wheat, Lucy 36
Wheatley, --- 50
  Ann 18
  Daniel 39
  George 61
  Honor 53
  James 74
  Leannah 18
  Mary 22, 50
  Sarah 18, 55, 62
Whily, Allen 72
Whitacre, Caleph 61
  Keziah 61
  Martha 52
White, Ann 61
  Carr 23
  Charles G. 70
  Charles Mason 70
  D.B. 70 (2)
  Elizabeth 45, 61
  Gamilla 70
  Goring 61
  Hamden 70
  Hannah 53
  Helen 70
  Jane H. 70
  John 26, 61 (2), 70
  John L. 70
  Mary 70
  Pleasant 7
  Robert, Rev. 70 (2)
  Sallie Warren 70
  Sarah 58
  Thomas 14, 41, 61
  William 23, 25, 62
Whitecotton, Harris 62
Whitely, William 13
Whiting, Betty 19
  Francis 19, 43
  Mary 49
Whitledge, John 73
  Thomas 73
  William 73
Whitley, Ann 49
  Selah 52
Whitten, Elizabeth 40
Wickliffe, Bettie 49

David 19, 33, 62, 76
Nancy 56
Robert 62
Wicks, Jean 24
Thomas 62
Wigginton, Benjamin 62
John 22
Mary 37
Wilburn, Edward 72
Wiley, Allen 2
Eve 2
Wilkins, Thomas 62
Wilkinson, John 62
Joshua 62
Willborn, Edward 2
William, Jonathan 72
Margaret 50
Williams, --- 72
---, Mrs. 39
Aggy 49
Amelia 51
Ann 6, 25
Benjamin 19
Betty 59
Catherine 25, 47
Elijah 25
George 25, 28, 62, 72
Hannah 49
Isaac A. 74
Joanna 52
John 6
John Pope 62
Jonas 73
Joseph 75
Litty 53
Margaret 31
Mary 49, 55
Nancy 52, 60
Paul 4, 22, 24, 62, 72
Pope 18
Richard 62
Richardson 25
William 25, 29, 62, 73
Winny 49
Williamson, Catherine 70
Elizabeth 10, 22
Hannah 10
James 10
Louisa F. 70
Louisa R. F. 70
Martha 10
Mary 10
Paul 22
Robert Bruce 70
Sarah Brook 70
Susan 70
Thomas Vowell 70
W. W. 70
William, Rev. 70
Williangham, William 62
Willingham, John 62
Willis, Richard 19
Sally 56
Willoughby, David 62
Elijah 62
John 62
Wills, John 61
Wilson, Alexander 62
Elizabeth 47
Nancy 50
Sally 58
Wine, James 70
Sarah G. 70
Wingfield, Thomas Smith 70
Winkfield, Honor 36
Winmill, Albert 70
Josephine 70

Winn, Betty 32
Hannah 32 (2)
Hester V. 41
James 14, 62
Jemina 74
John 41
John Noble 41
John Smallwood 41
Margaret 14
Martha 59
Mary 41 (2)
Minor 14, 19, 34, 62
Minor, Capt. 32
Richard 14
Sarah Ann 41
Thomas 41
Thomas Roley 41
William 14, 32
Zachary Cox 41
Winston, John, Col. 68
Minerva 68 (2)
Winter, Elizabeth 67
Winterton, Sally 47
Winwright, John 73
Wise, George C. 70
Withers, Abijah 33
Aggy 58
Albert 64, 70
Alese 42
Ann 46
Benjamin 32, 62
Betty 42, 62
Cain 28
Centy 28
Daniel 74
Elijah 42
Elizabeth 28 (2), 33, 42, 53
Enoch 28, 32, 33, 35, 42, 62
George Washington 22
Hannah 28, 44, 62 (2)
James 21, 22, 26, 27 (2), 30, 33 (2), 35, 42, 44, 62 (3), 72
Jemina 22
Jennette 42
Jesse 42, 62, 74, 76
John 22 (2), 27, 28, 32, 34, 35, 42, 62 (2), 72
Joseph 32
Lewis 42
Lucinda 48
Lucy 28
Mathew 42
Molly 42
Patty 28
Rose 30
Sallie W. 64, 70
Sally 28, 61
Seathley 56
Sithey 28
Spencer 42, 74, 76
Susan 42
Susannah 48, 50
Thomas 28, 32, 35, 72
Thomas, Dr. 70
William 22, 28 (2), 32, 42, 62 (3), 72
Wolf, Catherine 58
Wolfe, Jacob 62
Wood, Daniel 70
De 35
Dickerson 42, 75
Dickinson 62
Elijah 42
Elizabeth 62
James 40, 42, 62
John 5, 62

Joseph 72
Joshua 72
Louisa 53
Mark 62
Mary 42, 47
Nehemiah 72
Samuel 5, 12
Thomas 62
William 35, 42
Woodard, Lewis 75
Woodford, Catesby 24, 29
Mark 29
Mary 29
William 29
Woods, Robert 4
Woodward, Caty 46
Woodyard, Lewis 18, 75
Woodzell, Emma D. 70
George 70
Martha Clark 70
Mary 70
Wooks, James 37
Wrenn, --- 50
Daniel 62
Elizabeth 61
Isaac 34
Jeremiah 62
John 34
Thomas 62
Wright, Betsy 28
David 62
Elijah 62
Elizabeth 28, 45, 53
Frances 45
James 11, 12, 19, 28, 32, 38, 40, 41, 62
John 7, 28, 62
John, Capt. 12, 72 (2)
Joseph 2 (2), 73
Mary 28, 30, 53, 59
Milly 46
Rosamond 28
Sary 49
William 18, 28, 72
Wyatt, William 3
Wyer, Ann E. Powell 70
Anne Powell 66
H., Rev. 70
Henry 66
Henry, Rev. 70 (3)
Henry Halstead 70
John Powell 70
Walter Penfield 70

--- Y ---

Yates, Frances 39
Lewis 39
Nancy 39
William 39
Yorby, William G. 74
Young, --- 9
Bersheba 13
Caty 57
James 6, 43, 62, 72
John 29, 62
Mary 53, 57
Nimrod 62
Original 13, 15, 17, 18, 24, 28, 29, 72
Patience 28
Richard 44
Sukey 28
William 28, 29
Youngblood, William 62